——————— In a New Century ———————

In a New Century

*Essays on
Queer History, Politics, and Community Life*

John D'Emilio

The University of Wisconsin Press

Publication of this volume has been made possible, in part,
through support from the **College of Liberal Arts and Sciences**
of the **University of Illinois at Chicago.**

The University of Wisconsin Press
1930 Monroe Street, 3rd Floor
Madison, Wisconsin 53711-2059
uwpress.wisc.edu

3 Henrietta Street
London WC2E 8LU, England
eurospanbookstore.com

Library of Congress Cataloging-in-Publication Data

D'Emilio, John, author.
In a new century: essays on queer history, politics, and
community life / John D'Emilio.
pages   cm
Includes bibliographical references.
ISBN 978-0-299-29774-9 (pbk.: alk. paper)
ISBN 978-0-299-29773-2 (e-book)
1. Gay liberation movement — United States — History.
2. Gay rights — United States — History.
3. Gay activists — United States — History.
4. Gays — United States — Social conditions.   I. Title.
HQ76.8.U5D445   2014
306.76'60973 — dc23
2013033118

Contents

Contents

In a New Century

Introduction

Writing History, Making Change

Dr. John D'Emilio recently joined the staff of UNC–Greensboro in the history department. . . . D'Emilio comes to North Carolina from New York. UNC-G recently held a Gay Awareness Week celebration on the campus and I understand the fag doctor participated. Greensboro now rivals Chapel Hill and Charlotte as the leading center for faggotry in North Carolina.

The Landmark, Orange County, North Carolina, May 10, 1984

A nationally known gay and lesbian scholar, John D'Emilio, has been lured to the University of Illinois at Chicago in what is considered a recruiting coup among academics.

Chicago Sun-Times, Chicago, June 24, 1999

Fifteen years separate these two newspaper articles. Half a generation. The articles remind me of how much I have to be thankful for. The change that I have experienced in this short stretch of years staggers me.

At the time I moved to Greensboro, North Carolina, in 1983, at age thirty-four, I had lived my whole life in New York City. I had been one of those New Yorkers who was sure I would never leave. The strong ties of locale seemed a genetic inheritance. My mom lived her entire life in just three neighborhoods in the Bronx. In sixty-two years of marriage, my parents had only two telephone numbers. All my grandparents migrated

3

to New York from south Italian villages that hated to lose their sons and daughters. Once they arrived here, they put down roots that dug deep into the urban pavement.

When I started college, I moved out of the Bronx, to Manhattan. It was a short journey by subway. In those days, the two boroughs shared the same area code. But in every other way the distance was vast. The adult world I built for myself was as different from that of my parents as New York was from the Sicilian countryside. It was populated by political dissenters and cultural radicals. It was also, substantially, a gay world. Newly visible, intense, dynamic, its exuberance contagious, it enveloped me with magical warmth. Most strangers to New York find this hard to believe, but natives know that you can live among its packed hordes and still enjoy a palpable sense of community. Mine was bounded by the route of the No. 1 Broadway Local. Even with the hundreds of thousands who lived or traveled along its path every day, I knew I belonged. I knew the shops and proprietors, I enjoyed the comfort of familiar faces, and I almost never left my apartment without running into a friend or acquaintance.

I left New York with great sadness. In the months between getting hired at the Greensboro campus of the University of North Carolina and loading the U-Haul, my tear ducts worked overtime. I, who could not carry a tune, suddenly seemed to know every New York–themed song of the twentieth century. I'd be jogging along Riverside Drive and suddenly imagine Frank Sinatra crooning, "If I can make it there," and I'd start to cry. I'd turn the corner from my apartment building onto Broadway and start humming, "Give my regards to Broadway," and my eyes would fill.

So why then did I leave? Partly it was sadness of a different sort. Those last two years in New York, AIDS had invaded my world, and its presence was inescapable. It was impossible to be among gay men and not have the conversation turn to AIDS. Our fear and anxiety were poisoning the well, and, at the time, there was still a deep sense of helplessness.

But this makes the decision appear too reactive. I had also pursued this move with deliberation, even if I hadn't fully grasped how it would change my life. Years before, as an enthusiastic graduate student caught up in the fever of gay liberation, I had decided to research and write gay history. The work brought the satisfying pleasures of intellectual discovery. It also brought the thrill of watching my work and the work of others become a tool for community building. As I suggest in "Finding History, Creating

Community," there was a hunger then for words and images from the past. History was our confirmation that the worlds we were constructing in the present were not our momentary hallucinations but had roots and connections; our lives had strong ties to something that stretched way back in time.

The problem was that uncovering gay history did not pay the rent. I was getting tired of scrounging for money, of taking jobs that were certainly worth doing but that absorbed my energies and left me with too little time to do what I loved. The glory of academic life is that it pays someone like me—little Johnny D'Emilio from the Bronx—to read and lecture and lead discussions with students on the subjects that grip me and then have long summer vacations for sustained research and writing.

Of course there was a second problem. No history department in the United States had ever hired someone whose work was gay identified. It rubbed me wrong to think that my road was blocked for no good reason and that, by doing nothing, I was acquiescing to this. So for three years I applied for jobs, scads of them, until, implausibly, the University of North Carolina in Greensboro offered me a tenure-track position.

There's a story behind this hire, as there almost always is. Growing up, I had listened as my mother repeated endless aphorisms born of an ingrained Sicilian cynicism. "It's not what you know but who you know" was one of them, and her view of life drove me crazy. Well, follow this trail: Jim, who was then my lover of two years, had gone to college twenty-five years earlier with Patty, who remained his close friend. Patty was married to Loren, a straight-as-an-arrow college football star who had played in the Orange Bowl and then gone on to graduate school in history. Loren was on the search committee looking to hire a twentieth-century US historian at UNCG. Loren and Pat have always been appropriately reticent about what went on in those committee proceedings. But my gut tells me that I owed my job to his ability, because of the personal connection, to see beyond the label "gay history" and be able to say that "this guy has good credentials." In other words, I'm sure it was he who saved my application from the garbage bin in the early rounds of deliberation, so that I finally had the chance to present myself, in person, in an interview setting. With all that has changed in the past thirty years, even today too few historians are able to see beyond the label "gay" and imagine something of real value there.

North Carolina was not New York. I had grown up in a world populated by Catholics and Jews. In Greensboro, a city of 160,000 people, there were two synagogues, four Roman Catholic parishes, and more than three hundred Protestant churches. The ministers there must have had an informant in the telephone or gas company because, within a few days of settling in, Jim and I received visits from a parade of clerics—Methodist and Baptist, and Presbyterian and Baptist, and Episcopalian and still more Baptists. From the front porch of the house we were renting, I could see the steeple of what was reported to be the home of the largest Southern Baptist congregation in the state. And these folks were serious about it. On Broadway, three blocks north of where I had lived in Manhattan, one of the tall 1920s apartment houses sported a several-story-high message painted on the side of the building: "The wages of sin is death, but the gift of God is eternal life." But the sign had been there for decades. The luster had faded from it, and it never changed. Now, in Greensboro, there were billboard-size religious messages everywhere, and they changed with each Sunday's sermon.

Then there was the fast food. I was almost thirty before I ever walked into a McDonald's. The signs informed me that billions of burgers had already been sold. At the time I left New York, I'm not sure that a McDonald's or Burger King had even opened in Manhattan. But from the center of Greensboro a series of major avenues fanned outward, each becoming a Miracle Mile of franchises. McDonald's, Burger King, Wendy's, Kentucky Fried Chicken, Pizza Hut, Pizza Inn, Shoney's, Arby's, Taco Bell, and Biscuitville were all there, and they were packed with families.

On the other hand, Greensboro also hosted every Saturday morning a county farmers' market that set up shop just a mile from where I lived. The growing season was long in North Carolina. The first greens arrived at the beginning of April, and the farms were still producing in November. Summers were beyond bountiful, with weeks and weeks of fresh corn and tomatoes. Jim had been raised on an Iowa farm, and the return of real corn to his diet was a boon he had never expected. I learned that a half-dozen ears of fresh-picked corn, boiled not too long, with a couple of sliced tomatoes on the side, was all the dinner one could want. After a couple of years we began venturing beyond the farmers' market and into the fields just a half hour from the center of town. In May we'd come back with piles and piles of strawberries. In August and September, we picked bushels of tomatoes and bundles of basil that made enough sauce to last through the winter.

Even during the months when there wasn't much growing in the fields, the market was alive with country women selling their baked goods. Our favorite stall belonged to a generously proportioned woman from the next county who, as anyone approached, would begin to intone with her own unique syntax: "We have your zucchini bread, and we have your banana nut bread. We have your lemon pound cake, and your sweet potato pie, and your red velvet cake. We have your persimmon pudding."

Greensboro was also achingly beautiful, and that was a revelation to me. In the 1950s the various ladies' garden clubs had banded together and sponsored, over several years, a mass planting of dogwood trees. Tens of thousands were distributed around the city, and more were added in succeeding years. Every year the magic happened. Around the first week of April, the pale white blossoms would reach full bloom, and I would come out of the house to be dazzled by the splendor of it. It was as if the city had experienced a heavy spring snow the night before, but the flakes had all stopped falling twelve feet above the ground and were poised there, waiting to melt. Before long I found myself measuring the progress of spring by the sequence of buds in town. Crocuses prepared the way for daffodils, which heralded the arrival of hyacinth and tulips, which announced that the Bradford pears were soon to flower. If there were irises it must be final exam week and the beginning of May. When the crepe myrtle bloomed, summer was firmly here. Over the years Jim and I took note of which streets had the best of whatever was in bloom. I thought of it as spring's greatest hits, as we'd drive to see the forsythia on Aycock Street and the azaleas on Friendly Avenue and the irises on Cornwallis Drive.

Much as I came to love the flowers, I knew that the kind of gay scene I encountered would have a greater impact on the quality of my daily experience. I've said that I applied for lots and lots of jobs. But I did not apply to all of them. My job search had a geography, and its shape depended on whether I could imagine a gay life taking form there. I don't remember now what the state of gay travel publishing was in the early 1980s, but I somehow managed to discover that Greensboro had two gay bars, which seemed to me a beginning.

During my interview visit, one of the department members let me know discreetly that he was gay. Two weeks after Jim and I arrived, he took us to a Saturday afternoon barbecue in the country. It was held on an acreage owned by a lesbian couple. One was head of the dance department at the university, and the other, a former academic, managed properties in town and was very much a progressive community activist. They lived in a restored eighteenth-century farmhouse dripping with charm, with a tobacco shed in back, a stream, and a pond. The barbecue was sponsored by a local chapter of the Gay Academic Union, an organization I had helped found in New York ten years earlier. Fifty or more folks were there, women and men, a broad age range, most all of them white. The covered-dish spread was fabulous, as it would be at any potluck I attended in North Carolina over the next dozen years. Midway through the afternoon, there was an auction of gag gifts to raise money for the lesbian and gay health project in Durham.

For the next couple of years, GAU served as a gay home base, a place where I tried to build a social network and a political community, as I was accustomed to having. It was filled with good folks who were easy to be with in ways common to southern culture—warm and friendly, easygoing and jocular. They were creating something of a lesbian and gay oasis in the midst of a relentlessly straight environment. Yet the gulf between what I had known and what I was encountering was vast and deep. For instance, virtually no one was out of the closet. A few years earlier, one member of the anthropology department, Tom Fitzgerald, had bravely proposed and taught a summer session course on homosexuality, but it had never made its way into the permanent curriculum. The whole experience had apparently been disturbing enough that Tom had not continued with it, and, as time went on and the institutional memory faded, he was, de facto, less and less out. A faculty member whom I met at that first barbecue told me that, since she had gotten tenure, she was no longer afraid of being seen going into a gay bar.

Here's an incident from that first year: I'm at one of GAU's monthly meetings, which were held on Friday evenings at the Unitarian church (thank God for Unitarians everywhere). The church was located near the edge of town, down a long gravel path, surrounded by trees—a protected location, not on any main line of traffic. The program that night consisted of a couple of psychologists talking about mental health issues. As I sat there, it felt as if I had time traveled back to the 1950s, to the gay world I had written about in my dissertation. This could have been a meeting of the Mattachine Society or the Daughters of Bilitis, with an invited professional telling us that we were good and okay—except, thank goodness, in the 1980s we were now listening to a lesbian and a gay expert. Progress comes in small steps.

The culture of the closet remained strong in North Carolina in those first several years. The boundaries were policed as much by the gay community as by the straight majority. I remember when Jim, who had volunteered to be editor of the GAU newsletter, mailed out an issue in which he identified himself by name. He got quite a few phone calls from members who were agitated by this break with discretion.

In general, "gay" stood outside the framework of daily experience in Greensboro. During the first year, various faculty members held dinners, to which Jim and I were invited, as a way of introducing us to the social world of the university. I much appreciated these events, even as they were sometimes extremely awkward. At one of them, I was engaged in conversation with a knot of people. Jim was standing nearby, and I caught the sound of someone asking him how he was finding life in Greensboro. He mentioned several things (including rhapsodizing about the farmers' market), and then said, "But it's SO heterosexual!" For a tangible instant, every conversation in the room paused. It was as if a new word had been spoken, one never before heard. Moments like this have become emblematic for me of my whole time there. The utter foreignness of things gay quickly brought back an old sensation: the nagging, incessant awareness of difference that I sometimes think every gay man and lesbian of my generation came of age with. The less visible gay was, the more it preoccupied my waking hours. This feeling had gradually faded during my last decade in New York. Now it had returned.

Teaching was what I was hired to do. Many years earlier, I had taught part time at three different schools. I'd hated it. I was a bundle of anxieties standing in front of the classroom. It made me painfully self-conscious, and I wondered what I was doing talking so authoritatively to undergraduates who were just a few years younger than I was. In the intervening years I'd had the opportunity to speak on panels and lecture a good bit before gay community audiences, and it had suited me better. There was none of the coerciveness of the teacher-student relationship in those settings, and I could feel the encouragement and appreciation of my listeners.

Folks who don't teach tend to look at the teaching profession, especially at the college level, as a privileged occupation. And they are right. We get long summers off and vacations throughout the year. We work with very little immediate supervision. We have great flexibility in setting our schedules. We are getting paid to think. Once tenured, we have job security for life.

At the same time, entry into the profession is a psychologically brutalizing experience. Graduate school provided me not a jot of training or preparation for teaching beyond observing what our professors did in the classroom. My first year in Greensboro, I worked almost continuously from Sunday mornings until Friday afternoon, typically putting in twelve-hour days. Somehow, my school years had imparted the conviction that my knowledge was always inadequate. The core message of graduate training was not how much one knew but how much one didn't know. A huge amount of time went into organizing a series of courses I had never taught before, mastering enough material to fill the class hours, and shaping it so that I could communicate something intelligible to my students. But that's just the content. Meanwhile, there were living, breathing human beings sitting in front of me, bringing into the classroom each day the difficulties—academic, emotional, practical—that they were struggling with and that were preying on their minds. I soon learned that the issue of content was more easily taken care of than the matter of shaping an environment that put students at enough ease for learning to occur.

Most of my students were from North Carolina. For many of them, enrolling in UNCG meant coming to the city. Family ties were strong, and lots of my undergraduates could trace ancestral roots in their counties several generations back. Things I took for granted were new to them, and much of their life experience was outside my own. I remember one time, in my US history survey course, lecturing on the "new immigration" from southern and eastern Europe at the end of the nineteenth century. I could sense that the class hadn't gone well and decided, for the next meeting, to spend some time in a discussion of how their own ethnic backgrounds shaped their outlook even today. As I explained to them the questions I wanted them to talk about in small groups, a number of hands shot up, and several students asked, simultaneously, "What's an ethnic background?" The question floored me, and, laughing, I explained life in the Bronx, where no one I knew was an American, and everyone—Irish, Italian, Pole, German—was hyphenated. Soon, they were parsing North Carolina society in ways that made sense of their experience. "We're mountain people," said one. "We're country folk," said another. And they then proceeded to explain the cultural nuances behind those terms.

When I first started teaching, my undergraduate students were almost all born in the 1960s. They had childhood memories of the decade, and, through older brothers and sisters, some of them had shared vicariously in the cultural and political excitement of those times. Lots of them had attended racially integrated public schools when that was still a fairly new experience, and so they also had been touched directly by the historic force of the civil rights movement. Less than four years before I arrived in Greensboro, Ku Klux Klan members had massacred a group of demonstrators right in the heart of downtown. Despite videotapes showing the killings of the unarmed demonstrators, an all-white jury acquitted the defendants on every count. With events like these fresh in the minds of my students, it didn't require a major leap to have them cast a critical eye across the American past. All this made it easy to construct US history courses, which was my teaching charge, with a social justice emphasis. Notions of oppression, inequality, and organized resistance were not constructs from a distant past but ideas that were alive in the public culture around these students.

Mostly I taught fairly standard US history courses, even if I gave them a radical twist—the United States since World War II; a survey of US history; American foreign policy; the United States in the 1960s. Because of my own research interests, I found ways to integrate at least some material about sexuality into my syllabus—enough to open my students to topics they might not have thought about but not so much that it subjected me to the charges that faculty whose work focuses on identity too often face: "I thought this was supposed to be a course in history [or English or . . .] but all s/he talked about was women [or race or . . .]." I was able to place into the curriculum a survey-style course on the history of sexuality in the United States. And, in UNCG's Residential College, an experimental unit within the university that brought students together into a learning community, I could venture further afield and put together more imaginative seminars. Murray and Fran Arndt, a faculty couple who were at the heart of it, were keeping alive some of the communitarian values associated with the cultural radicalism of the 1960s. They had created at the Residential College a four-semester American studies sequence that all students took and that was team taught. The course alternated a week of lectures, delivered to 120 students and one's co-teachers, and two weeks in smaller, individually constructed seminars.

My second year in Greensboro, I taught in the post-1945 segment of the sequence and designed a seminar called "Sexuality, Power, and Politics." We had four units—on sexuality and Cold War culture; on race and sexuality; on feminist sexual politics; and on gay liberation and the conservative response to it—with readings and a writing assignment for each. For the unit on gay liberation, which I placed at the end of the semester, I asked students to write a "coming-out" letter to their parents. For the overwhelming majority, who were heterosexual, I was asking them to put themselves in the shoes of someone else. I wanted them to try to understand viscerally, through the exercise of imagining what they would write to their parents, the stigma and the oppression attached to being gay. In my innocence, I thought the point was simple and obvious.

My first clues that it wasn't came a few days before the assignment was due. Because the students at the Residential College lived together and took courses together, everything that happened there was grist for discussion. The week we started the unit on gay liberation, other faculty in the program began making observations like "Quite an assignment you devised there!" or "Interesting idea." The tone was not in any way hostile, but the comments were always accompanied by nervous laughter. Walking into class on a Monday morning, after the weekend in which many of them ought to have started the assignment, several students said they had questions about it. "Do we have to mail the letter?" one student asked. "What if my roommate sees it?" another wanted to know. "Do I have to put my name on the assignment?" asked a third. "But I'm not gay!" someone else chimed in.

Put me in unexpected and potentially conflictual situations and my unguarded spontaneous response is to laugh. The laughter is a cover for my own embarrassment and nervousness, but it also, fortunately, is disarming. With each of their questions, I would laugh and provide barely more than a one-word answer. Soon some of them were laughing, too. Finally, one of the students, who had been especially perturbed by what I was asking them to do, looked up and said, "This is the point, isn't it? It's a really scary thing to do."

I came to call instances like this one "teaching moments." They make the whole classroom enterprise thrilling and are the payback for the long, often tedious hours of preparation. Fortunately, I have had more than my fair share. Once, in my history of sexuality class, I lectured on the career of Margaret Sanger. I had discovered that biography was a good way into history for my students, and I had developed a set of biographical lectures to illustrate key issues or themes. Sanger deserves to rank way up there in the pantheon of important world figures in the twentieth century; she is certainly a lot more important than most American presidents. My lecture done, I opened the class for comments and discussion. Linda, a very sharp adult student who was working toward her high school teacher certification, erupted: "How could I have gotten to be forty years old and never have even heard of Margaret Sanger?" The younger students were taken aback by her vehemence and saw, in a flash, some of the truth of feminism.

I remember another time, teaching my post-1945 US history course. That semester, unusually, the enrollment was all male. We had reached the point in the semester, near to the end, when the topic was women's liberation. I'd already lectured a bit, and they'd read a few score pages of writings from the women's movement. Lots of it dripped with the anger that comes from the first articulations of oppression. It was heavy stuff to read, especially for a group of young white southern males. Leading a discussion that morning was like pulling teeth without Novocain. I kept probing and pushing until finally one of them let leak a pretty sexist comment. And then there was another, and another. Since there were no women in the room, I thought, "Why not? They're carrying it around. I might as well let it rip." The statements became more and more outrageous until even some of the students who a few minutes earlier had been on board began to get uneasy. Soon they, rather than I, were trying to answer their peers. Finally, one of them said, "But they're not as good athletes as we are," and another shot right back (this was the semester after the 1984 Summer Olympics), "Right, and I'm sure you can outrun Joan Samuelson in a marathon!" Everyone roared at that one, including its target, and it opened a space through the underbrush of their emotions for a thoughtful engagement of feminism.

Through all of these years, in the classroom and elsewhere, I had to navigate the "coming-out" issue. Coming out was not a one-time event. It had to happen again and again. For virtually all my students in the 1980s, I was the first gay man they had ever knowingly met. Because of my sexuality course and the book I had written, my identity was already in the air, but not quite named and clear. For those meeting me for the first time in a course, my identity just hung there, unspoken yet present.

In my third semester, I used an excerpt from my book, *Sexual Politics, Sexual Communities*, as reading for a segment of the course on sexuality during the early Cold War. On the day when the reading was due, a student raised her hand and asked, "Are you a homosexual?" It wasn't the question I was expecting. But, with a smile and without skipping a beat, I said, "Yes, I am gay," and moved on to the next student comment. That moment changed the whole tone of the course. Over the next week, I noticed that everyone had become more relaxed. The experience made me realize I had to figure out a way to address the coming-out issue without turning it into high drama.

Beginning the next semester, I began every course not simply by calling roll but by asking students to introduce themselves. I would pose a series of questions that allowed them to show themselves: "Fifty years from now, what would you like your legacy to be? What makes you a good friend? If you were president of the world for a day, what one thing would you change, and why? Tell us about the best day of your life." I explained that it was a good way for me to remember their names, and I told them that, as a "reward" for answering my intrusive questions, I would introduce myself by answering theirs. It worked better than I could have imagined. Their introductions helped create a sense of community, and their answers often produced knowing laughter and recognition from their peers. And their questions allowed me to show myself, too. My coming out happened organically, but it was not the main event. Instead, it was just one piece of information in a back-and-forth conversation.

Twice during my time at UNCG, the personal, the political, and the teaching came together in beautiful ways. I was asked to submit an "expert" affidavit in court challenges to state sodomy laws. I invited students to help in doing the background research for these affidavits. They threw themselves into it. Although neither of the cases succeeded, the work generated among them a sense of possibility for how history could be a tool for social change. And, years later, in 2003, the work of historians would make a difference in *Lawrence v. Texas*, the Supreme Court decision that did finally declare state sodomy statutes unconstitutional.

Occasionally in my years in Greensboro, I had a class that bombed. But mostly I loved my students and found teaching absorbing, exciting, even thrilling. If I could have moved the campus to, say, Fairfax County, just outside Washington, DC, and commuted every day from an apartment in the District, I'd have been content for the rest of my days.

But teaching in itself did not make for a satisfying life, at least not for me. Simply put, it was too difficult being gay in North Carolina in the 1980s. Difference may be invigorating, but not when there seems to be only difference, which pretty well describes the emotional texture of my social life there. It was hard rarely seeing my gay self reflected back, except in the person of Jim. Our isolation as an openly gay couple who viewed the world through the lens of gay liberation was debilitating.

During these years I made some efforts to find an academic job elsewhere, but hiring committees were still not especially amenable to the kind of work I did. Fortunately, my book on the homophile movement, plus other writing that I was doing, was opening doors of another sort. Especially after the publication of *Intimate Matters*, a book on the history of sexuality in America that I coauthored with Estelle Freedman, my closest friend, I had, for an academic historian, fairly high visibility. In the evolving world of the gay and lesbian movement, my detailed knowledge of the history of activism and of sexuality gave me a longer view on current movement efforts than most activists had. I had also had in my pre-Greensboro years some experience in social change organizations, both gay and not. So I began to look for ways to have a life more connected to what I passionately cared about—gay liberation and progressive social change—than I was able to imagine as a classroom teacher in a small southern city. Beyond the Triangle Area of Durham-Raleigh-Chapel Hill, with its top-notch universities and emerging high-tech companies, there was not much gay or lesbian activism obviously visible in the state during my first years there. And, a Yankee college professor was not the right person to try to jump-start it in Greensboro.

Those years in Greensboro coincided with an important transitional period for the gay and lesbian movement nationally. At the time I left New York, gay activism in much of the country was in low gear. No great changes seemed to be in the offing. The Reagan years were creating an environment inhospitable to progressive activism. The recession that national economic policies had induced was extremely hard on local community-based organizations, and the government funding that sustained much grassroots work in the 1970s was drying up. AIDS soon began to change all that. As the epidemic spread beyond a few urban epicenters, it mobilized gay communities. A whole network of service organizations sprang up, drawing in large numbers of volunteers and tapping money that had remained outside the orbit of activism. It took just a few years for the impulse to care for the sick and the dying to transmute into anger at government neglect. The boundary between AIDS activism and gay or lesbian activism was porous, and the rage induced by the epidemic unleashed a broader political impulse. Retrospectively, I think of the 1986 *Hardwick* decision, when the Supreme Court, in a split vote, sustained the constitutionality of state sodomy laws, as the key moment of revelation. Here we were, as a community, suffering under the weight of this horrific affliction and engaging in a heroic response, and a group of judges in black robes said it was okay for the police to invade our bedrooms and arrest us, which is just what had happened in the case of Michael Hardwick.

I can't quite reconstruct the sequence of events that led to my involvement with the National Gay and Lesbian Task Force. The best I can remember is that I got a call one day in 1987 from Sue Hyde, a field organizer for NGLTF, asking me to plan with her a "town meeting" on sex and politics. The idea grabbed my attention, and I said yes.

Sue had been hired the year before to direct a newly created Privacy Project at the Task Force. It was meant as a response to the *Hardwick* decision, and Sue's job was to work with activists in states with sodomy laws to build repeal campaigns. Sue is a great organizer. In the succeeding years I saw her operate in many a tense meeting, with feelings flying around the room and divisive political passions unleashed. She would sit there with legs crossed, one elbow resting in a hand, the other hand holding on to her chin, frowning slightly and nodding. After sufficient venting had taken place, she'd make an observation that, though it might not cause peace to break out in the land, would chart the way toward a next step. Looking at the list of states that still had sodomy laws (the Solid South, the Mormon-dominated mountain states in the West, and a handful of others), she defined her task not as lobbying for repeal but as building a strong enough infrastructure of grassroots groups so that repeal would someday be possible. Her town meetings on sex and politics were a way of provoking community discussion, of allowing the complex connections between public and private to come into view. They were especially on point in the mid-1980s, when AIDS had spawned a new outburst of homophobic responses to gay sexuality as menacing to the health of the nation.

The event was scheduled to coincide with the 1987 March on Washington, when hundreds of thousands of lesbians, gay men, bisexuals, people with AIDS, and their friends and supporters would be converging on the city. It was held in a large auditorium at George Washington University, and it was packed. Every seat was filled. Folks were sitting on the floor and leaning against the walls. Though I can't at this distance remember much about the specific content of the presentations (except for Jade McLeughlin's use of the memorable phrase "lesbian bed death"), the atmosphere was electric. Partly it was because of the weekend. Queers were everywhere in DC during those few days, and it was an odd and thrilling experience to feel oneself in possession of the nation's capital. Partly it was the psychic toll that AIDS was taking and the way this event, which affirmed gay sexuality, offered a vision of sex beyond the ravages of disease. And partly it was the moment, pregnant with activist energies straining to explode into life.

The weekend was a watershed. I had attended, over the years, any number of mass demonstrations, including some of the large antiwar events in the 1960s and the antinuclear march in New York City in the early 1980s. In numbers, this was at least on a par with any of them and, to my observation, seemed to dwarf them all. However, the issue wasn't simply size but the combination of events that weekend and what they symbolized. There was a mass public wedding of same-sex couples outside the offices of the Internal Revenue Service. There was a very large civil disobedience action in front of the Supreme Court. There were huge numbers of meetings that brought together lawyers from around the country, and church activists, and antiviolence organizers, and other interest groups. There was the display, for the first time, of the Names Project Memorial Quilt on the Mall. And then, finally, the march itself, organized by state contingents so that one could see, with utter clarity, how we as a people stretched the length and breadth of this country.

It is evidence of just how much the world has changed since then if, reading this, you find yourself wondering, "So there were lots of people from around the country. This is news that gays and lesbians are everywhere? What's the big deal?" In 1987 it was a big deal. It is one thing to say we are everywhere as a rhetorical device that a big-city activist wishes to be true. It is quite another to see contingents from Alaska and Montana and Maine and Kentucky and New Mexico assembling and marching to the rally site. The 1987 March signified the birth of a movement that was nationwide in its reach. It launched a period, of which we are heirs today, where gay communities have become visible way beyond a few large cities and university towns. And these communities have spawned organizations that help bind their members, giving them a voice and a presence in the public world.

Of all the national lesbian and gay organizations existing at that time, NGLTF seemed to me best poised to seize this particular moment. Lambda Legal Defense and Education Fund, a national legal advocacy group, pursued change through a strategy of litigation. The Human Rights Campaign Fund operated as a gay PAC, funneling money to friendly candidates for congressional office; it was just starting to add to its work a lobbying operation in Washington. The Task Force had always been hazier as to its mission and opted to shift gears as issues changed and new openings appeared. In the late 1980s, its staff consciously moved in the direction of "movement building" as its primary activity, seeking ways to build a stronger grassroots infrastructure of activism around the country and to maintain links between the national and the local. Jeff Levi, the executive director at the time, had been a key AIDS lobbyist in the first half of the 1980s. He saw how critical the developing network of local AIDS service organizations was in making Congress receptive to AIDS issues, as these activist volunteers visited the offices of their representatives and pressed upon them the urgency of the epidemic. He had hired Urvashi Vaid, an activist with ties to Boston's queer community, as communications director, and Urv was working the media in every way imaginable at a time when most media still ignored the community.

Jeff shaped the work of the Task Force around a set of issue-based organizing projects. Sue Hyde's Privacy Project focused on sodomy law repeal. Kevin Berrill worked on homophobic violence. Ivy Young developed a Families Project. Later, a campus organizing project was added to the mix. Each of them developed strong ties with grassroots activists who were working on these issues, and they provided materials, information, programmatic ideas, and tactical assistance—in short, help from the outside to local people who often felt themselves beleaguered and without much support. Peri Jude Radecic worked as a national lobbyist, making use of the ties that other staff developed locally to create pressure for hearings in Congress and to move legislation forward. They were a hardworking, talented, and very funny bunch of folks, as sharp a collection of activists as one was ever likely to find in a single place.

I was fascinated by the vision of the Task Force staff. In a country growing ever more conservative, they were still committed to building a movement for progressive social change. They did not believe in top-down models of activism but instead were trying to create synergy between local activism and national campaigns. Drawing on my knowledge of twentieth-century US history, I interpreted what they were doing as an attempt, on a smaller scale, to combine the style and mission of the NAACP, the staid, stick-to-the-rules granddaddy of civil rights organizations, with those of the Student Nonviolent Coordinating Committee, the militant 1960s group whose youthful members were willing to break every rule in the book. When Jeff asked if I would join the board of directors, I said yes without hesitating.

As a historian, I am used to writing about social movements. Along with journalists and other social scientists, I view the world of activism through a number of different lenses. We can emphasize the biographical, as Taylor Branch has done in his magisterial study of the civil rights movement. We can write about organizations as agents of change or about the clash of ideologies or about the impact of big disruptive events, like war or economic depression or assassinations. We can evaluate the success or failure of movements by looking at their ability to mobilize resources, take advantage of political opportunities, and craft alliances. But the internal dynamics of organizations often remain below the radar of the historian or else are considered too insignificant to be worthy of attention.

My five years on the Task Force board changed forever my understanding of collective movements. I came to appreciate how the invisible operations of an organization—the relationship between board and staff, the personality conflicts, the fund-raising strategies, a bad hire, and any number of other matters—have an influence that ripples outward into how the organization presents itself to the world, how it does its work, how it relates to other actors in a campaign. I came, in other words, to take seriously the microscopic elements of change, the small constituent parts that, ultimately, shape the whole.

The next five years combined high drama with a steep learning curve. When I first joined the board, meetings were chaotic affairs, with sharp words ricocheting around the room and discussions displaying a heart-stopping intensity. Often the emotions were so out of proportion to the matter at hand that I, a newcomer, knew I was listening to the replaying of very old emotional conflicts that had perversely attached themselves to a minor item of business. The board seemed intent on meddling in almost everything the staff was doing. What had attracted me to NGLTF—the work of the staff as it appeared from the outside—seemed endangered by the very group of people whose role was to oversee the organization.

Soon after I joined the board, Jeff announced that he was resigning as executive director, and Urvashi decided to apply for the job. An internal candidate always creates something of a sticky situation. If he or she is rejected, often the person will leave the organization. Such a candidacy also asks the board to put aside the bonds of personal relationships and to look fairly at the pool of candidates. Urv was smart, energetic, and charismatic. She held out an inspiring vision of NGLTF's and the movement's potential. She lacked a depth of management experience, but then so did most movement activists in those years.

The selection process was contentious, but the board ultimately hired Urv. At that time, few women, and virtually no persons of color, had been entrusted with the leadership of a major gay organization. Over the next several months, board officers acted toward Urv in ways that were consistently demeaning to her and subversive of her authority. They repeatedly questioned her judgment and engaged in a level of oversight that made it difficult for her to do the job. One of the board co-chairs was particularly egregious in his behavior. It seemed pretty clear that he, and the other officers, would never have treated a white male executive in the same ways.

Urv, along with some of my close movement friends, asked me if I would run for the position of male co-chair, thus challenging the current leadership. I didn't look forward to the factionalism this might unleash, but I also knew it was necessary. I tried to go about it with as much integrity as possible. I did not conduct a secret campaign of lining up votes but told the current co-chair that I was running against him, explained why, and sought to keep a dialogue going. I'm glad I did, but if I thought it would make life smoother, I was wrong. I won election handily but then had to endure for the next two years his public carping criticisms as well as some very direct and unpleasant personal attacks. One time, at a board meeting in Nashville, we were taking a break between sessions, and the former co-chair cornered me in a hallway. He proceeded to heap abuse on me and faulted everything I had done that day. I remember thinking, "Don't rise to the bait. This too will pass. His term will expire soon. It will pass, it will pass, it will pass." His was the kind of behavior that occurs in organizations all the time, where the pull of an individual's ego weighs more heavily than the mission of the group.

Taking on the board leadership of a national organization, even a relatively small one like NGLTF, is time consuming. Over the next couple of years it often felt as if I had taken on a second full-time job. I wish I could claim that my leadership transformed the culture of the board of directors. Meetings went hugely better, since I have good facilitation skills. As a board, we began, for the first time, to address seriously the issue of fund-raising. But mostly, I saw my role as keeping a lid on the irresponsible behavior of disruptive members and, by putting myself between them and Urvashi, absorbing as best I could the attacks that some of them were wanting to lob in her direction.

What made the time worth expending and the unpleasantness worth enduring were the heady accomplishments of those years. With all due respect for other movement activists, I do not think there has ever been such a collection of skilled, savvy, effective staff as was found at NGLTF in those years. Twenty-five years ago, family issues were not near the top of the queer agenda, as they are now. Ivy Young's work with the Families Project helped make that transition possible. Kevin Berrill had become Mr. Antigay Violence. For years he traveled around the country, meeting with grassroots activists and building alliances with other ethnic and religious communities concerned about hate violence. Kevin's efforts created a national movement out of what had previously been scattered local efforts. Peri Jude Radecic, who had come to the Task Force from the National Organization for Women, was skilled on Capitol Hill and smart in her mobilization of constituents. At every board meeting, she began her staff report by saying, "Well, the bad news is that I still haven't gotten you your civil rights. But the good news is that . . ." and then proceeded to list the amazing things she had accomplished in the preceding few months.

The staff benefited from the historical moment. The years I was on the board, from 1988 to 1993, were good ones for the lesbian and gay movement. AIDS activism was exploding everywhere, and the media-savvy tactics of ACT UP gave militancy and direct action a reach broader than at any time since the early 1970s. The impact extended to the gay movement as well, with organizations growing in size and more individuals than ever before willing to come out and take risks. For the first time, serious openings were occurring at the level of state and national government. A number of states passed gay civil rights measures. And from Congress came the first significant gay- or AIDS-friendly legislation. Within the space of two years, Congress passed the Hate Crimes Statistics Act, the Americans with Disabilities Act, and the Ryan White Care Act. Each was an indicator of the movement's growing influence in politics and the community's increasing incorporation into the social fabric. The Task Force was heavily involved in each of these achievements.

And then there was Creating Change. A conference intended to bring activists together from across the country, it premiered at the end of 1988.

New to the board and with a reputation as a historian of the movement, I was invited to give one of the keynote addresses, and I used it to provide a big picture of activism and what it had accomplished in the two decades since Stonewall. More than three hundred people attended the conference, and their response was positive enough that Creating Change became an annual event. It became a place where local organizers working on a particular issue could meet with their peers, learn from one another, debate strategy and tactics, and plot out cooperative campaigns. As with any such large gathering, it also brought differences to the surface, and, at virtually every conference, there was bound to be a moment when conflict erupted very publicly. Rather than being destructive, these moments were often cathartic. Another kind of catharsis often occurred at the plenary sessions, which brought everyone together to hear a featured speaker. I particularly remember the speech given by Vito Russo, a militant AIDS activist and the author of *The Celluloid Closet*, and the one by the Reverend C. T. Vivian, a close associate of Dr. King and a longtime activist in the Southern Christian Leadership Conference. Each of them, in different ways, communicated a message of hopefulness, one that validated the power of collective action to make change and that practically had the audience rising out of our seats and marching on the citadels of power.

In the middle of my time on the NGLTF board, I had a fellowship year at a research center in Palo Alto, California. The Center for Advanced Study in the Behavioral Sciences is an academic's idea of paradise. An invitation to be a fellow there was like getting a communiqué from God saying, "Come stay in heaven for a year." Each fellow gets an office atop a California hill that looks out across the Stanford campus, with its own lake and its buildings with their red-tiled roofs, to the South Bay and the mountains on the other side. For daily companions, one has forty other smart intellectuals, almost all of whom are blissfully happy at the prospect of an uninterrupted year in Eden. The center employed a chef who, each day, prepared gourmet lunches for us. In good weather, which was most of the time, we could eat outside, surrounded by the well-tended gardens. We had a budget for copying and student help to fetch and return our library books. Really, it was a little taste of heaven, a taste of privilege such as I had never experienced.

Along with my Task Force work, the time at the Center made my life in Greensboro seem ever more unsustainable. Living in northern California, within a short drive of San Francisco, where some of my closest friends lived, I had a chance to recall what a difference it made for me to be within reach of a vibrant queer community. In the Bay Area, I had an abundance of personal intimacy, intellectual stimulation, and political camaraderie. With Estelle Freedman, Allan Bérubé, and Nancy Stoller, three close friends and scholars who were very much social justice activists, I was in a year-long study group that pushed all of our work forward. That whole year, my mood was so euphoric that I managed not only to continue my work with the Task Force but also to shape and complete a book of essays and to launch a major new research project, a biography of Bayard Rustin.

Not that Greensboro was remaining fixed in time. It too was changing. An AIDS service organization had formed there in the late 1980s, though it was discreetly called the Triad Health Project. The local community had sent a contingent to the 1987 March on Washington, and the experience precipitated a flurry of activism after folks returned home. When police made arrests at a local cruising spot in the downtown, it sparked small protests. A countywide activist organization formed, and it quickly began a study of discrimination in employment. We succeeded in getting hearings before the Greensboro Human Rights Commission and the City Council about the need for civil rights protections and a city nondiscrimination policy, though the city manager and city attorney together managed to forestall any serious movement in these directions. Activism was also percolating in a number of other North Carolina communities in these years, enough to sustain an annual Pride Event that rotated among cities. Fifteen hundred queers marching through the streets of Charlotte, with its well-organized Southern Baptist clergy, is a lot more inspiring than watching several hundred floats wend their way through Boystown in Chicago or along Market Street in San Francisco.

I began to notice some change on my campus, as well. In the early 1990s, for the first time, a few students in my history of sexuality class were coming out—sometimes right at the start of the semester, sometimes as the class went on. One year, I shaped my seminar in the Residential College around autobiographies. I wanted to teach post-1945 US history through memoirs that focused on social identities and oppression—race, gender, class, and sexuality specifically—and have students do autobiographical writing on each of these themes as a way of bringing the course up to the present. Only one of the books I used, Paul Monette's *Becoming a Man*, was gay themed, but the seminar drew in almost all of the gay, lesbian, and bisexual students in the program. There were enough of them that it allowed for a dialogue to occur, not very common in those years, between gay and straight young adults.

Other markers of change extended beyond my undergraduates. By the '90s, there was enough of a gay studies literature in circulation that I started having students apply to our master's degree program because they wanted to work with me on gay history or the history of sexuality. One year, I had a sufficiently large group of students to be able to teach a lesbian and gay history course for the first time. It was startling to find my full intellectual and personal self in the classroom. The campus was also hiring junior faculty who, although their work was not queer focused, were young enough that they took being out of the closet for granted. Finally, we were able to form a faculty-staff group at UNCG, although success was its undoing. As the numbers who came to meetings grew, so too did the reluctance to press for any changes at the university until, finally, the group devolved into a now-and-then potluck gathering.

My unhappiness began to infest my home life. Even though Jim hadn't been able to come with me for my fellowship year in California, I went anyway. The long separation was especially hard on him. While I was having fun in paradise, he was at home, having to get used to a roommate to share household expenses. Then, once I returned to Greensboro, my dissatisfaction was so deep that I spent more and more time traveling. I attended Task Force meetings in Washington, visited friends in New York and California, scheduled research trips for weeks at a time in the summer, and went to professional conferences whenever I could. One year I counted more than a hundred nights away from home. Of course, this may have been a bit of a blessing for Jim because, increasingly, when I was home, I wasn't much fun to be with. I carped and criticized and found fault, magnifying small differences into major dramas. Jim's easygoing midwestern farm ways were no match for my New York meanness, and our verbal fights bruised him and only left me angrier.

When I look back on all of this, I think what was worst about it is that Jim wasn't having an easy time either. For instance, tenure protected me from any serious consequences for being out of the closet. Not Jim. He, too, was out. He didn't know how not to be. But it made life hard for him in the world of work. There was one work place in particular where the job particularly suited his skills and temperament and where he stayed for four years. But the homophobia kept extending its tentacles around him until, finally, he was unceremoniously let go, with twenty-four hours' notice. It was ugly, and three difficult start-and-stop years of short-term employment ensued. But I was so caught in my own woes that I had little emotional slack for his.

Whatever dissatisfactions I had with life in Greensboro, the university was always fair to me. I was appreciated and respected by my colleagues, asked to direct the graduate program in history, and put in charge of searches for new faculty. My tenure case sailed through, and I was later promoted to full professor after just a few years. Still, however well thought of I was on my home campus, I continued to strike out in my efforts to find another academic position. A full professor with three well-received books, I never once was a serious contender for any other job I applied for. I never received an interview at another campus during my twelve-year stay in North Carolina.

Finally, the moment came, after a particularly difficult stretch in my relationship with Jim, when I had to admit that my life was unraveling and that no effort at adapting, no matter how determined, would let me reach contentment in Greensboro. The cultural gulf was too deep. It was as if, green card in hand, I had to decide whether to take the next step toward citizenship. I knew that I couldn't. Jim, too, was ready to leave. Among my network of nonacademic friends and acquaintances, I put out the word. I wanted to relocate, and I was prepared to leave academic life in order to do it. A few months later, I got a call from Melinda Paras, the new executive director at NGLTF. She wanted to set up a policy institute at the Task Force. She imagined it as something of a "think tank" for the gay movement, something that brought together the research of academics and the energy of activists in creative, innovative ways. "Are you interested in building and directing something like this?" Melinda wanted to know. "Do you even need to ask?" I thought. It took a few more months for everything to fall into place, but in June 1995, a few weeks after classes ended, Jim and I packed everything, rented out our house on Magnolia Street, and moved to Washington, DC.

It would be hard to imagine a more dramatic contrast than that between the work culture of the academy, especially in a non-elite university, and that of an advocacy organization like NGLTF. Once I had made it through the first years of teaching and had a full set of courses prepared, the work demands were manageable. Every May, when the school year ended, I had a sense of closure, either for a job well done or, occasionally, for a class mercifully over. Each fall offered a fresh beginning. I could leave old mistakes behind and approach a new group of students with the intention of making this class sparkle. At the Task Force, and at many other organizations where staff see themselves as having a mission, the work is never done. As Peri used to tell us, "We still don't have our rights." At the end of every day, no matter how hard one has worked, there is an abiding sense of insufficiency. The "to do" list never shortens, and urgency often accompanies even the most routine work. Many NGLTF staff members regularly put in sixty hours a week and rarely took comp time to cool down. Plus, the budget was always so tight that there was never enough money to accomplish what needed doing.

In the two years that I worked there, these tendencies were magnified by the particular circumstances of the times. In 1994 the Republicans had captured control of Congress for the first time in forty years, and the "Gingrich Revolution" had arrived in town. Among many queer activists, particularly those at NGLTF, the feeling grew—and grew and grew—that Armageddon was approaching. The antigay rhetoric of the Christian Right was becoming ever more inflammatory, and it found a welcome home in the Republican Party. The breaking issue as I arrived in town was same-sex marriage. News from Hawaii was making the easily deluded within the activist community believe that gay marriage might arrive soon. But, instead, the right wing was using the prospect to launch a frontal attack. The new Republican Congress made it easy to pass a "Defense of Marriage" Act that Bill Clinton, a Democratic president, did not hesitate to sign. Moreover, in state after state, legislatures debated—and often passed—bills that embedded a new layer of homophobia in legal codes. In some states, antigay forces put referenda on the ballot, which provided the opportunity for large majorities to express their homophobia in the voting booth.

The job excited me in more ways than I could have imagined. No matter how stressful the work setting, no matter how intense the daily pressure, there was something exhilarating about my days. Even if everything that needed doing did not get accomplished, at least I had the sense that my work, including the most mundane tasks, was worth doing. I couldn't say the same of most university committee meetings. There were also shared moments that were unforgettable. I remember in particular the spring of 1996. We all knew that the Supreme Court would be handing down its decision in the Colorado Amendment 2 case. The voters in Colorado had narrowly approved a ballot initiative four years earlier that invalidated all local gay rights ordinances and prohibited any future ones from being enacted. In effect, it said to the gay, lesbian, and bisexual citizens there—and, indeed, to anyone who cared about gay issues—that democracy does not extend to you, that the democratic process is off limits when it comes to these matters. We knew that, if the high court sustained the constitutionality of Amendment 2, then similar ballot initiatives would pop up in many states and would likely pass. Every morning, in the office, we were on "court alert" for the first couple of hours until, finally, one day, we heard the good news. In clear unambiguous terms, the court declared Amendment 2 unconstitutional. Judge Anthony Kennedy, who drafted the opinion in *Romer v. Evans*, used words that struck a powerful chord in my gay soul and, I know, in the souls of others, too. "A state cannot so deem a class of people a stranger to its laws," he wrote. The sentence countered, so precisely, the feelings of alienation and difference that gay oppression bred into us.

Not many days had the zing of that one. And the times, as I said, were politically rough ones for NGLTF and for the gay movement more generally. Still, working there day after day for two years left me hopeful and excited. I felt a little bit like Rip Van Winkle, asleep for many years and then waking to a world that looks astoundingly different. The scope of gay, lesbian, and, increasingly, bisexual and transgender activism in the mid-1990s was breathtakingly broad. This was intensely obvious at the annual Creating Change conference, where attendees were now in the thousands. My job put me on the road a good bit and pushed me to network not only with academics doing useful research but also with gay and lesbian community centers, legal groups, statewide lobbying coalitions, local queer press, and many others who might have a stake in the work of this emerging policy institute I was shaping. As in almost every other sphere of life in these years, the Internet and the World Wide Web were reshaping how work got done and expanding exponentially access to information. Sitting at my desk, working through just the news clips that would reach me each day by e-mail, I felt as if I had a new grasp on how far the reach of the "gay revolution" in America extended. All around the country, one had the sense that lesbians and gay men were reconfiguring the patterns of everyday life, altering the practices of institutions large and small, re-making American habits of thought, and changing public culture. In the late 1990s, it wasn't cool to talk of radicalism or revolution or social trans-formation, but in fact the distance between the world as it existed at the time of Stonewall and what it looked like a generation later warranted such hyperbole.

I had another kind of Rip Van Winkle reaction to the experience of daily life in Washington. I lived in the Adams Morgan section of town, as mixed a residential area as one is likely to find anywhere. The blend of housing stock in the neighborhood was such that the prosperous and the struggling might live on the same block. White, black, and Latino faces graced the streets. There were families and young singles, gay, lesbian, and straight, all living in the same neighborhood. And not much evidence, at least overtly, of festering hostilities between them.

If I walked down the hill, to the Dupont Circle section of town, the mix shifted and the neighborhood became definably gay. I don't know what the headcounters at the Census Bureau would report, but I have often thought that an area needs only perhaps 10 to 15 percent of its residents to be gay men for it to have the aura of a "gay ghetto." Add a few bars to the mix, a gay bookstore, and a handful of other queer-identified businesses, and the pedestrian traffic of gay visitors from other parts of town will increase to the point that we seem to shape the character of the neighborhood.

But I say "we" advisedly. What became evidently clear, returning to urban life after a dozen years away, is that men in their twenties and early thirties shape gay male public culture. When I lived in New York, I was part of the "we." Now I was somewhat of an outsider looking in, observing a scene of which I was not fully a part. It was more than slightly unnerving to realize that age had made me invisible to most of the men strolling along the streets. But it was also bracing to observe what, to my eyes, was like a brand-new world.

Put simply, many gay men—and the worlds they moved in and through—had changed. Some of the change was superficial, literally about surface and appearance. Gym culture had become so much a part of the lives of many gay men that the bodies that were moving around the streets of DC were different in size, shape, and tone from what I remembered. Add to this the tattoos and piercings that were now commonplace among a younger generation, and it almost seemed as if I was of a different species, heading toward extinction. But there was something more subtle as well, something less easily definable. In New York in the early and mid-1970s, I can remember an excitement that came just from congregating in groups in Greenwich Village, whether outside a gay bar or at a busy intersection. Being together in public was a version of coming out, a collective assertion of identity that in itself seemed consequential. Now, two decades later, on the busy streets near Dupont Circle and in the surrounding neighborhoods, younger gay men held hands, kissed, waved at their friends, and chatted in groups, all in ways so lacking in self-consciousness that it seemed, dare I say it, normal. They were just going about the business of daily life in the city and engaging in social interactions that were completely unremarkable.

While the ability to live out one's gayness was all to the good, other changes seemed less welcome. Take, for instance, the Pride Marches that occurred in many cities each June to commemorate the Stonewall uprising in New York and that gathered activists all together, at one time, for an assertive march and rally. I marched for the first time in 1973 in New York, with a contingent of activists whom I knew well. The energy generated in us by this march through several miles of Manhattan streets was unforgettable, and it spilled over into the work we did in succeeding months. After that experience, I marched every year until I left New York, a decade later. In North Carolina, where annual Pride Marches began during the years I lived there, the size was much, much smaller, but that only made the act of marching feel even more consequential. Those of us who were out in the street were pushing the envelope of visibility. Now, back in a big northeastern city in the second half of the '90s, I discovered that the Pride "Parade," as it was now rechristened, had morphed into something entirely different. As the date approached for it in 1996, after my first year in Washington, I asked my colleagues one day at the Task Force whether we would all march together as an NGLTF contingent. They all looked at me funny, as if I was out of my mind, until Karen, one of the more militant staffers, simply said, "*Nobody* marches in the parade." I was dumbstruck. Nonetheless, when the day arrived, I was on the sidewalk along the route, determined at least to cheer the marchers on. Yet this was not like the marches that I had known. It *was* more like a parade, with floats and entertainment and crowds of onlookers drinking beer and cheering the participants on. Occasionally, a small contingent of activists from a small-town organization would appear, and for them it did still seem like an assertion of identity. But for almost everyone else, it was outdoor entertainment on a summer Sunday afternoon.

Engaging as the work at the Task Force was, by the second year it became clear that this was not for me. To the degree that I succeeded in building a policy institute, my main work would become managing staff, planning events, and raising money. The work that I was most passionate about and did best—research, writing, and public speaking—would be what others in the Institute did. And so, for the same reason that I had pursued an academic job years before, so that I would have time to "do history," I left the position at the Task Force after two years.

I applied for and managed to get a fellowship to allow me to return to my interrupted work on a biography of Bayard Rustin. The Rustin biography, which I draw upon for some of the essays in this collection, is without question the most fully satisfying and deeply engrossing major project I've engaged in. His life and career seemed to touch upon everything that matters to me. In the most expansive sense, he was a lifelong agitator for justice. His reach was extraordinarily wide—racial justice, world peace and nonviolence, socialism and economic justice. And he faced a gay oppression as fierce as anything one can imagine. Rustin's career offers inspiration, even as it also pushes one to ask tough questions about the vision, the strategy, and the tactics required to create a peaceful world in which resources are fairly and widely shared. With every other book I have written or edited, when the book was done I was ready to put it behind me and move on to the next project. With Rustin, I never want to leave him behind. I began giving talks about his life while still working on the book and have continued to take whatever opportunities come my way to engage in discussion about the issues that his career as an activist raises.

The fellowship allowed me to put off a return to Greensboro. But, I knew in my heart, and so did Jim, that we could not go back. During my third year in DC, I took the leap and resigned my faculty position at UNCG. Giving up tenure—aka lifetime job security—without another job is not something to do lightly, but it seemed necessary and right. I patched things together—small travel grants to do research, another fellowship for a second year of work on the book, some speaking gigs here and there—and spent down whatever savings I had. Meanwhile, I remained connected to the world that NGLTF had opened to me by continuing to help with Policy Institute projects and participating in conferences and other gatherings to strengthen activist networks. And I applied for academic jobs, hoping that it would go better and I would have more choices than I did two decades earlier when I first pursued the academic route.

This time around I did have a number of campus interviews and options. Sometimes I think it was a sign that times had changed, that there was more openness toward and acceptance of the kind of work I did.

At other times I wonder if having a residence in the nation's capital and experience at a "Policy Institute" gave more credibility to my CV than a Greensboro address.

The job I took was at the University of Illinois at Chicago (UIC). It was a moment in the school's history when it was pushing against academic routines. Stanley Fish, the recently arrived dean in the College of Liberal Arts and Sciences, was a high-profile academic who took special delight in upsetting orthodoxies, whether of the right, left, or center. One way this expressed itself was by putting resources into newer, less "traditional" academic programs, thus making it possible for units like Gender & Women's Studies (GWS) to do a significant amount of hiring. UIC's GWS Program offered me a position, and with it came the opportunity to teach courses related to LGBT studies and sexuality. As with my arrival in Greensboro in the mid-1980s, I became a brief news item, but, this time around, the reporting newspaper thought it was a hiring coup rather than a threat to the community's youth.

Even more than when I moved to DC, coming to Chicago, a city with which I had almost no prior experience, provided dramatic evidence of at least certain kinds of change. "Gay" was in the process of becoming openly institutionalized as part of the city's life. One might say that it had been invited into a newer style of machine politics that incorporated representatives from a wider range of identity groups. In the northside Lakeview neighborhood, commonly referred to as "Boystown," the city had recently erected rainbow towers for more than a half mile along its main thoroughfare, clearly designating it as gay. The city also sponsored a Gay and Lesbian Hall of Fame. Every year, individuals and organizations with significant histories of championing LGBT freedom were inducted into it, and the mayor himself presided at the ceremony. There was a city liaison to the LGBT community, and the community sustained a massive number of organizations that had a broad range of missions and appealed to varied constituencies.

Before taking these developments as heralding the arrival of a queer utopia, however, one needs to reckon with other sorts of changes as well. As in DC, the annual Pride March had been transformed into a festive parade. Its most notable features were the high number of corporate-sponsored floats, intended to let the hundreds of thousands of onlookers know that their gay dollars were wanted, and a similarly high number of floats sponsored by elected officials, who hoped by their participation to reap rewards at the ballot box. Sandwiched here and there were much smaller contingents of activists. Meanwhile, the streets were lined with massive numbers of spectators spanning the full spectrum of sexual and gender identities, many of them drinking themselves silly. Quite a large portion of them did not even know that the parade commemorated an uprising at the Stonewall Inn that, a generation ago, gave birth to a gay liberation movement that made such public celebrations possible.

Mainstreaming and corporatization were reflected as well in the developing plans for a community center to anchor the north end of Boystown and its rainbow towers. Government was providing a good deal of support by making a site available and affordable. But in this neoliberal twenty-first-century economy, the Center on Halsted, as it came to be known, had to rent half of its building to Whole Foods in order to be financially viable. While the building's beautiful gleaming structure with massive windows facing on to the street seemed overtly welcoming, its social service programming brought large numbers of queer youth of color, often gender nonconforming, to a neighborhood that had gentrified. Many of the "gentry" of the neighborhood were not always happy at the presence of the "common people." They were not exactly receptive to seeing these youth as part of *their* community and at times actively campaigned for police "protection" from what they perceived as "unwanted elements" in the neighborhood.

As I came to learn when I began doing research on Chicago history (a number of the short pieces I have written on Chicago are included in this volume), the city has a long history of neighborhood segregation based on race, ethnicity, and, of course, class. In the minds of many, gay often came to be identified with white, an association that some of the community's own institutions fostered. Look through Chicago's queer press from the 1970s and 1980s, for instance, when Boystown was coming into being, and one will notice how commonly the listings of bars, clubs, and other meeting places conspicuously left out South Side locations, where the largest number of African American Chicagoans lived.

One of the pleasures of teaching at UIC is that the campus departs in significant ways from that aspect of the city's history. The student body is amazingly diverse. Drawn heavily from the greater Chicago area, it is more working class than not, and it pulls in students from across a wide spectrum of racial and ethnic identities. I have had classes in which the students could trace their family origins to five continents. And, to give credit where credit is due, the GWS program and its classes seem especially effective at drawing in students that range across this broad population.

Working at UIC has offered almost continuous evidence of the way this new century departs from the previous one. In the fifteen years that I have been here, LGBT people and issues have become much more integrated into the daily life of the university. There is a staffed LGBT center that serves students, does significant campus programming, and works closely with other "diversity" centers. There are faculty members in a broad range of departments and schools whose research focuses on LGBT issues. And there are courses that students can take to introduce them to issues involving sexual and gender identity.

Although I have to confess to missing the standard US history courses that I taught for many years in North Carolina, the opportunity to teach these gay-centered classes has been a joy. My signature course, the one that has offered an inexhaustible supply of treasurable moments, is called "Sexuality and Community." I think of it as a kind of "Queer 101" class. In the first part of the semester, we do some history: from the "worst time to be queer" in the 1950s and 1960s through the era of gay liberation and lesbian feminism in the 1970s to the AIDS epidemic of the 1980s and 1990s and finally to the explosion in popular-culture visibility at the turn of the century. We use a range of materials—newspaper articles exposing "nests of deviates" hidden in the city; coming-of-age novels populated by rebellious young lesbians; angry political manifestos; art with a political message; and documentary films. We then move on to explore in depth some contemporary issues, ranging from marriage and family to the debates within religious denominations to questions of school policies and the struggles of youth.

The classroom experience has provided a mass of evidence for charting both changes and continuities over the past generation. When I began teaching at UIC, the relationship of most students to LGBT issues and identities reminded me in many ways of what I had experienced in Greensboro. A small number of students in the course of the semester revealed themselves to be gay or lesbian or bisexual or gender nonconforming. The great majority of the students did not, and they were taking the course because they were curious to learn about the topic. For all of them, I was introducing a history and a set of issues about which they knew nothing. The picture of intense oppression that I drew for them of the decades just before they were born made sense, because it was not so different from the world of the 1980s in which they had grown up. And the rebelliousness and the mobilizations for justice associated with gay liberation, feminism, and the fight against AIDS likewise hit a chord in them because these, too, did not seem so distant.

Just fifteen years later, the experience and outlook of most students are very different. More of them come out in class and do it quite easily. Almost everyone knows someone gay or lesbian. Many have gone to high schools with a Gay/Straight Alliance. Many have family members who are out of the closet. For some, the AIDS epidemic has struck close to home; they know someone, usually in their family, who is HIV positive or who died of AIDS. They have friends with lesbian or gay parents. And, through popular culture, whether it is Ellen DeGeneres or Ricky Martin or RuPaul or the characters in *Glee*, queer seems an integral part of their world. It seems so natural, in fact, so "normal," that the depth of oppression just a generation or more ago registers as unfathomable to them. Yet the political declarations of the Gay Liberation Front and Radicalesbians and ACT UP sit uncomfortably, as well. Why are they so enraged, why are they so hostile, today's students ask. I think of the current cohort of students as part of a post-Ellen, post-9/11 generation. Coming of age after Ellen's coming out, they take it for granted that LGBT people exist in society and are, in fact, everywhere to be found. But, in our post-9/11 world, so obsessed with danger and insecurity, a world in which political manifestos are associated with terrorism, the radical politics that opened the space for gay normalcy seems alien to many.

In a different way, however, the classroom offers evidence of an unfortunate continuity with the past. Despite all the changes, despite the visibility of LGBT people, students come to these classes and know nothing about the topic at hand. They have not heard of the Stonewall uprising. They do not know who Bayard Rustin was. The career and assassination of Harvey Milk are a revelation to them. AIDS and HIV are simply something that exists. And this ignorance is not related to their identities. Wherever they fit on the identity spectrum, all of this is news to them. I love the outrage that they display at these pieces of history that have been kept from them. But it also reminds me that, the increasing acceptance and normalcy of same-sex marriage notwithstanding, we are still a long way from a world where one can come of age with a sexual and gender identity that is not of the majority and not have it be a negative marker of difference.

The essays in this volume all come from this post-Ellen world of queer visibility and this post-9/11 world of heightened conservatism. They were all written after I moved to Chicago, yet they are informed by and draw upon my experience as both a historian and an activist in the 1980s and 1990s. Many originated as talks before a variety of audiences—some academic but more often audiences of activists and community people. A few have appeared before in anthologies on queer politics or history, and the set of Chicago stories initially appeared in the *Windy City Times*, a local LGBT newspaper. All of them reflect my continuing interest in sexuality, identity, and social movements and how historical insight can inform our contemporary approaches to them.

The essays in part I address activist audiences. In the first two, "The State of Our Movements" and "Beyond Queer Nationalism," I look at the broad sweep of LGBT activism since the 1960s, assess some of the forms that activism took and the gains that it has produced, and offer some suggestions about the future. The first comes from keynote addresses delivered at Creating Change conferences and the second from a talk to a national gathering of Point Foundation scholars, a group of students who are also community activists. "The Gay Movement and the Left" was written for a forum on the topic. It draws upon my own personal activist history and my knowledge of the influence of left-wing, radical perspectives on LGBT activism, and it asks why the left has remained relatively detached from queer politics. "Listening to Rustin" is an attempt to pull from the life of an extraordinary social justice activist some broader lessons about how to make change in the world. It was delivered at conferences commemorating the centennial of Bayard Rustin's birth.

In part II, I focus on the process of researching and writing history. Some of the pieces draw directly from my own experience. "Why I Write" is an autobiographical reflection on what has motivated me to do history and what has kept me passionate about it. "Putting Sex into History and History into Sex" explores how my own work has evolved thematically over three decades. In "History, Social Movements, and Community Organizing," I attempt to condense some core insights about what makes for good historical writing on these topics and argue that experience as an activist can enrich the history we produce. "If I Knew Then" focuses specifically on the practice of oral history, which has been an essential part of my work over several decades, and suggests how my appreciation and understanding of it has changed over time. In the last two essays in part II, I look more broadly at the emergence of community-based LGBT history projects in the 1970s and 1980s, reflect on what motivated them, and discuss how sharing historical knowledge became a means of building community.

35

The pieces in part III all focus on Chicago. The topics themselves are not necessarily unique to Chicago. Rather, they show the way that local episodes can illustrate broader themes in LGBT history: the opportunities that World War II offered for gender nonconformity, the depth of the Cold War persecution of gays and lesbians, the phenomenon of lesbian pulp novels, the rise of a new militancy in the late 1960s, and other such topics. While I believe these stories are interesting in their own right, I think they can also serve as examples of the basic truth that, all around us, in whatever community we live in or decide to write about, there are instructive stories from the past that need to be rediscovered and told.

The final set of essays attempts to draw out explicitly some lessons from history. It makes a difference, as I argue in "Remembering Bayard Rustin," that Rustin's place in history has been largely forgotten. It narrows and distorts our understanding of how change happens and how social justice goals are achieved. In "Some Lessons from *Lawrence*," I assess the significance of the Supreme Court decision that finally eliminated sodomy laws from US penal codes, and I argue in "Rethinking Queer History" that we need to see LGBT experience as thoroughly integral to the main themes and developments in US history. Finally, in the closing essay, I use history to offer a critique of the prioritizing of same-sex marriage as an activist issue and dissent from the inflated claims that most commentators have made about its significance.

History, as I frequently tell my students, is above all a story of change. The changes that have occurred in the past five decades around LGBT issues in the United States have been vast, and the new century gives us a vantage point from which to see the depth and breadth of these changes. But not all change is for the best, and change offers new challenges, as well. I hope the historical reflections in these essays provide a resource for understanding and assessing change, for taking stock of the kind of change that still needs to happen, and for having a better grasp of the ways to get there.

Part I

Strategizing Change

1

The State of Our Movements

Some Reflections

Twice in the past decade, I was given the opportunity to share my thoughts about the state of the LGBT movement and issues of strategic direction. In November 2005 in Oakland and in January 2009 in Denver, I spoke at plenary sessions of the National Gay and Lesbian Task Force's Creating Change conference, perhaps the largest annual gathering in the United States of LGBT activists. At the time of the Oakland conference, George W. Bush was in the first year of his second term as president. When we gathered in Denver, Barack Obama had been inaugurated just a few days earlier.

In the essay that follows, I've preserved the tone of speaking to an audience. I have edited the comments a bit to reduce repetition, but inevitably some observations recur in the two parts. The views expressed in 2005 naturally informed my musings in 2009, but the new context of an Obama presidency certainly shifted some of my emphases and, as I suggest in the remarks, opened me to new ideas and perspectives.

Oakland, November 2005

I started in the grassroots wing of the movement; there was no other wing, really, in the early 1970s. I became an activist by meeting in a living room

39

with other gay men, lesbians, and bisexuals, deciding to take action, and giving ourselves a name. I remember when the National Gay Task Force was formed in 1973, I saw it as a dangerous sign of the movement's growing conservatism because, I thought, "Why would anyone want to engage in a dialogue with a federal government run by Richard Nixon!" While Task Force staff got elected as delegates to the 1976 Democratic Convention, I and just about every other gay man I knew were demonstrating loudly outside the convention.

From the beginning, the world of ideas mattered to me. I learned in the 1960s that there is a politics of knowledge and that without control of our history, without the power to shape the ideas and the information about us that circulated in the culture, we were lost. I've devoted myself to that for thirty years. When I started, I couldn't get a job doing queer cultural and educational work. I taught and lectured in movement meeting places and wrote in the kind of movement publications that no longer exist. Now I have a tenured job at a major university and have to turn down publishing opportunities. My own personal situation has shifted dramatically—from margin to mainstream, you might say.

Much as I value the world of culture and writing, I know that ideas and images aren't everything. I remember getting very excited in the mid-1980s when I saw what was starting to happen at NGLTF. Suddenly it had a staff—people like Urvashi Vaid and Sue Hyde and Kevin Berrill and Ivy Young and Peri Jude Radecic—who were grappling with what it meant to have a politics of sexuality and who understood that a national organization was only as strong and as effective as its ties to a vibrant grassroots activism. The Task Force was trying to bind the local and the national, a politics of identity and a politics of power, tightly together. My excitement over that led me to a dozen-year-long history with the organization.

Let me say one thing more about where I'm coming from. I spent more than a decade researching and writing about the life of Bayard Rustin. It scrambled every answer I thought I had about making change and raised questions I still don't know the answer to. Rustin was a radical. His goal was radical transformation, not itty-bitty reform, and he believed it would come only through masses and masses of people activating themselves to pursue justice. But he also came to the conclusion that the fight isn't between transformation and mainstreaming. Instead, he urged his fellow radicals to figure out how to make mainstreaming one of the tactics in the radical arsenal, to figure out how coalitions could be built between those on the outside and some of those on the inside in the interest of social and economic justice.

So, that's a bit of where I'm coming from. Now, what do I think we are up against as a movement, and what do we have going for us? I'm going to start with some very broad-stroke answers.

What do I never forget that we are up against? First of all, a global system that produces and defends inequality, no matter what the cost.

Let me start by saying that not everything about capitalism is bad. Five centuries of it have created enough wealth and produced enough scientific knowledge that it is possible to eliminate hunger on the planet, to contain epidemic diseases, to guarantee literacy to everyone, and to do this in ways that preserve the environment for future generations.

Will capitalism ever do this? No. It puts profit above human need, and it will always put profit first until people acting together impose limits on it that can't be evaded.

What does this have to do with an LGBT movement? The inequalities that capitalism creates spawn religious and ethnic and national hatreds. Capitalism makes jobs disappear. It creates continuing and permanent insecurity. It requires huge militaries to defend itself. If any of you think for a minute that unbridled market capitalism will create a world in which queer people have a safe and secure place, you're a fool.

If that isn't enough to be up against, we also live under the rule of a political elite in this country whose primary goal is to starve the public sector to death. The goal of the governing Republican coalition for the past quarter century has been to come as close as they possibly can to dismantling every aspect of government except the military, the criminal justice system, and the national security apparatus. If it has its way, even the public schools (the rhetoric of "no child left behind" notwithstanding) will wither away. This has been their goal for twenty-five years, and there are no signs that they are finished.

Play out the implications of this for our communities: What does this mean for AIDS education, treatment, and research? What does it mean for our desire to have gay studies programs be part of public higher education and to have a queer-affirming comprehensive sex education curriculum be part of the public schools? What does it mean for those of us who, because of homophobia, are likely to age with fewer attachments to wide family networks and can count on almost nothing from a Social Security system that is already insufficient and endangered? Each of you can probably think of other examples of how the current political economy in this country is a threat to our survival.

Here's one more thing closer to home that we are up against, something inside our own communities: we are up against the unequal distribution of the gains of the LGBT movement.

It was never true that all of us were equally the victim of homophobia or that each of us was targeted by gay oppression in the same way. But, a generation ago, oppression struck so heavily, it was so thick and pervasive, that we all knew that there was danger out there, that it could come at any time, and that it could strike any one of us. Street queens and high-toned opera queens may have looked at each other across a class divide, but they also knew that the police could arrest any of them at any time.

Today that's no longer true. Large segments of the LGBT population—segments shaped by educational privilege, by skin color, by where you live, by how gender normative you are—do not have to give much thought any more to how oppressed they are. For some, life is ever so much better than it was the night the police came to the Stonewall Inn.

But read the Amnesty International report on police harassment of trans youth of color, and it will remind you, if you did not already know it, that oppression in its rawest and most brutal form is alive and well and affecting only some of us.

What does this do to community solidarity, to a sense of shared urgency, to how we set agendas in this movement?

That's the bad news, or at least some of it. But we also have a lot going for us, and we shouldn't ever forget it.

We have everything we have built over the past generation—the organizations, the community institutions, the bridges to other communities and allies.

We have every victory we've achieved. It matters that sodomy laws are gone, that the American Psychiatric Association has removed homosexuality from its list of mental illnesses, that many cities and states have added sexual orientation to civil rights laws, and that some have now added gender identity or expression. It matters that there are welcoming congregations, that many workplaces have partnership benefits, and that bookstores and libraries are filled with queer books.

We have each other. Look around the room. Look at the relationships we have built, the skills and experience we have accumulated. We have fought like the dickens to find each other, and many of us know that we would give our lives for one another.

We have our everyday acts of heroism and courage. We have our outrage at injustice, our unwillingness to remain silent, and our refusals to pass as straight. We have our presence in every institution and in every community, among the most oppressed and the most powerful.

With this context in mind, what do I think the LGBT movement has done right, and what has it done wrong?

When I first started thinking about this, I imagined coming up with two lists—a list of the things we are doing right and a list of the things we are making a mess of. But it wasn't that simple because the things that I thought were right invariably had a flip side, and the things that seemed to be a mess could not just be dismissed as failures. So, it's this sense of complexity and contradiction that I want to emphasize.

When I think about what is right with the movement, the first thing that pops up is the visibility we have achieved over the past generation.

Imagine that the only type of visibility is a headline that reads "Police Raid Den of Perverts and Arrest 50." Imagine that the only type of visibility is a movie in which the lesbian character commits suicide. Imagine that every time someone is publicly identified as queer, it is a story of tragedy or scandal or shame.

This is what life was like for us fifty years ago. The visibility we have achieved in the past generation is like the air and water we need to sustain life. What we have achieved is phenomenal.

But then I think about the particular visibility we have achieved, and I think, "We've got a problem." Try to attach particular faces to that visibility. Think about two of the most visible representations of who we are—Ellen and Will. Think about some others—Melissa Etheridge and Tony Kushner, Rosie O'Donnell and Barney Frank. I love them all! But they are just a few examples of how "gay" has come to mean "white" in America.

Think about what happens when gay means white. It makes gay a form of wealth and privilege. It shouts to communities of color that gay is white folks. It allows queers of color to be stigmatized in their home communities as turncoats, folks who have gone over to the other side. It fractures our strength and makes coalition building a much more difficult task. It points us toward single-issue, lowest-common-denominator gay agendas. It gives the lie to the slogan "We are everywhere" and makes our rainbow flags symbols of opportunism. Until we shift decisively the colors of our visibility, visibility will be at best a double-edged sword.

What else is both right and wrong with the movement? The fight for access to marriage.

I remember a conversation I had in 1995 at the NGLTF offices with Marjorie Hill, who had been the liaison of Mayor David Dinkins to the queer community in New York. Marjorie was describing what happened when she mentioned in the office that she and her partner had decided to have a wedding. Suddenly coworkers who had kept their distance from this very public lesbian could not stop talking with her. They gave advice; they asked questions; they shared experiences. In my intro-level gay studies course, I always show the documentary *Chicks in White Satin*, about a lesbian couple's decision to have a wedding. Even some of the straight male students in the class get teary-eyed.

With marriage, we have found an issue that pierces the homophobia in the hearts of heterosexuals like no other issue of ours has. The campaign for marriage has created an arena in which our joy, our exuberance, our pleasure with each other is on public display. Marriage has made millions of heterosexuals shed tears of happiness for us. Marriage inserts us into the center of social life and cultural ritual instead of our being forced to the margins, separate and outside.

But that's only one side of the story. The fight for marriage equality is also one of the things that is most wrong with the movement. The rhetoric of the marriage campaign and the frenzy of the marriage enthusiasts have created the illusion that same-sex marriage is a panacea, the magic bullet that will end homophobia and oppression and will, finally, bring equality. Marriage has made court cases, lawyers, and litigation seem like the cutting edge of social change. Marriage has allowed a small number of individuals to hijack the movement's agenda. Marriage has eclipsed most other issues on the LGBT agenda—issues like AIDS prevention and services, issues like the rights of queer youth to self-determination—issues, in other words, that really are matters of life and death. Worst of all, the campaign for marriage equality has done what no other queer campaign of the past generation has done. It has generated a whole new body of antigay law.

Let me suggest one thing more that is both very right with the movement and very wrong: the strength of our national organizations.

We are living in a world of illusion if we think we can achieve our biggest and most ambitious goals without strong and powerful national voices. National institutions shape our worlds. Congress, the military, the Department of Health and Human Services, the American Medical Association, the National Collegiate Athletic Association, and many others deeply affect our status and well-being.

I'm glad that the budgets of Lambda Legal and NGLTF are large and growing. I'm happy that there is a national Gay, Lesbian, Straight Education Network, and a National Center for Lesbian Rights, and a national Gay and Lesbian Alliance against Defamation. These organizations give us continuity and expertise and shared memory as a movement. They allow us to penetrate institutions that once were uniformly hostile to everything queer. Thirty-five years ago, there were no stable national organizations, and we were not better off because of it.

But our national organizations can be as wrong as they are right. Agendas get set at the top and flow down. The movement is divided between full-time professional staff and the rest of us. Our large national organizations, as well as some of the well-established local ones, can make it much harder for young adults to make their way into the movement. I think it has been a tragedy that our national organizations have mostly shied away from having chapters or affiliates as a way of making sure that links between local and national are strong and that communication is continuing, rather than weak and haphazard. And sometimes an organization can get so large that it becomes easy for its staff and board to think that "what's good for the organization is what's good for the movement."

What should we be focused on in the years ahead? When I ask myself, "What is to be done?" I find myself focused more on ways of strategizing and thinking rather than on a specific set of tasks.

For instance, I think we have to create agendas and set goals that bring individuals, organizations, movements, and communities together across lines of identity and oppression. Building unity doesn't have to mean compromising integrity or giving up our deeply felt needs. It does mean thinking beyond what Urvashi Vaid has sometimes called our "lavender bubble" and reaching for the most inclusive vision of justice we can conjure up. Instead of thinking "AIDS funding," we should think "national health insurance." Instead of thinking "same-sex marriage," we should think "security for all families and households." Instead of "queer studies programs," why not "affordable public higher education for everyone"?

I also think that a persistent tension in our movement—between what I will call queer nationalism and mainstreaming—has to go. We need to build movement organizations and community institutions at the same time that we are burrowing our way into mainstream institutions. Neither separatism nor integration alone can work as a strategy for change.

But, really, if there were only one notion I could implant in everyone's brain, one thing I could wish for, one thing I could make everyone do, it would be this: "Start drawing up NOW your forty-year plan to end oppression!"

A little more than forty years ago, in November 1964, the right wing in this country experienced the biggest political defeat in its history. Barry Goldwater, a hero to conservatives, was trounced in the presidential election. Everyone thought the Republican Party was near death. But they picked themselves up, made their long-term plans to capture the political system in this country, and have succeeded more brilliantly than any of them imagined. Their success did not happen by accident. It happened because some of them drew up long-term plans. They took themselves *that* seriously.

So, start making your forty-year plan *now*. Take yourself that seriously. Make a forty-year plan for you as an individual, for your organization, for your community, for our entire society, for the globe. Make it in cooperation with your best friends and comrades, with the members or staff of your organizations. Set out your longest-range goals—where you want things to be in forty years—and work back from there. Compare your plan to the plan of others. Work to reach agreement. And then go do it!

Don't kid yourself: while we are sitting around *not* making a forty-year plan, someone else is, and, trust me, we will not like that plan.

Denver, 2009

I have been asked to talk today about the possibilities of the moment, the opportunities and challenges that have opened to us as a result of Barack Obama's election and a Democratic majority in both houses of Congress. Across the political spectrum, almost everyone is claiming that a new political moment has arrived, even if no one is sure exactly how to define the moment.

Before I get to what I most want to say, let me open with a couple of admittedly contradictory comments.

If all of us—queer activists and our close allies—just go about doing what we individually and collectively ordinarily do, there will be lots of victories at the national level over the next four (and, I hope, eight) years.

At every level of the federal bureaucracy are folks who will be responsive to us. Across a range of issues, there will be lots of non-headline-making decisions that will be queer friendly. There are also decent chances that, with the exercise of some intelligence in our organizing, bigger victories like the repeal of "Don't Ask, Don't Tell" and passage of an inclusive Employment Nondiscrimination Act can be achieved.

On the other hand, these are not ordinary times. The length, depth, and breadth of the current economic crisis cannot be predicted. When we gather at Creating Change a year from now, perhaps we will know that the worst is behind us. But perhaps not. Already, LGBT organizations around the country are firing staff, which makes it harder to do the work they ordinarily do. If the economic crisis spreads and deepens, it may sweep all other issues aside.

But this is not what I want to talk about right now.

A few days after 9/11, I stopped reading newspapers and watching the news on television. I had just started a fellowship year free from teaching so that I could finish a biography of Bayard Rustin. After five days of compulsively watching television reporting and buying newspapers, I knew that nothing good would be on the horizon for a very long time to come. For the most part, I put news of the nation and the world aside, and I went about my business of researching, writing, and teaching history.

Last year, sometime in the spring, I flipped over and became obsessed by the news again. It was around the time of Obama's so-called race speech. It became clear to me that Obama had a really good chance of winning the nomination and, given the unpopularity of Bush, a really good chance of becoming president.

My obsessive fascination with Obama and political news was not because I judged him to be especially progressive. His platform seemed very centrist to me, what one might expect of a liberal Democrat. Neither was it because, as an orator, he surpassed any one I had heard in a long time and left me enthralled whenever I listened to a speech. It was not even because he was African American, though that made the prospect of his election especially thrilling.

No, the fascination had something to do with the content of the rhetoric, the core message that framed any particulars of his platform. Obama had a way of talking about the nation, without embracing a chauvinistic nationalism. He had a way of talking about America, without sounding jingoistic. He had a way of asking everyone to think beyond partisanship, without it sounding phony or hypocritical to me. He spoke a rhetoric that asked us to recognize how we are bound together, without pretending that there weren't differences of opinion and experience. For someone like myself, who came of age during the Vietnam War, when "America" was coming to mean aggression and destruction abroad and when appeals to unity masked attempts to suppress dissent, my attraction to Obama's oratory was nothing short of astounding.

In particular, I found myself gripped by someone whose language, assumptions, platforms, and formulations stood almost completely outside the language, assumptions, platforms, and formulations that typically come with identity politics. In fact, he rarely even explicitly acknowledged identity politics.

For most of my adulthood, something like 80 to 90 percent of my energies have been organized around identity politics, either my own or as an ally to others. I am not alone in this. Since the 1960s, identity politics has been the most dynamic force in US society. Social movements have been organized around them. Mass political mobilizations, party politics in the United States, and political rhetoric all have been filtered through the lens of identity. Beginning with a politics of race, ethnicity, and national origin, moving into a politics of gender and sexuality, and expanding further to include a politics of disability and physical difference, identity politics has made things tick in the United States.

The changes that identity politics has wrought are extraordinary. The depth, breadth, reach, and range of these movements are almost beyond our ability to catalogue. We could spend the rest of the day just making lists of all the legal, institutional, cultural, and social changes that have grown out of identity-based movements, and we still would not have exhausted the list of what has been achieved. The changes have been so great in so many arenas that historical memory of what things were like is being lost to a younger generation. For instance, when I lecture to my undergraduates on the 1950s, which I describe as "the worst time to be queer," they find the conditions of just fifty years ago unimaginable.

So, from one angle, when I think about identity politics, I think, "Hooray! Let's drink a toast to identity politics!" But, unfortunately, there are also two other undeniable though not often acknowledged results of forty-plus years of identity politics.

First of all, in every identity-based movement, the benefits have not been equally distributed. In fact, they have been wildly unevenly distributed.

For instance, Barack Obama, an African American man, is now president of the United States. Yet in the neighborhoods that surround where he lived in Chicago are countless young black men who have few prospects beyond drugs, gangs, violence, and prison. Or, to make the point very personal: I'm a tenured college professor in Chicago with a comfortable salary and secure employment. Yet, in this same city, young transgender people of color are still mercilessly harassed by the police.

Is this inequality of outcomes accidental? Is it an unintended consequence of identity politics? Or is it perhaps inherent, organic to that framework of interpreting the world and political organizing? Do our attempts to remedy some of the deficiencies of identity politics through what we speak of as intersectional politics smash that framework and rescue us from its limits? Or will it too be something that distributes benefits unequally? Identity politics has helped make the student bodies of elite educational institutions like Harvard and Princeton admirably diverse. Yet, at the same time, our urban public school systems are being financially starved into a state of collapse and are increasingly populated overwhelmingly by students of color. How will identity politics remedy that?

Second, although it is comforting to imagine identity-based movements as the basis for a multi-movement progressive coalition, bigger than the sum of its parts, few of us acknowledge that two of the most wildly successful identity movements of the past generation have been movements of the right. There is the movement of evangelical Christians, certainly a fiercely identity-based movement. Think, for instance, of how successful it has been in obstructing movement toward reproductive justice and how consistently it has opposed any movement toward LGBT equality. There has also been the identity-based movement of the filthy rich. Since the election of Ronald Reagan in 1980, the filthy rich and their supporters have so dramatically remade the tax system in the United States that the gap between them and the rest of us is much larger than it has been at any time in the past eighty years. The dismantling of a progressive federal income and corporate tax structure has led to the starving of the public sector, especially those programs that aim at economic democracy.

It is useful, and sobering, to put these two movements in the category of identity-based politics. When I think in these terms, it helps me to see that even when my kind of identity politics is motivated by fierce outrage at injustice and inequality, the "me" or "us" of an identity movement always implies and calls into existence a "them." Is it possible that even when identity politics comes from a progressive political stance, it unleashes a fractured oppositional political process rooted in antagonism? Such fracturing plays not to justice but to self-interest and resentment and competition. When you unleash those emotions in political combat, the good guys seldom win, because resentment and competition and self-interest are not the stuff of social justice.

For me, this is the kind of rethinking that Obama's public rhetoric has provoked. This is what most excites me about the Obama moment. It is about a call to reconstruct how we think about and frame goals, agendas, priorities, and campaigns. It is not about denying differences or aspiring to a phony unity rooted in pretense but about framing agendas and pursuing goals that pivot around notions of a common good in which all share the benefits. A common good: the very phrase seems deeply moral to me.

So at this moment when we are going to achieve victories and make gains, large and small, just by doing the things that our organizations normally do, can we also creatively rethink our goals? Can we move along a path that stands outside the particularities of identity—or interest group—politics? Are there ways we can frame our queer agendas so that they put us smack in the middle of broad-based campaigns that speak to a common good?

Take, for instance, the issue of youth. In the past decade or so, queer youth around the country have displayed a great deal of initiative and energy. Gay/Straight Alliances have sprung up in thousands of high schools, a phenomenon almost unimaginable to folks of my generation. At the same time, the increasing visibility of queer youth has made them especially vulnerable to verbal harassment and physical violence.

We have a network of organizations that work on issues of youth and schools, that support the efforts of the young people themselves, and that work toward measures that will create "Safe School" environments for students who identify as LGBT. This is all to the good. But do we really imagine that any amount of training of school personnel to be LGBT sensitive can make safe a school that teaches abstinence-only sex education? As long as the federal funding policies of the Bush administration that reward schools for teaching abstinence-only sex education remain in place, goals of LGBT safety and acceptance will remain illusory.

Fighting for comprehensive sex education funding is something that will benefit all young people. It is not, strictly speaking, a gay identity-based issue. Yet LGBT youth will benefit immensely from successful efforts to institutionalize comprehensive sex education.

Or take the issue of AIDS prevention. With fifty thousand new HIV infections in the United States every year, the epidemic remains urgent and of crisis proportions. The population is disproportionately young, low income, of color, and men who have sex with men. Though AIDS was never solely a gay issue, its close association in this country with gay men marked it from the beginning as "not mainstream."

At a time of great economic crisis, when the nation is debating how to stimulate the economy in ways that provide long-term benefits, why isn't the funding of community-based AIDS education and prevention near the top of the list? It would provide jobs in communities that need jobs. It would reduce long-term health costs. It would preserve large numbers of young people as healthy, productive members of society. I can hardly imagine a more productive use of federal dollars. Can the rhetoric of a common good become the vehicle for seeing AIDS prevention as a priority in this new era?

I am not suggesting that all of you drop what you are working on and fight for comprehensive sex education or funding for community-based AIDS education. I am saying that I think Obama's rhetoric offers us the opportunity and the challenge not to think in the particularities of identity or in terms of group self-interest but to imagine our goals and dreams and agendas in the context of a common good. To the degree that we are able to do that, we may have more traction in this new political world. We will be contributing to the demise of a fractured, antagonistic system of political mobilization that may not have served us as well as some of us think it has.

2

Beyond Queer Nationalism

Changing Strategies for Changing Times

The mission of the Point Foundation is to provide scholarships for LGBT college and graduate students who not only are doing well in school but also show a commitment to community involvement and to goals of social justice and social change. In 2008 I was invited to be one of the plenary speakers at its annual conference, which brings together all its scholarship recipients. Because it was the fortieth anniversary of 1968, a year of tremendous upheaval in the United States and around the globe, and because the media were giving so much attention to events of that year, I decided to frame my remarks around a contrast between then and now. How had change been achieved, I asked, and are the strategies and mindsets of the past still appropriate today?

I make my living studying and teaching history. I do it because I love history. I can't stop myself from thinking like a historian. What I mean by this is that I find myself frequently drawing comparisons in my head between past and present, between then and now. I think about the passage of time, about what has changed and what hasn't.

This is a good time to be a historian. We are living at a moment when it is hard not to be aware of history and historical change. We have just lived through a presidential primary season unlike any other in American history. The final two candidates standing for the nomination of a major political party were an African American man and a white woman. If you have any sense of history, you cannot help being stunned and awed by such an outcome.

We're also living through the fortieth anniversary of one of the most tumultuous years in US history. Events of great magnitude are being remembered in the press almost constantly. Nineteen sixty-eight was a year when the war in Southeast Asia finally took the turn that led the United States eventually to disengage from a deeply unpopular conflict. Nineteen sixty-eight was a year when a president's popularity sank so low that he was repudiated by his own party and did not even try to run for reelection. It was a year when disorder and chaos, protests and rebellions, swept across the United States. Two charismatic public figures, Martin Luther King Jr. and Robert F. Kennedy, died by assassination. Riots and rebellions tore cities and college campuses apart. The world watched on television as police in Chicago went berserk and attacked demonstrators, journalists, and unsuspecting citizens during the Democratic Party's national convention. Radical feminists protested outside the Miss America pageant in Atlantic City, and women's liberation consciousness-raising groups were springing up all over the country faster than one could count them.

Let's use that year, 1968, as a measuring point of change for LGBT people over the past four decades:

- In 1968 forty-nine out of fifty states had sodomy laws. The government criminalized homosexual behavior, even in private between consenting adults. Today there are no sodomy laws; the Supreme Court declared them unconstitutional in 2003 in the case of *Lawrence v. Texas*.
- In 1968 no elected official in the United States was openly gay, lesbian, bisexual, or transgender; today there are more than five hundred.
- In 1968 not one government jurisdiction prohibited discrimination based on sexual orientation or gender identity. The federal government actually banned the employment of anyone who was gay, lesbian, or bisexual. Most states did the same thing in their licensing and certification of professions. By contrast, twenty states now ban discrimination based on sexual orientation, and thirteen ban discrimination based on gender identity. And many more cities and counties have civil rights protections, as well.

- In 1968 there was not a single LGBT character on television; now, just in the twenty-first century, there have been more than a hundred recurring characters on network television and almost two hundred on cable.
- In 1968 at most three universities had LGBT student groups. There were no queer studies programs or courses, no campus LGBT offices and staff, no resources of any kind except for the campus psychiatrist, and he might have told you that you were sick. Today at least 130 colleges and universities support LGBT offices with staff; almost a thousand campuses have LGBT student groups; and there are so many courses offered that it is impossible to count them.
- In 1968 not a single high school in the United States had a gay/straight alliance or anything like it; today, forty years later, more than 3,500 high schools have such groups.

I could offer many other examples. One could fill a whole book with such examples. The point is that much has changed. So much has changed in such a short period of time, as historians measure time, that it is almost impossible to grasp. If you have lived through all of it, as I have, it is difficult not to be hopeful about the capacity of human beings to make constructive change in the world and to move whole societies and cultures. Change like this is extraordinary.

All this change did not just happen. These changes occurred because individuals, acting both alone and together, made the decision to do something about the conditions in which they lived. Can we learn something that might be useful to us today by exploring the underlying strategies used to make change? Might it be helpful to think about the way that these changes have made the present different enough that it is time for new strategies and new ways of thinking about how to make change?

Discovery

Try to imagine 1968. Imagine someone in the United States coming of age, an adolescent who has some vague inkling of being different from her or his peers. How do such young people discover their identity? There is no Internet, no Facebook, no Google, no websites to browse in the library or in your room at night. There is no "gay studies" section at your local bookstore, although you might come across on the book rack in your local drugstore a salacious paperback about lesbians. Cable television, with its edginess, does not yet exist, and there is nothing on the networks to give you a clue. Your local newspaper might occasionally contain an article about homosexuality, but most likely it details the raid of a bar, described as a nest of perverts, and the arrest of its patrons.

In other words, for those who thought their sexual or gender identity was different from that of their peers, different from almost everything they saw around them, it was going to be a long, slow haul to acquire information, to get a sense of what these feelings meant, to find other people like themselves, and to discover places to meet and socialize. Almost every memoir or autobiography that we have from men and women of that generation speaks of this long initial period of confusion and loneliness and isolation.

Coming Out

In the wake of 1968, in the wake of the upheavals that were rocking the nation, what might you do to transform this painful, lonely, and isolated stage of discovery? You become visible. You declare yourself. You come out!

Today, coming out is so normative, so much what we are all supposed to do as proud queers, that it is easy to forget how revolutionary this once was. The impulse to come out grew very much out of the late 1960s. It was a time of mass movements in which many people were embracing their identity rather than trying to assimilate into a white, middle-class, Protestant, heterosexual mainstream. It was the era of black power, of La Raza, of Native American rebellion. The early gay and lesbian liberationists were part of that '60s generation. Their message, their strategy, was to come out. Come out everywhere and to everyone. Wear it on your sleeve. Declare yourself boldly and proudly. Make it an issue all the time. Come out to family; come out at school; come out at work; come out on the streets. And come out with others, together, for support. Parade around, have public demonstrations, and show yourself.

In fact, in the 1970s most did not come out. It was still too scary; the risks were all too real. But the actions of the few who did come out had a tremendous ripple effect. Especially in the largest cities and in university towns, visible queers made it easier for those who didn't declare themselves to their family, friends, and coworkers to find nonetheless a public gay world and to absorb pride by proxy.

Building Community/Building a Nation

Suppose you were one of those who did come out. It does not solve all your problems. It is still an unsafe world. Oppression is not imaginary. What does one do next?

The strongest impulse was to create organizations and to build community—to build, really, something of a "queer nation." Because of the visibility and dynamism of racial and ethnic nationalist mobilizations in that era, it was only natural that queer activism would follow a community-based, nationalist model.

From the '70s on, this mostly unnamed nationalism expressed itself in a mania for organization. In 1968 there were maybe fifty LGBT organizations in the United States. By 1975 there were perhaps a thousand. Today there are more than triple that number among high school students alone. A city like Chicago has more queer organizations in the twenty-first century than existed in the whole United States in 1968.

Some of these organizations were explicitly political and activist. Their members planned demonstrations against police harassment, against negative media portrayals, against businesses that discriminated, and against politicians who refused to support legislative protections. But most of the organizations that formed in the 1970s were about constructing community, creating bonds of association, and fostering ties and connections between people. Or, put another way, LGBT folks who were coming out in the 1970s were going about the task of queer nation building.

They did it in so many ways. Take religion. Christianity and Judaism had long histories of hostility toward homosexuality. Religion was often the first place that young people felt the sting of oppression, of being labeled bad. In the 1970s, in one community of faith after another, LGBT people joined together. They formed organizations, like Dignity among Roman Catholics and Integrity among Episcopalians, that attempted to achieve change in the theology and practice of their faiths. But they also came together in congregations of their own making. Each week they would meet for services, bonding together as a community. After service, they would go out together in the neighborhood, creating a visible queer presence.

Other examples of this community, or nation, building abound. Sports leagues proliferated. Men's and women's softball teams played in cities around the country and, like their religious peers after services, socialized publicly together after the games. Activists opened community centers, permanent places where LGBT people came together. These centers often housed services, like counseling and clinics, that fostered an ethic of caring and service, of building bonds and connections between people. The 1970s witnessed the rapid founding of a gay and lesbian press. In city after city this emerging community had its own newspaper, and these newspapers had listings of events and maps that showed the location of bars and organizations so that the geography of the queer nation became more solid. There was a flourishing of entrepreneurship, of bookstores, restaurants, travel agencies, mental health professionals, medical practices, and other such businesses rooted in a common identity. In professional associations, academics, social workers, nurses, doctors, lawyers, and police officers came together to create networks of solidarity and support. In the space of a decade, a rich and complex community infrastructure emerged so that, at least in larger cities, some individuals could almost live in a queer world, a queer nation. It still might take a while for young people coming of age to figure out issues of identity and then to find this world, but, once they did, it was richer, denser, and more embracing than ever. And it encouraged a stance of pride and coming out that, in turn, further strengthened this new imagined nation.

Politics in This "Queer Nation"

What did the politics of this new queer nation look like?

There were moments of real debate. In the year or two after Stonewall, when the radical spirit of the '60s was still very alive, a debate erupted. On one side were those who thought that gay liberation was part of a much broader struggle for human freedom and that therefore we should all work together across lines of identity. On the other side were those who argued that the focus needed to be on gay issues alone. The debate between those who wanted to pursue a multi-issue coalition politics and those who sought a single-issue nationalist politics was often fierce. But, for the most part, the single-issue position became the dominant face of the movement.

What did that lead to in practice? It meant campaigns and mobilizations to work on sodomy law repeal; to lobby for local civil rights statutes protecting against discrimination; to remove homosexuality from the American Psychiatric Association's list of mental illnesses; to change the military ban; and to burrow into institutions like religious bodies and schools and professional associations in order to win gay-and-lesbian-friendly policies. This single-issue politics accomplished a good bit. The APA did eliminate its classification of homosexuality as a disease. The federal Civil Service Commission dropped its blanket ban on the employment of lesbians, gay men, and bisexuals. Half the states repealed their sodomy statutes. A few dozen cities enacted antidiscrimination statutes.

But these gains extracted a price. The single-issue focus made it more difficult for those LGBT folks who belonged, so to speak, to two or more nations to feel at home in this movement. Many of those for whom battles against racism and against sexism were as much a part of their being as were campaigns against homophobia refused to put those passionate claims aside. As a result, the public face of the organizations that engaged the political system and that received media attention was almost always white and very often male.

Two decades after Stonewall, in the late 1980s, at the height of the AIDS epidemic, another round of queer militancy emerged. Activists were again demonstrating in the streets. They were occupying the offices of newspapers and government bureaucrats and corporate executives. As in the early days of gay liberation, these bands of activists extended across the queer spectrum of color and gender and identities. And, once again, the old debate of single-issue or multi-issue politics emerged. Do we focus solely on AIDS, or do we fight to change the whole health care system? This time, the outcome was a bit more complex, a bit more ambiguous. There were more efforts to develop coalitions and some effort to place the epidemic in a broader political economy of health. The demographics of the epidemic helped ensure that the infrastructure of organizations among LGBT people of color would emerge stronger and have more permanence. But, overall, a single-issue "nationalist" perspective and strategy won out again.

And here we are today, four decades after the Stonewall Rebellion. At the local level, the face of LGBT organizations and the LGBT community has become more diverse. Yet it is fair to say that coming out and a community-based nationalist politics are still the underlying conventional wisdom. It is the way things are, the way things are meant to be.

But stop for a minute and think "history." History is a story of change. So much has changed in these forty years. Isn't it fair to ask whether the old conventional ways make the most sense? Does the world that we live in today—the challenges that we face today—require the methods and the outlook and the strategies that were developed for the conditions of forty years ago and that have essentially been repeated over the succeeding decades? Are the stage and the experience of self-discovery as isolating, as long, and as dramatic as they once were? Is coming out as much of a before-and-after moment? Is it as life changing and life defining? Does community building—what I am calling "nationalism"—still need to be the defining task? Will the goals that we still need to achieve on the road to both equality and justice best be achieved through a single-issue nationalist politics?

Take the life stage of "discovery." I do not want to minimize or dismiss the struggles that each individual may still experience today. I am sure that each one of you here has stories to tell. But it is also true that the experience is not the same as it was forty years ago. The cultural resources for learning about LGBT life and identities are infinitely greater than they were then. Invisibility is not the issue that it once was, and in this age of the Web the means to break through isolation are much more accessible.

Coming out is also a vastly different process for many today. We could probably spend the night doing cross-generational sharing about coming-out experiences. But one thing is certain. For most young people today, the divide between before and after is not as deep and as wide as it used to be. The prospect of crossing that divide is not as terrifying. Many skip the stage of living in the closet and leading a double life. Some are never in the closet to begin with.

What about the nationalist process of building community? As someone who remembers the time before and who has devoted a lot of energy over the past thirty-five years to building organizations and institutions, the community-building impulse is precious to me. And, although nationalism has never appealed to me, either ethically or as a political philosophy, in practice I have lived out a good bit of my life as a nationalist.

Many of the institutions that were built continue to need support in the form of infusions of staff, volunteers, and donations. Many of these institutions will win your generation's patronage. They are a wonderful gift that an older LGBT generation bequeaths to a younger generation. But, at the same time, there is growing evidence that the younger generation is not so interested in the older generation's gift! For instance, as a number of mainstream religious bodies become more open and welcoming, what is the appeal of a separate space for worship? Isn't it interesting that the form that high school organizing has taken is as gay/straight alliances? And, when one can buy books online and when the large chains stock LGBT books and an LGBT customer is not afraid to bring one to the cashier for purchase, will we continue to need and patronize our community bookstores?

As to political mobilization and agendas, consider the single-issue nationalist character of so much LGBT activism and strategy. Does it make sense for some of the key issues and challenges that we face now and in the years ahead?

The AIDS epidemic, for instance, is all too alive and well. Does an LGBT-focused agenda make sense when fully half of the cumulative case load in the United States is no longer L, G, B, or T? Can AIDS be effectively fought in an environment in which the federal government and many states support an abstinence-only model of sex education? How will a single-issue nationalist approach effectively deal with AIDS, even among us?

What about the issue of youth and violence? This is one area in which things have actually gotten worse in the past forty years. Increased visibility and the ease of self-discovery at earlier ages coexist with homophobia. This has meant greater vulnerability for young people who come out or seem "queer." In high schools where abstinence-only sex education is the norm, what is the likelihood of acceptance for LGBT students? At a time when school districts are starved for funds and the federal government finances religiously based charter schools, can we really imagine safety for LGBT adolescents? Does the LGBT community perhaps need a program for the revival of public education in the United States and for a revolution in the content of sex education curricula? These are not the issues of a queer nationalism, yet can we imagine real success without them?

Finally, let's think for a minute about the issue of marriage. We are living through a moment of great excitement in the campaign for marriage equality. The achievement of marriage in California this year is significant. But look at what the single-issue, marriage-for-gays-and-lesbians campaign has also done. It has given us, for the first time in forty years, a new body of antigay law. More than half the states now have constitutional amendments that define marriage as the union of a man and a woman. Roughly forty states have recently passed laws saying they will not recognize same-sex marriages performed in other states. As couples from those states go to California or Massachusetts to get married and as they file lawsuits back home challenging those laws and those constitutional amendments, their cases will ultimately be ruled on by some of the most conservative courts, including the Supreme Court, in the history of this nation.

Instead of the single-minded focus on marriage, can we learn something from the other nations that do have marriage equality? In all of the countries in which same-sex marriage is legal, marriage is not the source of significant state benefits. Benefits like health insurance and pensions for seniors had already been separated from marriage. In some countries, like Canada, the law barely distinguishes between married couples and co-habiting couples. Instead of prioritizing the right to marry, should we be fighting for public policies that value all family forms and make benefits a function of personhood rather than marital status?

I don't have answers to these questions. But I do know that, as a historian, "change" is the name of the game. Change is the fundamental law of society and culture. Your generation is different from mine—not completely different, not unrecognizable to each other, but different enough that you will set your own agendas. You will have your own goals and your own aspirations and your own challenges. Our history is there for you to learn from. One can only hope that it is not there to be unthinkingly copied and repeated.

3

The Gay Movement and the Left

In 2008 *New Politics*, a socialist journal, invited a group of writers and activists to contribute to a forum titled "The Gay Movement and the Left." Contributors included Bettina Aptheker, Martin Duberman, Jeffrey Escoffier, and David McReynolds. The impetus for the forum was the discovery by Christopher Phelps, a historian of the left, of a 1952 document, "Socialism and Sex," within the records of the Socialist Party. The forum was an opportunity for me to reflect on my own experience and on the ways that gays and lesbians with leftist views have played a critical role in the LGBT movement. These reflections led me to ask why the left has often been so hesitant about embracing this struggle for justice.

The Jesuits trained me well. My high school speech and debate coach taught me how to speak in complete paragraphs and to construct what he described as a "seamless" argument. Many years later, a close friend and fellow historian used the same word in reference to my historical writing.

This essay first appeared as "Can the Left Ignore Gay Liberation?," *New Politics* 12, no. 1 (Summer 2008): 28–31.

He described one of my books as a "seamless" narrative. Well, that skill, if I have it, has eluded me as I've tried to compose my contribution to this symposium on gays and the left. So, instead, I offer a series of disconnected but, I hope, relevant observations.

I have been teaching an undergraduate history course on the United States in the 1960s for almost twenty-five years. Since important elements of the spirit of "the '60s" lasted well into the '70s and were passed on by older brothers and sisters, for a long time my students came to the course already at least partly versed in that decade's history. But a few years ago I noticed that something decisive had shifted. I now have to explain that liberal and left are two different political categories; that at many points in the '60s they were bitterly opposed to each other; and that "radical" in the '60s meant something other than a wild fundamentalist, whether Christian or Muslim.

The change brought home to me what I suppose I already knew but didn't want to admit: that the left in the United States today is so inconsequential that groups of working-class college students at a public urban university don't even know what the term means. That is, they think that liberals are the left. Why do I mention this? Because I find it hard to grab hold of the premises of this forum. Instead of asking, "Should the contemporary left campaign on this issue as part of a program for American society?" I'm pulled to ask, "Why should a gay and lesbian movement, whose component parts number thousands and thousands of organizations in the United States, give a second thought to a 'left' that, for the overwhelming majority of Americans, is hardly known to exist?"

As Christopher Phelps reminds us, the Mattachine Society, the group whose founding launched a history of continuous queer organizing in the United States, owed its birth to a group of men with ties to the Communist Party. In the late 1960s and early 1970s, critical figures in the radical gay and lesbian liberation movement—Carl Wittman, Charlotte Bunch, and Allen Young are three names that come to mind, but there were many more—had roots in the New Left activism of the era and brought those experiences and perspectives with them as they helped radicalize gay and lesbian politics. Then, in the late 1980s, ACT UP chapters around the country had not only angry twenty-two-year-olds at their overflow meetings but also alumni of the radical social movements of the 1960s and 1970s who invested AIDS organizing with militancy and with a politics that called attention to systemic inequalities and oppression.

So, yes, in a sense, the left can claim a critical role in what I consider the three most compelling, historically significant moments in the gay and lesbian movement. Yet the movement's headiest periods have neither been initiated nor carried out by left organizations and their leadership. Rather, it has come from gay, lesbian, bisexual, and transgender activists whose worldviews were shaped by various left traditions but who worked outside the left.

Wonderful and important as those three transforming moments were, none of them lasted long. After each of them, as gay activism resettled into more mainstream, reformist, and civil rights frameworks, individual activists who saw themselves as leftists either went back to the left or tried to keep a left analysis or program alive within the gay and lesbian movement. My own direct experience of this history (rather than my retelling of it as a historian) came in the 1970s in the wake of the gay liberation moment. I joined one of the many pre-party formations that grew out of the upheavals of the '60s. The one I chose, the New Action Party, was completely unsuccessful in its aspirations to become a political party, but it did provide me with wonderful mentoring from impressive community organizers who were older and more experienced than I.

At the same time, I was part of a collective in New York called the Gay Socialist Action Project. We organized "actions," convened educational forums to talk about left analyses of gay oppression, and mobilized visible gay contingents for events like the 1976 counter-Bicentennial demonstrations or protest rallies outside the Democratic National Convention in New York City that summer. There were equivalent gay men's groups in cities around the country—San Francisco, Chicago, Boston, DC, Los Angeles, and, I'm sure, others. I would be hard pressed to claim that these grouplets did many things of earth-shaking consequence. Leftist labels in themselves tended to marginalize us. But we did function as a system of support and self-education among ourselves, cracking a political isolation that tended to deepen with the rightward shift of the country. The connections between us helped shape how some of us were able to be activists within the gay and lesbian and, as the '80s moved into the '90s, bisexual and transgender movement.

Here's how this process played itself out with me. At some point, I decided to devote my activist energies to the National Gay and Lesbian Task Force. Of the various national gay groups, it was the one that seemed most attached, even during the Reagan years, to the spirit of gay liberation. And it seemed to attract, to both its staff and its board, folks who were now labeling themselves "progressive." In concrete terms this meant an allegiance to community organizing and grassroots mobilizations rather than to inside-the-Beltway lobbying. It meant an approach to gay politics that always argued for interconnections between issues and between various forms of oppression. Thus, when I chaired the board of NGLTF, we issued a statement opposing the Gulf War in 1991. Later, when I became director of its Policy Institute, we issued position papers and took stands on things like affirmative action, welfare reform, and immigration restriction. From inside the GLBT movement, activists who thought of themselves as leftists worked consistently to magnify the movement's lens so that segments of the movement at least stood for a vision of social justice broader than a single-issue politics contained within a civil rights framework. But, again, we didn't do this as members of a left organization. We did it from within the GLBT movement, as activists who had a left-inspired vision of what social justice might look like.

At some point in my twenties, I began to identify as a leftist. I did it for a combination of reasons. I came to believe that capitalism (the private ownership of the means of production) would always produce inequality and exploitation. I longed for an economic structure where everybody had enough (vague to you reading this, but clear to me what this means). I wanted a social structure in which other systems of oppression and inequality would become artifacts of the past. Because I didn't think that the latter (no racism, no sexism, no homophobia) would ever happen under capitalism, a democratic socialist vision of a future society became mine.

And, as I read more history, especially about American radicalism, I was taken by the way that fighting for the underdog, fighting for those who were persecuted and mistreated, seemed to be what motivated the people who called themselves leftists.

So imagine now how disorienting it is for someone who thinks the left fights against injustice to read one of the questions guiding this forum: "Should the contemporary left campaign on this [i.e., gay] issue as part of a program for American society?"

It is almost certain that in the 1950s more gay men and lesbians than leftists were the target of government investigations and were fired from their jobs. In the 1960s, when leftists were enjoying expansive possibilities for organizing mass protests, gay men and lesbians were routinely arrested in mass sweeps by the police in major American cities. In Chicago, Mayor Daley's police force arrested a lot more homosexuals than radicals. When the Chicago police murdered Black Panther leader Fred Hampton, there were tons of protests, as there should have been. When, the following year, police shot and killed James Clay, a black transvestite, there was not a peep of protest. Between 1961 and 1973, something like 58,000 American military personnel died in Southeast Asia. The war became the central obsession of both the government and a broad left. Between 1981 and 1993, more than 58,000 Americans died of AIDS. The Reagan-Bush government had other things to occupy their attention, and the left, if there was one, did not make AIDS a rallying cry.

The point of the preceding paragraph? It is hard for me to understand why, at this point in time, adherents of a political tradition committed to fighting against oppression, to championing the underdog, and to promoting justice and equality would still be asking whether they should campaign on "this issue." What needs to happen to a group of people before it becomes obvious to everyone that they are the targets of systematic oppression?

In the early 1980s I published an essay titled "Capitalism and Gay Identity." It was an attempt to theorize a materialist basis for the emergence of gay identities, communities, and politics in the United States across the twentieth century. A key piece of the argument proposed that gay and lesbian communities formed on social terrain outside the family and kinship networks. It was the system of wage labor at the heart of capitalist social relations that allowed same-sex desire to congeal into an identity and that made it possible for groups of such people to come together. I also argued that the success of gay and lesbian liberation depended on fighting to expand that terrain, but not in the harshly individualist ways of the capitalist market. Rather, it depended on constructing a society in which the boundaries between family and community were porous, a social democratic society, if you will, that offered security for all regardless of an individual's relationship to a heterosexual family unit.

A GLBT movement in the conservative climate of the twenty-first century fights for equal marriage rights, and it becomes a mobilizing tool for the right. I suppose the left could stand shoulder to shoulder with those gay activists fighting for marriage rights. Or, it could propose and then organize around a comprehensive "family agenda" that promises security for all the complex family forms that exist in the United States today.

In this first decade of the twenty-first century, gay and lesbian life seems so visible and normalized. Ellen is a big star. Mayor Richard Daley Jr. presides each year over the induction of new members into Chicago's Gay and Lesbian Hall of Fame. President Bush jokes with Representative Barney Frank about Frank's boyfriend. But, at the same time, young people who come out or who betray signs of transgressing gender and sexual identity boundaries are subject to a level of ridicule, harassment, and violence that was rare a half century ago, when the closet reigned supreme. I suppose the left could add the issue of queer youth to its program for American society (actually, I wish it would, since these young folks could use all the allies they can get). Or the left could make the systematic dismantling of public education by the right over the past generation the scandal that it is, offer a comprehensive program for financing the education of our children, and have respect for all young folks by the schools, regardless of sexual or gender identity, be a nonnegotiable item.

I know there is something ridiculous about proposing in two short paragraphs big, complex, almost-impossible-to-imagine-achieving programs. But the point is that there isn't a single significant element of American politics and policy—family, schooling, health care, national security—in which issues germane to GLBT folks don't surface organically. But the issues will only surface among leftists if the left, whoever and whatever that is today, opens its eyes and ears to see and hear the queers all around them. If the left is fundamentally about constructing a society without exploitation and oppression, I do not see why or how gay issues would not be part of its program for American society.

4

Listening to Rustin

Lessons from an Agitator for Justice

The year 2012 was the centennial of Bayard Rustin's birth. Though not well known today, Rustin was one of the mid-twentieth-century's most important activists in the United States for social and economic justice. The centennial year provided the opportunity to hold events across the country to reflect upon his life, his accomplishments, and his continuing relevance to contemporary struggles for justice and equality. I was fortunate to be able to speak at a number of these events, and this is one of the talks I developed. It is an effort to distill from more than a half century of Rustin's activism the key lessons that he offers. Rustin was an extraordinary individual who also provoked controversy because of his ideas and his actions. But, whether one agrees with his strategic vision or not, his experience and his commitment require that we think seriously about his ideas and his choices.

In so many ways, there could not be a more appropriate time to reflect on Bayard Rustin's life than in this centennial year of his birth. In an era when terrorism is a national preoccupation and the United States has been at war for a decade, when the Occupy Movement has called our attention to economic inequality and is searching for ways to make change, and when mass incarceration and restrictive voter registration laws systematically undo key triumphs of the civil rights movement, Rustin's life has much to say to us.

Rustin devoted the better part of his years to evangelizing for non-violence as a solution to conflict and a route to justice. For decades he was on the frontlines of the black freedom struggle in the United States and the global struggle against colonialism. He always argued that neither peace nor social justice was possible as long as the world's resources were controlled by a small, privileged owning class. Rustin's life speaks to just about any question one might ask or any dilemma one might face about how to make progressive change in the world.

I say this not because Rustin's life is simple. His story is not a classic morality tale pitting the forces of good against the forces of evil. Instead, it is full of tensions and ambiguities. There are times when Rustin is heroic and inspiring, but there are also times when his choices are puzzling and infuriating. There are times when his wisdom elicits respect and his courage elicits awe, but there are also times when his frailties are all too apparent.

Rustin was many things to many people, but he was never easy. For instance, he was an uncompromising pacifist who chose jail during World War II, yet later in life he campaigned for the sale of military jets to Israel. He was proudly and defiantly black, and he accepted no restrictions on his person. He waxed eloquent about his experiences in Africa and the independence struggles he witnessed. But he had no patience at all for a politics of racial justice rooted in nationalism and identity, and from the late 1960s on he made withering critiques of key elements of African American politics, such as community control of schools, affirmative action, and the establishment of black studies programs.

To take another example, Rustin was a genius at organizing protests. He engaged in his first protests while still in high school in the early 1930s, and his last arrest came in the mid-1980s in support of striking workers at Yale. He planned actions that involved a handful of brave individuals in life-threatening circumstances and actions that involved almost a half million. He articulated a theory of "social dislocation" in which he argued that activists had to make the cost of doing business as usual too high for those in power. Yet at other times this master of protest argued that activists had to get out of the streets and off the picket lines and instead play by the rules of the political system.

As one final example of the difficulty his career offers us, Rustin was more widely known to be gay in the decades before gay liberation than almost anyone of his generation. His sexuality was a matter of public record, and he suffered tremendously because of this. And yet, near the end of his life, when gay liberation was transforming the meaning and experience of being gay in America, Rustin refused to contribute to the first anthology of writing by black gay men. "I have always believed sexual orientation to be a private matter," he wrote Joseph Beam, the book's editor.

Rustin's life is not easy but difficult, not simple but rife with contradictions, not clear but hard to pigeonhole. If we are looking for a hero to venerate—a black hero, a gay hero, a Gandhian hero—Rustin is not that figure. Wherever we might place ourselves on the political spectrum, Rustin will at some point make us sputter in anger. But he will also force us to think. He will make us question our assumptions. If we take him seriously (and his work and his accomplishments force us to take him seriously), his life requires us to reflect on our own truths about how to build a world worth living in.

For the rest of this essay, I ask that we listen to Rustin's life. I am not claiming to channel Bayard Rustin. I am not claiming to endorse the things I describe. But I am trying to offer as best as I can his views of what is required to build a world in which every human life is treasured. His particular issues might not be your particular issues. But his long life as an agitator for justice and a campaigner for peace shines a light on the choices and dilemmas that many activists will inevitably face.

At the top of Rustin's list of lessons is the bedrock conviction that *nonviolence is the only way*. He came to this conviction first through the Quaker influence in his youth and then through the excitement of learning about and studying what a man of color in India was doing to the mighty British Empire through the application of nonviolent resistance. For twenty-five years, from 1941 to 1965, Rustin worked as a staff member for pacifist organizations whose commitment to nonviolence was complete.

Rustin applied nonviolence steadily, conscientiously, and self-reflectively in the black freedom struggle. He brought nonviolent direct action to A. Philip Randolph, one of the most respected African American leaders of his generation, so that it became part of Randolph's "March on Washington" movement during World War II and the campaign to desegregate the military during Truman's presidency. He brought non-violence to the founding of CORE, the Congress of Racial Equality, and its pioneering direct-action work in the 1940s. He brought it as well to Montgomery, Alabama, in 1956 and to the mentoring that he subsequently did of the young Dr. Martin Luther King Jr. as King rose to national prominence. Rustin was central to the transformation of Gandhian non-violence in the United States from the cherished possession of a few initiates to its embrace by masses of Americans.

With the benefit of retrospective wisdom, we know that nonviolent direct action had a relatively short run as an articulated philosophy at the leading edge of social change in the United States. It vibrated with the most creative energy for roughly a decade stretching from the Montgomery bus boycott in the mid-1950s through the sit-ins and freedom rides of the early 1960s to Mississippi Freedom Summer in 1964.

Advocates of nonviolence have often been labeled mushy-headed or hopelessly impractical or naively idealistic, and sometimes they were. But Rustin was not one of those. To Rustin, real nonviolence in the tradition of Gandhi was determined, forceful, and resistant. It brought conflict to the surface. In the short run, it was likely to provoke even more violence.

Rustin knew what he was talking about because he had put himself there. In 1942, traveling by himself on a Tennessee bus, he refused to move to the back, was arrested because of that, and then had to run a gauntlet of white police officers in a Nashville police station. In 1944 he challenged segregation in a federal prison and was badly beaten by a white inmate. In 1947 he found himself trapped in a North Carolina house that had been surrounded by enraged white men armed with clubs, who were throwing rocks through the windows and threatening to lynch Rustin and the other occupants. In the middle of the Korean War, he faced down an angry crowd in Times Square in Manhattan when he gave a soap-box oration in favor of peace. These examples could be multiplied many times over.

What made this kind of violence productive for Rustin was the stance of the resister. By his attitude and his response to the attacker, Rustin was inviting reconciliation. In 1964 Rustin spoke to a large group of young civil rights activists getting ready to head down to Mississippi for the summer. Three civil rights workers had disappeared. Bombing, arson, and shootings by white supremacists were the facts of daily life, and these actions were being encouraged by white political leaders. Here is what Rustin told these young activists: "When I say I love James Eastland, the segregationist senator from Mississippi, it sounds preposterous—a man who brutalizes people? But you love him or you wouldn't be here. You're going to Mississippi to create social change—you love Eastland in your desire to create conditions that will redeem his children."

Debates about nonviolence took place in the black freedom movement, in the struggle against colonialism in Asia and Africa, and in the American antiwar movement. These debates often pitted allegiance to a utopian vision of peace and brotherhood against a hardheaded realism about oppression and injustice. Rustin never saw it that way. He embraced nonviolence and remained permanently wedded to it precisely because it was practical and necessary and promised success. He believed this because he knew and understood that every act of violence had consequences, and no act of violence was ever self-contained. A war to destroy Hitler and fascism produced the passions and hatreds that led to Cold War militarism and the nuclear arms race. A war that ended slavery produced the passions and hatreds that led to the Ku Klux Klan and lynching and Jim Crow. Anticolonial wars of independence produced the passions and hatreds that led to military dictatorships and ethnic massacres. Palestinian suicide bombers and Israeli tanks inevitably lead to more suicide bombers and more tanks. Riots in Harlem and Los Angeles and Detroit and Newark in the 1960s and campus disorders around the country in the name of peace in Southeast Asia produced backlash from whites and from patriots that made racial justice and peace more distant goals.

However just the cause might be, violence and destruction always generated a counter-response that never exhausted itself. Rustin embraced nonviolence because he saw it as the only way to break this cycle. For him, nonviolence was simultaneously a moral philosophy of right living, a political strategy for making change, and a psychological theory about human beings and how to change them. In the course of a long life of activism, his conviction grew stronger that nonviolence was the only way to make permanent constructive change.

Yet that same long life as an activist led him to the second lesson he might offer us: *nonviolence might be the only way, but pacifism will not get us where we want to go.*

Rustin's personal pacifist stance against war never changed. He always said he would refuse to fight. He believed that war was always wrong even though, in many situations, it was the best thing that good people could figure out to do. But long years of activism in the American peace movement led him to conclude that pacifism would never bring peace.

Just as his certainty that nonviolence was the only way came from his engagement with it, so too his certainty about pacifism came through deep involvement. Rustin spent twenty-seven torturous months in federal prison during World War II because he refused to fight in a war. He called for open resistance to conscription when the Truman administration and Congress enacted a peacetime draft. During the early Cold War, when McCarthyism silenced debate about military policy, Rustin led peace caravans through American cities and towns. At the height of the nuclear arms race, he defied government orders to take cover during civilian defense drills. He helped devise and implement the campaigns against nuclear testing in the Nevada desert, the south Pacific, and the Sahara in Africa. He helped coordinate a San Francisco-to-Moscow peace walk. He had working relationships with pacifists across four continents. It was because of all his experience as a pacifist that he came to the conclusion that, while peace was a nonnegotiable goal, pacifism was politically ineffective.

Why did he come to that conclusion? One reason was his impatience with pacifist foolishness, with the tendency, never suppressed for very long, to engage in the grand gesture, in symbolic acts of moral witness. Rustin himself was a master of this. At one point during the Korean War, he wrote, "Let us resist with our whole beings!" If we do not, he continued, "the stones themselves will cry out!" He could believe in such posturing the first time, the second time, even the tenth time. But by the hundredth time, he was growing skeptical. Is the goal to make a point, or is the goal to end war? The San Francisco-to-Moscow peace walk that he helped organize in 1961 made the participants feel holy and righteous. It convinced them that they could sacrifice just like a soldier in battle. But did it bring the world a day closer to world peace? Rustin's answer, eventually, was no.

Rustin did not just reject the tactics of pacifism. He rejected pacifism as a movement. He believed that pacifism as a strategy was doomed to fail because he came to believe that war was a by-product of other, more critical, phenomena. War was a sideshow, so to speak. It was always the result of something else, always caused by some other structural injustice. For Rustin, the road toward peace did not run through organizing against war. *To achieve peace*—and this is a third lesson he offers—*one must work for justice.*

This is not a new phrase. I have seen bumper stickers with this slogan for at least twenty-five years. I also do not want to claim that the concept originated with Rustin. But his work, as much as anyone's, gave the idea currency in the United States.

Rustin worked in a particular sector of the American peace movement. It was almost completely white, thoroughly male dominated, and heavily drawn from an educated middle class. The Fellowship of Reconciliation (FOR), where he worked for twelve years, had its base among Christian ministers and believed strongly in prayer and moral witness. The War Resisters League (WRL) was a secular equivalent, more militant and anarchist, but it still saw opposition to war as the heart of its mission.

When Rustin joined the staff of the FOR, in 1941, its new executive secretary, A. J. Muste, was trying to change its tenor. Muste came out of the militant wing of the labor movement. He had been a communist in the 1930s. He argued that the only true pacifist was a revolutionary and that it would take a revolution in social and economic structures to bring an end to war. Muste tried to hire a young staff with the same inclinations.

Rustin was a key figure in the effort to implement this vision. For him, the defining revolutionary issue in the mid-twentieth century was the black freedom struggle at home and the larger anticolonial movement of which it was a part. Rustin built the bridge that linked pacifists to A. Philip Randolph's black-led working-class movement in the 1940s. He linked pacifists to the experiments with direct action that the Congress of Racial Equality was engaging in, as well. When he moved to the War Resisters League, in 1953, he brought the same impulse and drive. He connected these white pacifists to the Montgomery bus boycott, to building the Southern Christian Leadership Conference, to campaigning for school desegregation, and to developing nonviolent strategies for resistance to European colonialism. Rustin threw himself into this. He tried to reallocate the resources of pacifists to the black movement because it seemed obvious to him that every step toward racial justice was in fact a step toward world peace.

Overall, the record of this sector of the peace movement was at best mixed. If one reads the internal correspondence and the minutes of the boards of the FOR and the WRL, the tone is unmistakable. These pacifists often did not get it. They loved the big moments when nonviolence was in the spotlight—actions like the Montgomery bus boycott or the March on

Washington. But they also begrudged the diversion of resources from war and peace, which to them really mattered, and toward what they considered an important but secondary issue outside their core mission.

Rustin had to justify his time with the civil rights movement. He always did his work on the sufferance of a pacifist leadership that might call him back to task at any moment and often did. A dramatic incident illustrating this disconnect came in August 1965. On the twentieth anniversary of the dropping of the atom bomb on Hiroshima, David Dellinger, an important figure in the American peace movement, was picketing outside the White House in protest against the escalation of the war in Vietnam by the Johnson administration. Rustin, meanwhile, was inside the White House attending the signing of the Voting Rights Act. A century after the Fifteenth Amendment was ratified, legislation finally made the promise of the franchise real for African Americans, and President Johnson's role in this was decisive. Dellinger and a lot of other white pacifists never forgave Rustin for his implicit support of the president at a time when Johnson was making war.

Rustin's commitment to pacifism never wavered. But he believed that the contribution pacifists could make to peace was their understanding of nonviolence. He wanted them to apply it in movements for social justice. For Rustin, social justice was the route toward peace, not the other way around. For Rustin, justice was the prize, and peace was like a beautiful afterglow.

This brings me to the fourth lesson to be drawn from Rustin's activist life. *Because he believed that justice was essentially indivisible, he also believed that any identity-based politics was a long detour away from the prize.*

This is the lesson that most challenges the direction of progressive politics in the past generation. Since the mid-1960s, struggles for social justice in the United States have overwhelming coalesced around identity, from black power and other forms of racial-ethnic politics that arose in the late 1960s, to feminism and gay liberation, and to a disability rights movement more recently.

Rustin was a dissenter from this. This may sound like a strange claim to make about him, an African American man whose deepest passion and longest commitment was to the freedom struggle of his people. Yet he was as vehement a dissenter from identity-based politics as one could find. He always said he hoped that, if he had been born white, he still would have made the cause of racial justice fully his own. He believed people had to fight for racial equality or any other great political goal not because it benefited them but because it was right.

Rustin believed that the rhetoric of black power as well as the nationalist impulse that arose alongside it was a disaster. He was unsparing in his public criticism of activists in SNCC (Student Nonviolent Coordinating Committee) and CORE who propounded it. He saw the rise of a politics of racial identity and racial solidarity as a tragic historic reversal, a route to powerfulness and defeat. In Rustin's eyes, "black power" did not merely harden the resistance of white antagonists of racial justice. It also simultaneously weakened the commitment of white liberal supporters. It let them off the hook, as Rustin said again and again, by making the work of liberation the responsibility of the oppressed alone. Black power and gay power and Chicano power might be splendid rousing slogans. But they had the paradoxical effect, Rustin thought, of intensifying the isolation of the oppressed and magnifying the separation and division between peoples. And isolation and separation were markers of oppression, not freedom.

Rather than an identity-based politics and the divisions it fostered, Rustin pressed for a coalition politics. This is perhaps the fifth piece of wisdom we can extract from his life. Rustin believed that *coalition will get you there faster, and coalition is not for the faint of heart.*

Just like "If you want peace, work for justice," this notion of coalition has become standard wisdom among most progressive activists. In fact, identity politics has spawned it, as if activists instinctively understood that we had to reach beyond the separate boxes that identity puts us in. But Rustin argued for coalition earlier, and he argued for it differently. Rustin's coalition politics is not the coalition of American interest groups, the coalition of the urban political machine: "You scratch my back, and I'll scratch yours." It is not the coalition politics that has developed out of contemporary theories of intersectionality, where the multiple identities that an individual embodies can lead to a more capacious understanding of both oppression and justice.

Rustin began articulating the primacy of coalition at a particular moment, right after the 1963 March on Washington, when he saw a coalition spontaneously take shape. It was propelled by the civil rights movement. But it included elements of the white religious community, whose justice traditions were being reawakened by the civil rights movement, and elements of the intellectual class and the labor movement, as well. Rustin thought of this as a "coalition of conscience," and the use of that phrase is telling. It was a coalition based on ideals and values, not on self-interest or identity.

When Rustin spoke of a platform beyond civil rights for the coalition to work toward, he thought in terms of universalizing goals, of an agenda whose benefits extended to everyone. It might include elements like minimum-wage legislation, a guaranteed annual income, jobs for all, quality public schooling for everyone, and universal access to health care. When Rustin started pressing his ideas for coalition, he had to convince some mainstream civil rights organizations that a decent minimum wage was in any way relevant to the struggle for racial justice.

Coalition was necessary, but it was not for the faint of heart. Principles drove you into coalition, but compromise is what made coalitions work. Sometimes those compromises had to be made within a coalition, among its partners. But more often those compromises had to be made in relation to the institutions and individuals who exercised formal power. Compromise is not easy for people driven by passion and principle. Coalition might mean working with the Johnson administration on one issue, while disagreeing with it on another. Rustin believed there was a distinction between expediency (selling out or abandoning a principle for a short-term gain) and compromise (making concessions in order to move an agenda forward). And compromise was not, on Rustin's part, an argument for incrementalism: a little bit of change here and a little bit of change there will all add up eventually to a brand-new world. Rustin believed that big victories could get achieved and had to get achieved. But movements were more likely to achieve those big victories through a series of smaller ones. Coalitions would move their agenda forward if they made the compromises that brought those smaller victories first.

For Rustin, the goal of coalition building was to maximize power. He wanted to shift the balance of power in society in decisive ways. It was this concern with power that led Rustin to another conviction, another lesson that his life as an agitator for justice offers us: *Protest is a means, not an end. It is a tactic, not a strategy or a principle.*

No one knew protest as well as Rustin did. He protested alone. He protested in small groups. He protested with masses of people. He protested across six decades. He protested on four continents and in every hemisphere. At various points, he told Americans of conscience to go out into the streets and stay there until the government protected its citizens from violence. He told them to occupy buildings and stay there, to bring the business of government to a grinding halt until the wheels of justice started to turn.

But, at other times, Rustin advised against protest. In some circumstances and at some moments he saw protest as counterproductive. He saw it leading to reactionary political outcomes. He saw it antagonizing likely allies, promoting confusion rather than clarity, and producing the illusion of victory rather than the real thing. Especially in the mid-1960s and especially among younger activists, he saw protest degenerating into attention-grabbing gimmicks rather than functioning as a carefully crafted tactic designed to move an agenda forward. Protest, he felt, was becoming a form of militant posturing that obscured the powerlessness of the protesters.

For Rustin, protest was not a value in and of itself. It was not something one did to prove one's courage or display one's moral integrity. Protest was a tactic thoughtfully deployed in pursuit of long-range goals. In the biggest sense, the long-term goal for Rustin was the creation of a just society, a society in which everyone was treated with respect, everyone had a say in the decisions that shaped his or her life, and everyone shared in the wealth that society produced. Sometimes protest brought this vision closer. But sometimes protest was nothing more than the acting out and confirmation of the powerlessness of those in the streets.

The last lesson I want to extract from Rustin's life has to do with the issue of hope. In this past decade in the United States, we have lived through a time when our national leaders have told us that the surest route to safety, security, freedom, and justice is through war. We are living at a time when the gap between the rich and the rest is greater than ever, when our national government seems to exist only to serve the wealthy, and when every bit of good that government has done in the past century is being carefully, methodically, and systematically dismantled. In circumstances like these, where is hope to be found?

Rustin had great staying power. His activism extended over a half century, circled the globe, and encompassed a broad swath of social movements. He built relationships with thousands of activists and mentored two generations of fighters for justice. He shifted ground. He changed tactics. He rethought his priorities. But he never withdrew from the fray.

His staying power is especially remarkable because of what he lived through. He came of age as a political being during the Great Depression. Despite the suffering and the hardship, despite the threat of a rising fascism in Europe and Asia, it was an exciting and hopeful time. People were in motion. They were dreaming great dreams. And they were achieving important things. But then he watched the world turn. He lived through the descent into world war and the reaction afterward when the reforming zeal of the 1930s was crushed by the witch hunts of the McCarthy era and the United States became a permanently militarized society during the Cold War.

Rustin was there for the reawakening that came in the second half of the 1950s, on the sidewalks of Montgomery, across the breadth of Africa, and among the voices raised against the insanity of a nuclear arms race. He watched this grow and spread and grow even more in the first half of the 1960s. And then he watched the country turn once again. For Rustin, the decisive moment was Nixon's election in 1968. He saw it as a terrible defeat for everything he believed in, a shift as terrible as the ending of Reconstruction in 1877. He saw it pointing toward the place the United States has arrived at several decades later.

Though this shift was crushing for him, he never gave up. He never threw in the towel. He never went home to tend his own garden. When he was interviewed late in life by younger activists seeking wisdom and inspiration, he said that what he had come to believe in the course of a long life was that the gods did not require us to succeed in our endeavors. They simply required that we not stop trying. In taking that stance, Rustin was saying that hope is not something one goes looking for. It is not something that someone else can give us. Instead, *hope is something that each one of us is able to create and renew each day by our own actions in the world.* This, perhaps, is the core message of Rustin's life, and it is a very hopeful and empowering message.

Part II

Doing History

5

Why I Write

In 2003 graduate students in the history department at
Columbia University organized a conference, "Why We
Write: The Politics and Practice of Writing for Social Change."
Their invitation to me to speak at the conference was an
opportunity to return to the campus where I had been both
an undergraduate and a graduate student. It was also an
opportunity to reflect upon the unexpected circumstances
of my life—that, against the odds and much to my surprise,
writing became a major part of what I do in the world.

One can never predict what a simple invitation to give a talk can provoke.
Thinking about this panel and the theme of the conference has made me
realize how lucky I am and how blessed I have been. I have had a solid
quarter century of writing of things that I care about passionately and that
at least a few other folks care about, too. Every day I carry with me the
certainty that the heart of my work, my writing, has made a difference in
the world.

This essay first appeared in Jim Downs, ed., *Why We Write: The Politics and Practice of
Writing for Social Change* (New York: Routledge, 2005), 11–16.

But why do I write? I write because someone—a fellow graduate student—told me one day that I was good at it. More than three decades later, I remember the moment as if it had happened yesterday. A small group of Columbia history students was meeting at my Riverside Drive railroad flat to put together the next issue of *Common Sense*, our rabble-rousing newsletter. Except for my desk, which was a six-foot-long plank stretched across a pair of two-drawer file cabinets, everything else was close to the ground. My bed was on the floor. My dining table was a painted wood board resting on milk crates. My sofa was the mattress of a twin bed pressed against a wall with some pillows as backing and a paisley-patterned sheet as covering. Several of us were squatting on the floor and hunched over the table, rulers in hand, painstakingly creating headlines by pressing letters, one at a time, onto the mock-up of our newsletter. Richard, meanwhile, had wandered over to my desk, where he stood reading pages of my not-yet-proofed master's essay. He looked down in my direction and, with a mixture of surprise and admiration, said, "You write so well!"

Richard and I had only a passing acquaintance. He was a year ahead of me in the program. He had no reason at all to flatter me. No one had ever said such a thing to me before. It was shocking and revelatory. It opened up for me the possibility that writing—not simply research, or study, or teaching—was something I might do.

Why else do I write? I write because reading history books saved my life, and I have been bold—or foolish—enough to think that maybe my writing could do the same for someone else.

The northeast Bronx, where I grew up, was more than a world away from the Morningside Heights campus of Columbia University. The combination of fervid anticommunism and Roman Catholic moral absolutism made for an environment in which certitude was a fundamental principle. The description of God in the Baltimore catechism ("He always was, always will be, and always remains the same") extended to every aspect of life ("It always was this way, always will be this way, and always remains this same way"). This was not a comforting world view for a boy on the edge of adolescence with his first inklings of an unorthodox sexuality.

One of the main ways I dealt with this discomfort was by getting lost in books. Many of those books were novels filled with characters whose lives were thoroughly unlike anything I knew. Heroic courage, undying passion, bottomless grief: the emotions and the experiences took me beyond the dulling sameness of everyday life. But novels were make-believe. They were engines of pleasure that, in the end, didn't count for much in the hard-nosed practical world of my youth. History, by contrast, was real. It happened. It mattered. The lesson I took from the history books I read (not the social history of ordinary people and popular insurgencies but narratives of royalty, empire, generals, and war) was that change is the essence of life. What once was will not be again; nothing ever remains the same. The comfort I extracted from this was indescribably sweet. I wanted to tell it to the world.

But these are not the only and perhaps not even the main reasons why I write. Most of all I write because my life intersected with a vibrant social movement that made writing a powerful, vivid, and compelling activity. At the time, this intersection seemed serendipitous, almost accidental. Later it came to seem overdetermined: How could a young gay man shaped by the student protests and antiwar activism of the late '60s, sporting the long hair, beard, and sandals of the counterculture and living in New York City, not be swept up by the drama of gay liberation? Later still I came to view my involvement as far more intentional on my part. After all, I chose my friendships, made decisions about how to spend my time, returned again and again to meetings, conferences, and demonstrations, and came out in settings that helped guide me along particular paths.

My impulse to write the kind of history that I do had almost no connection to professional aspiration or ambition. My imagined audience wasn't then and still hasn't become the academy or the world of formally trained historians. In the 1970s, to write gay history and to have a career as an academic historian seemed self-evidently mutually exclusive. These two activities were so incompatible that to choose gay history as my subject matter meant that I simultaneously searched for a public other than university students and professional scholars.

That public was coming to life in the 1970s. It was small in numbers, yet it also had a discernible social weight to it. And it was growing.

The gay male world of the 1970s was different from both what came before and what exists today in large urban centers. I remember gay bars in New York City during the late 1960s. Heavy doors and darkened windows protected patrons from any peering eyes outside. These were nighttime places, free from at least some of the dangers that socializing in daylight might have posed. Just a few years later, everything seemed new and uncontainably exuberant. Crowds of men spilled out of bars, milled around on the sidewalk with an utter lack of concern about what the police might do, and brazenly cruised the streets of Greenwich Village.

Exciting as this new world was, it sometimes appeared desperately fragile, rootless even. Many of the men populating these bars led vibrantly queer social lives even as almost no one who was straight knew that they were gay. They stood uncertainly poised on the threshold of the closet door. Around them, in the bars, on the streets, and in the pages of a new queer press that was distributed on newsstands and handed out in bars were a smaller number of men propagating a new ethic of coming out, of self-revelation, of unabashedly wearing one's gayness everywhere.

In those years, queer activism was easier to fall into than it is today. It seemed natural, as much a way of being as a set of activities. It had not yet been professionalized into full-time paying jobs that only a few community members held. Nor was it neatly compartmentalized under the rubric of middle-class volunteerism, a few hours spent each week or month with an organization that served the community. Instead, it could be expressed on the spot by responding to one of the many flyers that circulated all the time, announcing a rally or a march. It displayed itself through the conversations one chose to initiate among straight friends and coworkers or the proselytizing about coming out that one did at bars, in bathhouses, or on the streets in the course of one's own socializing. It took form for me in part through the reorientation of my work life. More and more of my time was spent contributing, in effect, to movement building and social change in ways that felt almost effortless.

Gay stuff hadn't come to saturate mass culture, the media, and the arts as it has now. Gay also hadn't yet gone glossy, with the pages of our publications imitating *People* and other worshipers of celebrity ("42 Music Stars on Gay Marriage," shouts the cover of an *Advocate* that lies in my study. "We're for It!"). Instead, the queer community of those years sustained a set of publications that were oppositional. Some of them had wonderful names like *Fag Rag, Sinister Wisdom, Gay Sunshine,* and *Amazon Quarterly*. Their cheap newsprint made them ephemeral and, hence, all the more precious. They were produced by staffs that weren't paid, and their pages were filled by writers who weren't compensated. Circulations were in the thousands. They were among the few places where gay men and lesbians could find reflected back to us the stance of pride that we were trying to project into the community and the culture at large. They were looking for material to print that had substance and that was accessible.

Writing gay history seemed a way to participate in making this new world. In a decade when Alex Haley's book, *Roots*, and the television series made from it sparked a national preoccupation with finding and claiming one's cultural antecedents, history tapped especially powerful emotions in gay men and lesbians, few of whom had come of age with any sense of a past that was about them. History filled a hunger, an aching need.

This emergent community made spaces for these newly uncovered stories about the past. Almost all of the first histories to make it into print, books like Jonathan Ned Katz's *Gay American History*, John Boswell's *Christianity, Social Tolerance, and Homosexuality*, and my own *Sexual Politics, Sexual Communities*, were rehearsed as performances or lectures or classes for community audiences before taking publishable form. In a number of cities, local community-based history projects dug up documents and artifacts and images, and their members combined these into slide talks, films, panel discussions, and books. Periodicals like the ones mentioned, as well as *The Body Politic* out of Toronto and *Gay Community News* from Boston, opened their pages to accessibly written pieces about the gay, lesbian, and transgender past. A writer could see his or her words translated very quickly into action, wielded as a tool for building new lives and communities. It was a great motivation for writing, and, for me, it made writing a passionate pursuit.

When I think about the large projects that have consumed me over the years—projects that have fed into or been fed by smaller ones—they have all been firmly situated in a present moment that compelled me to look at the past and write about it. I was drawn to what became *Sexual Politics, Sexual Communities* in order to offer a more capacious historical tradition to those of us who were gay liberationists in the 1970s and who often felt as if our activism had no antecedents. I wrote *Intimate Matters* with Estelle Freedman in the 1980s because of the fierce sexuality debates that were fracturing feminism, because of the reactionary conservatism of the Reagan years and its impact on sexual politics, and because of the urgent need to think expansively about sex in the context of the first years of the AIDS epidemic. I have fed and deepened my thinking and writing about the history of social movements and the politics of sexuality by long immersions in the kind of worlds that I write about. Over the years, this sort of reciprocity has kept me wanting to write.

The book that I have just finished—a biography of Bayard Rustin, a Gandhian activist, radical pacifist, and civil rights strategist—has absorbed me for a dozen years. It is bigger, measured by numbers of pages, than any-thing I've written before. The motives that drew me to Rustin's life were more complicated than those that sparked other projects. The push to write about him came from the emotional residue still lingering from my time as an undergraduate here on Morningside Heights in the late 1960s; it came from experiences in the classroom with undergraduates who wanted explanations and insights about the 1960s that I didn't have; and it rose out of the dilemmas that I saw queer activists confronting at the height of AIDS politics in the early 1990s. Without my intending it, the work on Rustin has been framed by the two Gulf Wars. I began the project the month after the first one started, and I finished the book the month before this one began.

The issues that Rustin's life puts before us have never seemed more compelling to address. He believed that war would never bring peace and that violence would never bring justice. He saw nationalism as a destruc-tive force in human affairs. He believed that economic insecurity and in-equality made a sham out of political democracy. When I ask myself "why I write" in the context of this book I've just finished—in the midst of this war my government is waging, in a political moment as repellent as any I've experienced in my lifetime, when our national government's devotion to no one but the rich and powerful isn't even masked—I also ask myself, "How do I make use of these words?"

I imagine spending the next couple of years on the road with Bayard Rustin. I see myself taking him or at least my account of his life to a range of venues: bookstores, community centers, and university lecture halls; radio talk shows and web pages; newspapers, magazines, and organizational newsletters. I want to use this writing as an opportunity to create spaces, real and virtual, where audiences can coalesce and conversations can occur so that together folks can reflect about issues of war and peace, racial and economic justice, and forms of democracy that are both local and global.

As I plot these activities, I realize that the reason I have continued to write is that it's the way that I've found to keep issues like this at the center of my life.

6

Putting Sex into History and History into Sex

While the previous essay allowed me to reflect on the shift-ing motivations behind my writing, this essay represents an attempt to explain how the interpretive focus of the history that I have written has shifted over the course of a genera-tion. What was I trying to accomplish when, in the 1970s and 1980s, I first started writing about gay history? How have I come to understand the history of sexuality and the history of social movements differently as I continued to write and research? This essay originated as a talk given at UCLA in 2007.

Virtually all of my work has concerned either social movements or sexuality. Often it has been located at the place where those two topics intersect. I am interested in how the disenfranchised, the marginalized, and the excluded, by acting together, make change and intentionally become a force in the world. I try to understand sexuality not as something private, not as some-thing understood primarily through biology or individual psychology, but as something social, cultural, and political and, in many ways, very public. I am fascinated by what sexuality can reveal about cultural outlook, social arrangements, and the unequal distribution of power and privilege in a society.

When I began this kind of work, in the mid-1970s, it was very much connected to the gay and lesbian movement of those years. Activists often framed their task as one of freeing a group of people from oppression. Since silence and invisibility were the tropes deployed by the movement to indicate oppression, as a young historian I went in search of this group of people to make them visible and to restore their voices.

The product of this effort was *Sexual Politics, Sexual Communities: The Making of a Homosexual Minority in the United States, 1940–1970.* It was a study of the pioneering generation of gay and lesbian activists who, between the 1940s and the 1960s, seeded the ground that flowered into the much larger movement of the 1970s. At the time the book was published, it was a new and interesting story. Most people, other than the participants themselves, did not know about it. It was also a story that intersected with some of the "big events" of the era: World War II, McCarthyism, the civil rights movement, the Beat generation, the emerging counterculture, and the sexual revolution.

It turned out to be a more complicated story than a simple recounting of the early stages of a group's political mobilization. It became a story of consciousness as well, a story of creation, of the *making* of a minority. A self-conscious social group came into existence where there had not been one before. By 1970 the terms "gay" and "lesbian" had much greater solidity in American culture than before. They had congealed as social categories in a way that had been much less true even a generation earlier.

This study of the pre-Stonewall movement was one part of a larger collective enterprise. It included the work of British sociologists and historians, including Mary McIntosh, Jeffrey Weeks, and Kenneth Plummer, and of historians and social scientists in the United States, among them Jonathan Ned Katz, Elizabeth Kennedy, Esther Newton, and Allan Bérubé.[1] Together, and with the validation that came from the translation into English of Michel Foucault's work on the history of sexuality, a "social construction" school of interpretation emerged. It emphasized the plasticity and malleability of human sexuality. In other words, sex changes, and consequently this made it a subject for historical investigation.

But what shapes sexuality? How does it get shaped? Why does it assume the forms that it does? What connections does sexuality have to other structures, institutions, and discourses?

In an attempt to pursue such questions, I found myself moving from the task of recuperating the history of a group of silenced and invisible

90

people to an exploration more generally of an aspect of human experience and social life. This led me to write pieces like "Capitalism and Gay Identity," in which I attempted to link economic structures and the social form that same-sex love and desire took. It led me to write "The Homosexual Menace," a look at the mobilization of state power and the elaboration of a state-generated discourse about sexual perversion during the McCarthy era. Most of all, it led me to write, with Estelle Freedman, *Intimate Matters: A History of Sexuality in America*.

We intended *Intimate Matters* to be a broad interpretive synthesis of what was then just a developing area of study. We took our own research, combined it with the published work of others, and fashioned a preliminary narrative of the history of sexuality in the United States. We looked at shifts in the meanings of sex. We identified some of the ways that the social regulation of sex had changed. We examined the moments when sexual issues became particularly salient as sources of political conflict.

Many themes emerged, but, to me, most significant was the close and inextricable relationship between sexuality and inequality. In so many ways, sexuality had been implicated in the production and reproduction of hierarchy. It had helped to structure patterns of inclusion and exclusion, and it had served as a location of both oppression and resistance. Take, for instance, the matter of prostitution in the first two decades of the twentieth century. Rhetoric about white slavery and an international traffic in women saturated the campaigns against prostitution. It served to expand the reach of nativist thought and broaden the sentiment to restrict immigration. Or, consider in the post–World War II era the way mothers on welfare were commonly represented as young and African American. This discourse linked a particular combination of class, race, and gender with immorality and thus served as a boundary-drawing device separating moral productive Americans from those who were not.

The work on *Intimate Matters* was but one piece of a much broader intellectual shift that was occurring in the 1980s in feminist scholarship. This reorientation can be traced in important anthologies of the time, like *Powers of Desire* and *Pleasure and Danger*.[2] It can be tracked as well in the intellectual and political debates within feminism that came to be called the "sex wars," when some writers and activists were pressing for sexuality not to be seen as coterminous with gender. Rather than absorbing sexuality within the analytic framework of gender, some were attempting to look at it as a domain of analysis in its own right. Perhaps the best and clearest statement of this was the essay "Thinking Sex" by the anthropologist Gayle Rubin.

After *Intimate Matters* I think I had the sense that "Okay, I did my part. Here's a broad outline of this history. Now you all can fill it in." I moved on to something else, a project that prioritized my interests in movements for social justice and that zoomed in on the 1960s. I thought that the life of Bayard Rustin, a radical pacifist, a Gandhian advocate for racial equality, and a socialist, would be a good vehicle for exploring the 1960s with a fresh eye.

Rustin is a very significant figure in mid-twentieth-century America. His life story can function almost as a synopsis of progressive movements for peace, justice, and equality from the 1930s to the 1960s. Through Rustin's career one can trace the transformation of American pacifism from a philosophy espoused by a tiny core of devoutly religious activists on the margins of the nation's consciousness to a movement that critiqued the nuclear arms race, conducted demonstrations across the globe, made it feasible for nations to cease atmospheric testing of nuclear weapons, and helped galvanize a massive opposition to the Vietnam War in the 1960s. Following Rustin's life allows one to see the Americanization of Gandhi and his philosophy of nonviolent active resistance to oppression. Rustin more than anyone else insinuated nonviolence into the heart of the black freedom struggle. He helped shape the career of Martin Luther King Jr. and the rise of the Southern Christian Leadership Conference as a major activist organization. His skill made the 1963 March on Washington such a resounding success, and the March helped to incorporate collective mass action into the accepted repertoire of political expression. Through Rustin, one can observe the articulation of coalition politics and multi-issue organizing before the birth of theories of intersectionality.

Writing about Rustin links the 1930s and the 1960s, two eras of mass mobilization in the United States. It demands that one explore the relationship between the Old Left and the New Left as well as the impact of McCarthyism on the progressive tradition in the United States. Rustin's life makes it clear that one cannot adequately interpret the 1960s without understanding the 1940s and 1950s, as well. His career brings to mind Jacquelyn Hall's presidential address to the Organization of American Historians, when she offered her conceptualization of a "long civil rights movement."[3]

These are all vitally important topics, and my biography of Rustin naturally touched on them. But Bayard Rustin was also a gay man, and,

92

because I brought my own intellectual history to the writing of *Lost Prophet*, the book inevitably took on a particular flavor. I like to think that I was open to certain kinds of questions to which many others might not have attended. And so, if I started out as a young historian in search of a group of people and if I moved on to study a broad sphere of human activity, with Rustin's life I found myself engaged in a project in which I put history into sexuality and put gay into history.

Putting Rustin's Life into the Orbit of Gay History

It might seem odd to say this, but Rustin's life and the history in which it is embedded stand outside the orbit of gay history as it was then and, more often than not, still is constructed. GLBT history has focused most strongly on those areas of experience where gay has been most densely packed: the pre-Stonewall movement; the community of working-class lesbians in Buffalo; gay New York; the creative moment of the Harlem Renaissance; communities and networks of educated middle-class women who loved other women; moments, like World War II and the McCarthy era, when mainstream sources of power and authority clashed directly with an emerging GLBT community.

The periodization of lesbian and gay history that has taken shape describes two contrasting class-based worlds at the end of the nineteenth century: a middle-class world that affirmed romantic friendships among women and among men and a working-class world of gender crossing in which same-sex relationships were structured around gender polarities. These gave way in the early twentieth century to urban communities that were progenitors of today's visible gay and lesbian communities. These emergent communities experienced a short period of openness in the decade or so after World War I. But this was followed by a long period of repression that commenced in the 1930s, continued through the 1960s, and helped construct the closet as metaphor and experience. Yes, there were efforts at resistance, but it took the Stonewall rebellion and the birth of gay liberation to usher in the beginnings of a new world in the 1970s.

At first glance, Rustin's life perfectly comports with this interpretive periodization. He moved to New York City in the 1930s in search of more freedom. From the 1940s through the 1960s, the era of the closet, when to step in any way into visibility risked bringing the force of the state and the opprobrium of society down upon one's head, Rustin's sexuality brought him trouble again and again and again. In 1944, while serving a term in federal prison as a conscientious objector, Rustin's efforts to organize inmates to resist racial segregation were disrupted when prison administrators charged him with sexual misconduct. The next two years were physically, emotionally, and spiritually harrowing for him. In the postwar years, Rustin got tangled in incident after incident: an arrest for solicitation in New York City, another arrest for being in a park after closing hour, a beating in Louisiana when he misread a potential sexual encounter, and, finally, in 1953, an arrest in Pasadena on a lewd-conduct charge. The Pasadena arrest led to a conviction and sixty days in the county prison farm, as well as his very public labeling as a sex pervert and a homosexual.

Rustin managed to avoid any other incidents after Pasadena. But, in this era of intense persecution, he was no longer able to control the circulation of information about his sexuality and thus was vulnerable to the use that others chose to make of it. The American Friends Service Committee debated again and again whether the group could use Rustin as a lecturer and trainer in nonviolence and pacifist education. In 1958 the American Legion in Montana protested a lecture by Rustin at a state college campus and circulated information about Rustin's sexuality that made it into the press. In 1956, when he traveled to Montgomery, Alabama, to provide help in the early stages of the bus boycott, his presence there agitated the interlocking circles of activists in the peace, civil rights, and labor movements, and efforts were made to get him out of Montgomery. Later in the decade, Rustin was not chosen to be director of the Southern Christian Leadership Conference, even though he had probably done as much as anyone to move Martin Luther King Jr. in the direction of creating his own organization and to shape the organization that King did create. In 1960, when he was in charge of planning massive demonstrations outside the Democratic and Republican national conventions, he fell victim to the scheming and rumor-mongering of Congressman Adam Clayton Powell and NAACP director Roy Wilkins. Neither of them wanted Rustin's influence in the civil rights movement, and they used his sexuality to isolate him. In 1963, after he had been chosen to organize the March on Washington despite all this, Rustin found himself attacked as a sexual pervert on the floor of the US Senate by Strom Thurmond, who put evidence of Rustin's Pasadena arrest into the Congressional Record.

On the surface, all of this looks like the sad old story of gay oppression tempered somewhat by the historian's revisionist tale of oppression marked by resistance. Bad things happen to Rustin again and again. But, like the homophile activists who started a movement against great odds, like the working-class lesbians of Buffalo who fought the police to create a public space for themselves, and like the black drag queens of Chicago who, in the 1950s, were having annual public parades, Rustin survived and endured. Despite twenty years of incidents, Rustin kept rising again: he may have been down, but he was also never out.

But Rustin's experience is so much richer than this. It isn't his sparring with a prison warden or an encounter with the Los Angeles County police or the ranting of Strom Thurmond that is the heart of Rustin's story. Rather, it is the engagement with a world of comrades and colleagues. This continual engagement pushed Rustin to fashion a stronger, less apologetic, identity. It forced the progressive activist circles in which he moved to fashion some kind of accommodation to the queer in its midst.

In an age when the topic of homosexuality was not openly discussed in mixed circles, reconstructing this process was not easy. The most extensive documentary record comes from the World War II years when Rustin was in prison. Fragments of a compelling correspondence among Rustin, his lover Davis Platt, his pacifist mentor A. J. Muste, another work associate, and a friend suggest a very dramatic story. Labeled by the prison system and put in isolation, Rustin struggled with a powerful, aching loneliness. He wrestled over whether to attempt to live as a heterosexual or to accept an ascetic discipline of celibacy and find some way to tame his homosexual longings.

Because Rustin worked for the Fellowship of Reconciliation, a Christian pacifist organization, the correspondence was framed within a religious discourse. Interestingly, those on the outside condemned not his homosexuality but the ethics of his sexual relationships. As one of his friends expressed it: "I would still be not at all concerned at the physical side of things if I felt a continuity and a sense of real love for another person. You know how it has been—relationships have been intense, perhaps, but basically very casual for you. It is not the physical side, but the promiscuity and carelessness which bothers me." Muste also took this approach. "On the question of a-typical relationships," he wrote, "my position has not changed. I insist people must be understood and loved. I keep my mind open." But his mind was not open to the promiscuity and duplicity of Rustin's sexual life. "I know there is that in you," he continued, "which shrinks from a decision here because you want personal security, love, warmth, being wanted. We all do, and God, what we don't do to get these things. But you are not getting them. . . . [I]n you there are depths and gifts which will bring you security, warmth, exhilaration, ecstatic joy, if only you give up what amounts to a death-wish almost for insecurity, for a surface tickling of yourself and an exploitation of others." Muste wanted a commitment from Rustin. He wanted a promise to end the promiscuity. If that required saying no to relationships with men, so be it. And yet Rustin, despite the enormous emotional stress, despite the awareness that his sexuality was in some sense doing him in, refused to make such a pledge. "There is nothing more I can say on this," he finally writes back to Muste, and there the correspondence ends.

Eight years later, Rustin found himself languishing in a Los Angeles County jail, devastated by his arrest and conviction on a public-sex charge. But, in response to a letter from one of his colleagues at the Fellowship, even at this lowest moment Rustin deflected attention from his sexuality. "I have gone deeper in the past six weeks than ever before and feel that I have at last seen my real problem. Sex has never been my basic problem," he wrote. "Pride, self . . . I was as selfish as a child. I am sure that in a way I must have known this. Now I feel it and know that pride must be overcome."

When he returned to New York and was sent to a psychiatrist to help him pull his life together, the psychiatrist did not engage in the kind of therapeutic practice that the prescriptive scientific literature of the era would suggest. He did not try to "cure" Rustin of his homosexuality. Instead, he pushed Rustin to face the rage that he lived with and not to act it out through reckless sexual activities that would only get him into trouble. Rustin came to serve in this period as a mentor to a younger generation of gay men who were active in progressive social change. He offered an intellectual defense of homosexuality that helped shepherd these younger men through the process of coming to terms with their sexuality.

After 1953 it is meaningless to speak of Rustin as being in the closet.

In looking for "the road to Stonewall," should we be looking in new and different places? Should we broaden our search beyond the work of homophile organizations or the social worlds created by bar life and the resistance that police harassment helped to shape? If we pull Rustin's life and the history of which he is a part into our framework of GLBT history, what do we find? It is certainly not a story of the closet. Nor is it a story that revolves primarily around the poles of oppression and resistance. Instead, it is a much blurrier story of engagement, of a give-and-take, of the majority struggling over whether and how to accommodate the queer in its midst. How do we tease out or measure the significance of this? Because the codes of discretion and habits of indiscretion often have not left an explicit documentary trail, it is not easy to do this.

Let me point to at least one indicator of historical influence. In the early 1960s, the Society of Friends produced a study, *Toward a Quaker View of Sex*, that departed from seven hundred years of Christian teaching about homosexuality. It became the opening statement in a continuing debate within Christian communities of faith about the morality of same-sex relationships. Rustin was an active Friend. He attended international Quaker conferences and was widely known. He was a subject of controversy in the 1950s. Can we see in the production of this document traces of his life and the impact it had?

As the movements of which Rustin was an integral part grew after the mid-1950s, the circles of debate, reflection, and disclosure inevitably extended ever more widely. In a sense, through Rustin's presence, the world of progressive social change entered a two-decades-long conversation about sexuality. His presence in a room—or his absence and the question of whether he should be invited into the room—forced an encounter with homophobia, a disruption of the normally unspoken assumptions about the heteronormative order of things.

I am not trying to replace a stark picture of oppression and a few brave resisters with a rosier picture. Rustin paid a very high personal price for this engagement. To his daily inescapable confrontations with white racism was added the stigma that attached to a gay identity. But putting Rustin's life and the worlds of which he was a part into the story of gay history allows us to piece together a different narrative.

Pulling Rustin's Gayness into the Narrative of Mid-Twentieth-Century America

Now let me reverse direction and look at Rustin's story from a second angle. What different understandings might we come up with if we pulled Rustin's sexuality into the narrative of mid-twentieth-century America?

Here we enter the tangled world of the 1960s and interpretations of that decade. The story of the 1960s has often been framed as a story of declension, of the rise and fall of American liberalism, or of the rise and fall of dynamic movements for progressive social change. There are the "good '60s" and the "bad '60s." The good '60s are about sit-ins and freedom rides, about wars on poverty and about the Peace Corps, about idealistic students and a hopeful, unifying rhetoric. The bad '60s are about war in Asia, about campus and urban rebellions, about the National Guard and the police attacking citizens, about assassinations, and about angry, polarizing rhetoric.

The moment when the worm turned came at mid-decade, between 1964 and 1966, when the leading edge of both black protest and the white New Left came to see Democratic Party liberals as the problem, as an obstruction, an entrenched interest, the source of the injustice they were fighting. Instead of making common cause, instead of engaging political differences in coalition, much of the left, both black and white, came to target liberals. The attacks from the left, along with the internal stresses created by Johnson's war policies, eventually led to the fracturing of New Deal liberalism and the beginning of the long decline of its institutional political power. Not coincidently, these political developments also opened the door for the rise of a new right-wing movement. Conservatives, who seemed beaten beyond recovery after the 1964 election, began a march toward political dominance. This moment, when liberalism and the left seemed to head in opposite directions, emerges in most writing as an intensely critical one in the history of American politics.

Interestingly, Rustin was absolutely and unequivocally arguing for the opposite of what happened. At the time, he was saying in every venue he could find that the left must work in coalition with liberals inside the Democratic Party. He argued that the left needed to adjust to its growing strength. It needed to imagine itself as not forever consigned to protest from the outside but instead as able to reshape from the inside the allegiances, the commitments, and the agenda of the Democratic Party.

It is important to understand here that Rustin, at that moment, was a unique figure. He was not just one more voice on the left mouthing off about strategy. His connections were as broad as anyone's. They encompassed the peace movement, the black freedom struggle, the labor movement, and the anti-Stalinist left. He had relationships with thousands of activists from around the country, built over time and spanning generations. He had proved his commitments across more than two decades. He had a reputation as a practical skilled organizer and as a theorist whose ideas about strategy grew organically from his experience. He was just coming off the great success of the March on Washington, which he had organized. Rustin ought to have commanded attention and credibility. At the very least, his ideas deserved a respectful airing.

But Rustin's political theorizing, what he described in a 1965 article as the need for a transition "from protest to politics," initiated something other than reasoned discussion. It set off a process in which he was publicly attacked and reviled not by Southern segregationists, not by J. Edgar Hoover and the FBI, but by his own long-standing comrades on the left. They attacked him not for being a sexual pervert but for being a turncoat, a betrayer of the revolutionary enterprise. Rustin survived two decades of trouble over his sexual identity only to find the fatally irresolvable conflict in his life coming over his political ideas.

One could make the claim that the attacks leveled at Rustin are entirely explicable within the categories of left-wing political discourse. The invective and the specific charges in some ways were not ad hominem but quite formulaic. Staughton Lynd, for instance, described Rustin as "a labor lieutenant of capitalism." But as I sifted through the evidence and tried to make sense of the dramatic turnaround in Rustin's political fortunes (from "Mr. March on Washington" almost to pariah), my historian's intuition made me wonder if something more was at play. I wonder to what degree Rustin's experience of a marginalized sexuality left him open to new political formulations. I wonder to what degree the continuing stigma of his sexuality left him isolated and therefore more vulnerable to political attack. I wonder whether the hard edge of criticism directed at his political views reflected a displacement of sexual antagonisms and anxieties.

Let me offer some examples of what I mean. Rustin was very unusual in arguing among radicals for this move into mainstream politics. Michael Harrington is the only other leftist of any stature making this political case. Rustin, I'm convinced, had grown completely impatient with left-wing notions of revolution and with the left's entrenched psychological commitment to outsider status. Other heterosexual male leftists may have experienced political marginality in relationship to power, but they also felt themselves embedded in a community. Even as Rustin was of this world, he was also simultaneously outside it. Did this different angle of vision make him receptive to breaking with conventional wisdom on the left about how to make change? Did it make him receptive to new political ideas?

Political ideas, especially about strategy, do not gain credence and weight simply by their cogency. Ideas do not exist in a vacuum; they have institutional contexts and institutional bases. At the time that Rustin was arguing for this engagement with mainstream party politics, he was without an institutional home. He had no institutional structure to mobilize behind him. He was operating essentially as a freelance organizer, moving from project to project. He lacked an institutional capacity to implement his ideas.

But how could that be? Rustin was one of the best organizers in the country. He had just pulled off what seemed like a miracle by organizing the March on Washington in just seven weeks. Early in 1964 he organized a one-day boycott of the New York City public schools, perhaps the largest racial justice action ever taken. Given this talent, Rustin's free-floating status can be explained only by the sexual stigma he carried, by the continuing discomfort that it provoked for many. Even as the civil rights movement in 1963 defended him against the attacks of a Strom Thurmond and publicly embraced him, many of those in it were unwilling to draw him too close. How might political outcomes have been different if Rustin had been able to argue his political views from inside the Southern Christian Leadership Conference?

One of the frustrating aspects of studying history is that the "what if" questions and the "if only" speculations can never be answered because the past cannot be replayed. We will never know if the political road that Rustin was proposing might have led in productive directions. We do, however, have a revealing analogue. At almost the same moment that the left was rejecting the strategic notion of reshaping the Democratic Party in more progressive directions, the right was formulating a plan to capture the Republican Party and reshape it in more conservative directions. They succeeded only too well, and they succeeded in part through the contribution that the left's attack on liberalism made to the disruption and discrediting of the Democratic majority.

So, to restate the argument—or perhaps the question: How would the narrative of GLBT history have to change if we were to make it take account of so much history, like the world of Bayard Rustin, that occurs outside its current boundaries? And how might the contours of mainstream narratives of twentieth-century US history look different if we were to pull gay experience and the workings of homophobia into the story? These are questions worth considering.

7

History, Social Movements, and Community Organizing

The campaign and election of Barack Obama in 2008 put the attention of many Americans on the topic of community organizing: What is it? Who does it? Why does one do it? What does it lead to? Many students naturally shared this curiosity and enthusiasm, and, at the University of Illinois at Chicago, where I teach, the graduate students in the history department responded by doing their own form of community organizing. They pulled together a conference in spring 2009 on the topic of social movements and community organizing. These were my remarks to the attendees.

This is a good time to be studying the history of social movements and community organizing. The 2008 election brought to the White House a man who proudly affirms his experience as a community organizer. Many of the faces at the inauguration of President Obama recalled the last great era of progressive social movements, when large numbers of Americans marched on Washington as part of their work for racial justice and an end to an unpopular war. We are also in the midst of the most serious economic downturn since the Great Depression of the 1930s, and we know from its history that economic crisis can provoke major social and political upheaval.

In reflecting on what I have learned about writing the history of social movements, I am reminded of my years in a Jesuit high school for boys. My Jesuit teachers were very engaged in the world. They cared about social justice, and they communicated that message in lots of ways. They were also devoted to logical argument. In the school's speech and debate society, they taught us that all subjects, all topics, all lectures—everything, really— can be divided into three parts. So, as a tribute to these first memorable teachers who communicated a passion for taking action to make the world a better place, I want to offer three lessons on the road to writing powerful histories of popular mobilizations and collective political action.

Lesson #1

If you want to write smart, insightful histories of social movements and community organizing, read sociology!

Why do I say this? History is very likely the most under-theorized discipline in the humanities and the social sciences. When history departments offer methodology courses, it usually means that students will read varieties of history. They will study works of social, political, and intellectual history; or they will compare and contrast works of local and national history; or they will read books that have used different bodies of evidence, such as private correspondence or census data. When I ask myself, "What is historical methodology," I usually settle on two things. Something uses historical methods if it explores change across time, and the best methodological advice to give a researcher is to "read everything." Read every newspaper, every government document, every letter, every diary, and every organizational newsletter. Read everything one can find that relates, however tenuously, to the topic. When you stop turning up anything new, anything that offers a new perspective, the time has come to start writing. These are the methods that I learned as an undergraduate history major and that were reinforced when I was a graduate student in history, required only to take history courses. They were the methods that I in turn impressed upon students in the years when I taught in a college history department.

Yet, at the same time, through good fortune and circumstance, I also stumbled outside my disciplinary field and wandered into rich intellectual territory that has made me a better historian. In the first half of the 1970s, I was part of an effort to build a new organization, the Gay Academic Union, the first such organization of its kind in the United States. All of us involved in the GAU saw knowledge as a tool for social change, and we wanted to build a large body of gay and lesbian scholarship. Though I was a historian in the making, the scholarly literature on such topics was slim to nonexistent. The result was that we came together across disciplinary lines, read widely across fields of knowledge, and engaged in lively discussions that reflected our different ways of constructing knowledge and understanding the world. Later, with a group of like-minded activists that I met through the GAU, I was part of a Marxist study group. Over a period of two years, we plunged into the writing of Marx and Engels, slowly building up to a several-months-long reading of Volume I of *Capital*. The analysis and interpretive framework were revelatory to me, and it was akin to having a conversion experience. I felt as if I understood the process of historical change in a way that I had not before. I felt as if I finally had a theoretical scaffold from which to hang my evidence. Or, to describe it another way, dialectical materialism became the architectural style of my historical edifice, and my research and evidence were the furnishings for the house. It proved very intellectually invigorating. Out of it came my essay "Capitalism and Gay Identity," which has probably enjoyed a wider readership than anything else I have written.

A few years later, I had the opportunity to attend a summer-long seminar at the Center for Advanced Study in the Behavioral Sciences. The participants were drawn from the broad spectrum of the social sciences. Our readings reflected that range of disciplinary backgrounds. I found myself encountering for the first time what was then called "new social movement" theory. Produced especially by sociologists, this writing tended to look closely at the social movements of the 1960s and 1970s and to construct theoretical frameworks for understanding the conditions that give rise to social movements, what makes them succeed or fail, why they develop in certain directions and not others, and other such matters. I would not claim that, having read a wide swath of this literature, I became a convert to one school of interpretation as opposed to another. Its influence on me was more diffuse. But it was critically important nonetheless, and over the years it led me to produce a number of essays about social movement history.

Theory allows us to move beyond rich storytelling (a valuable thing, to be sure). It lets us reach toward interpreting, toward generalizing, toward seeing broad patterns beyond the specific events, people, organizations, communities, and campaigns that we are studying. Let me give an example. In *The Dividends of Dissent*, Amin Ghaziani studies four national GLBT marches on Washington, stretched across three decades.[1] It is a historical study, but not in the way that I or most other historians would do it. Rather than construct a continuous narrative that covers the marches from conception to outcome and impact, he focuses on the process of organizing the marches themselves. In every case, the process was deeply, deeply factionalized. Participants engaged in bitter, almost blood-curdling conflict. Such conflict within and between movement organizations is not unfamiliar to historians. Think, for instance, of the history of the Student Nonviolent Coordinating Committee, of the Students for a Democratic Society, and of second-wave feminism. Historians have recounted, often in painstaking detail, the ways that factionalism and infighting disrupt the forward march of a social movement and destroy organizations. But Ghaziani reaches a different conclusion. Using social science theory, he interprets factionalism as generative and productive. It allows a variety of ideas to surface and lets different goals and strategies compete for followers. It is a totally fascinating take on his subject, one that leads to interesting reflection, and not one toward which most historians, caught up in the drama of the evidence of our sources, might easily gravitate.

Here is another example, drawn as much from my involvement in GLBT activism as from my study of it. For many years I found myself puzzled by the inability of the movement to have a national organization with local chapters. Other social movements had done this. Think, for instance, of the National Association for the Advancement of Colored People, the National Urban League, and the National Organization for Women. In the 1960s, Students for a Democratic Society, the chief organization of the white student New Left, had scores of campus chapters. In each case, the combination of national and local under one roof facilitated the growth of activism. When I served on the board of the National Gay and Lesbian Task Force, this often frustrating state of affairs generated many conversations about strategy and tactics. We tried and tried and tried to think of ways to make this happen, but we never got anywhere.

Then, years later, I came across path dependence theory, a staple of political science but also creatively used by economists and legal theorists. According to this line of thought, simple events and choices, coming out of particular conditions and moments, open a path that historical actors continue to walk down. Events and choices that might not have been deeply thought out nonetheless continue to influence future choices and events. They constrain the range of possibilities forever, despite the wishes of historical actors. Gay and lesbian liberation exploded into existence at the end of the 1960s, when grassroots activism was bubbling up in many forms. The movement took form through the proliferation of local organizations, rooted in the goal of solving local problems like police harassment and in providing support for coming out. By the time some activists began to consider a national organization, there was no way they could form chapters without being considered interlopers by local activists. Decades later, I and my comrades could forever beat ourselves over the head about our failure to create a national organization with chapters. Or, more productively, we could ask ourselves what paths were still available to create a movement in which there were cooperative ties between local and national. And that is exactly what has tended to happen in the past two decades. Through national conferences that bring together local activists to share experiences and lessons learned and through loose federations of local and state organizations working on common issues, the GLBT movement has managed to forge stronger relations between local and national.

So, lesson #1: read sociology! By which I mean: move beyond the evidence gathering that constitutes historical research methods, and find yourself theoretical tools that speak to the events, topics, movements, and communities you are trying to understand. Wear your theory lightly so that you continue to tell compelling stories, but wear it nonetheless.

Lesson #2

If you want to write smart, insightful, credible histories of community organizing and social movements, then join a community organization or become an activist in a social movement.

I write these words, and I immediately see a bright red light, flashing a warning in front of me. It is trying to alert me to the danger this advice poses to my "objectivity." Won't joining a movement and becoming a participant compromise my ability to write good history? Won't I be too invested in my conclusions or in particular kinds of conclusions if I have attachments to the organizations and mobilizations and issues that I want to write about?

There are dangers. Some of the early work on Students for a Democratic Society was produced by people who were close to it, and they present it, even when taking issue with some of its actions, as God's gift to humanity, as the key site for productive activism in the United States. More recent work, produced at a greater distance, has more of a critical and detached edge. If we are too close, as participants or as partisans, there is the danger of writing the history that we wish had happened or arriving at the conclusions we wish were true. So, yes, beware of how your emotional investments may compromise an ability to make hard interpretive choices.

Despite this danger, I am absolutely convinced that my own long history of involvement in a variety of movements and organizations and campaigns—sometimes as volunteer activist, sometimes as paid staff in an organization—has made me a better historian. It has allowed me to write histories that I believe are more insightful, more thoughtful, and more nuanced. I am convinced of this, though I also will admit that I can't prove it.

Nonetheless, I have example after example of issues that surface when trying to research and write the history of community organizing and social movements that I know I understand better because I have experienced these issues firsthand in one organization or another. For instance, working for progressive activist organizations has made me acutely aware of the scarcity question. So much has to get done with so few resources; too often the lack of resources subverts the loftiest goals. From the outside, it is easy to be sharply critical of the failures of movement organizations. But, from the inside, it often seems amazing that so much can happen through the force of passion and commitment alone. Social movements and community organizations regularly perform miracles.

Then there is the matter of human irrationality and how it plays out. Oppression and deprivation exact a toll. Yes, oppression can make people heroic. Suffering can generate compassion and generosity and lots of other wonderful human qualities. But oppression also hurts, and it can make people absolutely nutty. It can generate conflicts—infighting—that make no sense at all. The conflict will often get expressed in ideological terms, but it is really about people acting out the internalization of oppression. It has been both fascinating and disturbing to watch this phenomenon play itself out in organizations and do its damage. From a distance, historians can attribute the ruptures and divisions to serious differences in outlook. Up close, it looks very personal.

More constructively, close involvement in movements allows one to experience the almost magical power of individuals. Yes, the collective, the group, the cause itself, is important. But it is also revelatory to watch how much difference an individual can make. I don't mean the charismatic power that some individuals possess, like a Dr. Martin Luther King Jr. I mean the individual as an on-the-ground, inside-the-organization leader. Leadership is important, and there is a vast difference between good leadership and bad leadership. The power of individuals in social movements and in community organizing is less about the great speech and more about how an individual can effectively mobilize a group of people to work together effectively.

One of the first things I observed during my early years as a gay activist was the huge gap between the stated purposes of an organization and what is actually going on. Social scientists refer to this in terms of instrumental goals (the goals and mission of an organization) and expressive goals (what the individual gets out of it emotionally). Organizations in identity-based movements often function more as a home, as a safe haven from the daily assaults of an oppressive society, than as a group marching determinedly forward to transform society. But this can also be true of other movements, as well. Has the pacifist movement, without realizing it, had an investment in remaining small so that it can serve as a perfectionist, utopian community for its members? Without an appreciation gained from direct experience in movement groups, I am not sure I would have noticed this from the archival record that has been left behind.

Finally, participation feeds my commitment to research and writing. Involvement in organizations devoted to social, political, and economic change makes me want to study movements and learn more so that I can be a more effective activist. And studying movements of the past feeds my commitment to engagement in the here and now.

So, lesson #2: join a social movement or a community organization. It will make you a more insightful historian.

Lesson #3

Think big!

Let's be honest. In choosing to research and write about popular mobilizations and community organizing, our motivation is very often a passion for justice and equality. We have a strong urge to write about the dispossessed, the outsiders, the underdogs, the forgotten, the subalterns.

We want to put them front and center, to give them their due, to return their lives and their hopes and their dreams to the historical record. Of course, we will write critical, thoughtful history. But there is no question who or what we are putting at the heart of our story.

This is fine and good. But we owe it to our subjects, and we owe it to our allegiance to a truthful and useful history (and the one is the other), to embed their stories of organizing, mobilizing, and sacrificing in the biggest possible context.

Let me illustrate what I mean with gay history as an example. The first long generation of us who wrote in this area certainly made an effort to embed our work in larger contexts. In writing about the pre-Stonewall movement, I made a nod toward Cold War anticommunism as an important setting for my story. In *Gay New York*, George Chauncey acknowledges the complex process of urbanization that was occurring in the early twentieth century. In *Men Like That*, John Howard makes regionalism a critical part of the setting.[2] But, in the end, all of us ended up writing queer-centric histories. What moves our stories forward are the actions of our subjects, the men and women about whom we cared passionately.

In my research on Chicago's queer past, I have found myself pushing against this queer-centric framework. One of the most important changes that occurred in the 1970s in many cities around the country was a substantial decline in police harassment. This decline made it possible for more geographically stable and visible urban communities to develop, which in turn made it easier for others to find and participate in community life. The common explanation for this change is the militancy of a new breed of radical activists after Stonewall; their public demonstrations against bar raids and arrests forced the police to change their practices.

Chicago was one of the cities that saw a decline in raids, bar closures, and arrests. But it would be hard to claim that activists were primarily responsible. In Chicago, the police were one element of Richard Daley's political machine. In return for being loyal members of the machine, police had a relatively free hand to do as they wished, to engage in graft involving bars and liquor licenses, and to exact retribution against recalcitrant bar owners who refused to be extorted. Daley was not going to deny police their perks. It took outside pressure to make that happen, and the outside pressure suddenly materialized after Richard Nixon, a Republican, was elected president in 1968. Under Nixon, the US Department of Justice had no reservations about exposing the corruption of a key element of

Democratic political power in the Midwest. Thus, police practices were exposed; scores were arrested, tried, and convicted; and law enforcement in Chicago had to retreat. One important side effect of this much-larger-than-gay political story is the flourishing of a new kind of gay neighborhood and gay community in the 1970s and 1980s. Does my willingness to have the biggest plausible frame for my story minimize the importance of gay men and lesbians in history? I don't think so. Instead, I am connecting their story to national politics.

So, lesson #3: if you want to write the best possible history of community organizing and social movements, think big. Think as big as you possibly can.

8

If I Knew Then

Doing Oral History

Oral history has been an essential component of LGBT history from its beginnings. Interviews with informants about their experience have allowed for much richer accounts of public civic life and activism as well as for accounts of the social life and intimate experience of individuals who, as the title of one book suggests, have been "hidden from history." In 2012 Nan Alamilla Boyd and Horacio N. Roque Ramírez edited *Bodies of Evidence,* an anthology of original essays on the practice of queer oral history. My afterword to the collection allowed me to draw on my own experience and reflect on the different ways that oral history has figured in my work.

Oral histories have played an important part in my work since I started doing history. Between 1976 and 1980, for what became *Sexual Politics, Sexual Communities,* I interviewed about forty men and women who had been active in the pre-Stonewall homophile movement. Then, in the

This essay first appeared in Nan Alamilla Boyd and Horacio N. Roque Ramírez, eds., *Bodies of Evidence: The Practice of Queer Oral History* (New York: Oxford University Press, 2012), 269–77.

1990s, I conducted a comparable number for *Lost Prophet*, my biography of Bayard Rustin, a radical pacifist and civil rights activist who was also a gay man. Now, in my current work on the history of sexuality in Chicago, I am using oral histories done by others. In all these projects, I also pored through a large body of documentary evidence, some in archives and some in private hands.[1]

Oral histories functioned differently in these endeavors. In the case of the history of pre-Stonewall activism, I could not have produced a dissertation and, later, a book that was up to snuff without the interviews to which so many activists graciously consented. The archived materials at that point were slim; the private collections were hard to track down and unprocessed. For the Rustin biography, I faced the opposite situation. I could have spent a lifetime exploring every archive that touches upon Rustin's life and still have felt there was more to learn. But there were also absences in the written record, most obviously in relation to Rustin's sexuality, and the oral histories remedied some of that. In my current Chicago research, the oral histories of other researchers have functioned as an archival source.

In 1971, when I started graduate school at Columbia, the writing of US history was in upheaval. The radicalism associated with the social movements of the 1960s was affecting the production of US history in at least two important ways. One set of historians was revising the past from the top down. A New Left school of researchers was reinterpreting foreign policy as a story of imperial expansion and writing studies of political economy under the rubric of corporate liberalism. Another set of historians was reshaping an understanding of the past from the bottom up. New social historians churned out books and articles on topics ranging from seventeenth-century New England towns to daily life within the antebellum slave community to worker militancy in turn-of-the-century industrial cities. Both groups shared a critical distance from heroic narratives of US history, and both saw writing and disseminating these histories as transformative acts, capable of supporting progressive political change. Although not all of my peers approached their studies from this perspective, enough did to make graduate studies brim over with excitement. The sense of radical potential that some writers attribute to oral history today was something that, a generation ago, I attached to historical research itself.

Oral history and the new social history might seem to be natural bed-fellows, but, interestingly, oral history hardly figured in my graduate school reading. The new social history that appeared on my comprehensive exam lists covered eras too far in the past for there to be living interview subjects, though certainly students of slavery were mining the life histories collected in the 1930s as part of the Works Progress Administration. We did learn about the Columbia Oral History Project, started in the late 1940s by Allan Nevins and, as we were told, the first of its kind in the United States. But its purpose and focus were so far removed from the radical spirit of the new social history that oral history seemed less than compelling. The Oral History Project meant to remedy gaps in the written record created by the shift toward telephone conversation as a main mode of communication. Because presidents, cabinet secretaries, members of Congress, and other Important Men increasingly relied on the telephone instead of the memo or letter, interviewing had become a necessary form of research.

Still, the existence of the Project at Columbia and the endorsement of the method by someone as respected as Nevins gave oral history legitimacy. In comparison to the novelty of a dissertation on a gay topic, the fact that I expected to do interviews created scarcely a ripple in the history department. And, since this was before I or anyone I knew had ever heard of an institutional review board with the power to block the interviewing of research subjects, a need to gain its approval affected me not at all.

In the fall of 1976, I set out on a research trip to California, where I conducted about three dozen interviews in four months. The interviews primarily covered events that had occurred ten to twenty-five years earlier. In reconstructing that experience now, I am acutely aware that I am drawing upon memories of my own older than the ones I extracted from my informants. As virtually any practitioner of oral history can attest, memory is complicated. The issue is not merely how well or accurately we remember. Rather, we all have investments in our stories of the past. They are influenced by present-day agendas, some conscious and some not, that shape the telling. What investments do I have today in recounting my experience with oral history? Writing about it seems even trickier because, as will become apparent, I can't be the "good historian" and simply go back to the record—my transcripts—as a way of checking my recollections.

When I departed for California, I had already worked my way through runs of *ONE Magazine*, *The Ladder*, and *The Mattachine Review*, the main homophile publications of the 1950s and 1960s. I had pored through two file cabinets of records from the New York Mattachine and had read the small number of works that touched on pre-Stonewall activism. I intended during my stay in California to do both document research and interviews. But the boundary between the written and the oral was porous. For instance, I interviewed Jim Kepner in his apartment, the same space where he made available to me piles of clippings and folders of documents. Even when I worked in libraries, interview subjects like Dorr Legg and Don Slater were nearby, since they ran the libraries that housed the documents. To them, the history I was researching was still alive, in part because they quite literally lived with it. How did that influence their interviews and distinguish them from those who had left behind the experience of homophile activism?

My dissertation adviser had given me two bits of advice about doing oral histories. "Know as much as possible before going in to the interview," he told me. "And don't be too directing." The latter, which suited my personality, was rendered easier initially by how poorly I was able to comply with the former. Diligent as I had tried to be before approaching these activists for interviews, I still knew precious little about these organizations and their work.

With each successive interview, my ignorance diminished a bit, and this can serve as a reminder that doing oral history is itself a process that evolves in the course of a project. As I learned more, I could conduct my interviews differently. I was especially aware of this after I interviewed Jim Kepner. He had made himself the unofficial historian of the homophile movement. He had accumulated massive documentary material; he stayed in touch with people; he remained engaged in activism. Kepner also had an encyclopedic knowledge of the events, organizations, and people that constituted the movement.[2] Interviewing him was like opening an almanac and having the pages turn by themselves, with very little effort expended by me. After more than twelve hours of conversation with him, I was better equipped for future interviews. I continued to be nondirecting and open ended in my initial engagement with a narrator—"tell me about" rather than "did you"—but as the number of subjects I interviewed grew, I had a better sense of places that I hoped an interview might go, and I would intervene gently to steer the conversation in a direction.

A theme that courses through most of the writing about the practice of oral history is power. Power figures into every relationship, and it does not travel in only one direction. Power is also dynamic; it can shift over time. Heading into my interviews, I was a graduate student in my twenties, still uncertain as to whether I had a "real" dissertation topic. I was dependent on the power of my subjects to say yes or no to my request. I was also dependent on their power, given my initially paltry knowledge of the events under scrutiny, to tell me whatever version of their stories they chose to construct. Put most bluntly, I desperately needed what they and only they knew. But, once the interviews were over, my research done, and my book published, the tables would turn, and they would be dependent on me, the interviewer who had now morphed into author. I was interpreting their stories. I was selecting from their memories and arranging them in a way that made sense to me, without their continuing input. To become a historian, I needed them. But, if I became one, their place in history would be at least partly constructed by me.

That is one way of describing the relationship between my subjects and me, and there is a certain truthfulness to it. But if I had to reconstruct where I think we actually were then, I would describe the relationship with most of my subjects as one of mutual gratitude.

Why my gratitude? A key element of gay liberation rhetoric in the 1970s was its delineation of pre-Stonewall oppression. The queens of Stonewall rose up, and those who followed their lead burst out of the closet, rebels against the intolerable conditions of queer life. As I encountered men and women, all of whom belonged to the generation of my parents, aunts, and uncles and all of whom had lived under this earlier regime, it was hard not to be awed by their bravery. Regardless of how I measured the success of their work, they had set out on a path that, considering the objectively oppressive conditions in the 1950s and early 1960s, made the courage of my generation less impressive. These were the pioneers.

Why their gratitude? In the past three decades, accounts of homophile-era activism have appeared in so many books that it is hard to appreciate today how thoroughly the Stonewall generation refused to acknowledge or validate this early activism.[3] A small number of the homophile generation—Frank Kameny, Barbara Gittings, Jim Kepner, Del Martin, and Phyllis Lyon come quickly to mind—had made the transition into the 1970s, and they continued to build their activist resumés. But most had not, and most felt thoroughly neglected and unappreciated. To have someone of the next generation affirm, as I was, that their work mattered and that it needed to be told as history was gratifying.

In one sense, I could describe these interviews as an exercise in creating cross-generational ties. Certainly, for many years afterward, I carried with me a sense of those connections. I lived with those interviews and those subjects, metaphorically, for a long time. Through writing I did for a radical gay publication such as *The Body Politic* and through history talks I gave to community groups in the late 1970s and early 1980s, I held out the left-wing origins of the Mattachine as a tradition from which my generation of queer leftists could draw. And my feelings for some of them were passionate. I am reminded of something I wrote about Harry Hay and Chuck Rowland: "I could say that I fell in love, though that phrase barely touches the depth and variety of feeling that I have for them."[4]

At the same time, partly because I was writing a history of a national movement whose participants were dispersed rather than of a local community bound by place, I was at most a momentary visitor in their lives. It would be interesting to test out whether the appealing, almost utopian, hopes for oral history, especially queer oral history, as a tool for building intergenerational community are able to materialize and be sustained. How would one need to conceptualize and implement an oral history project for it to realize such a vision? Did the oral histories, for instance, that Elizabeth Kennedy and Madeline Davis conducted for their community history of lesbians in Buffalo leave such a legacy behind in a way that, by contrast, my interviews of homophile activists did not?[5] Is the current Twin Cities Project in Minneapolis-St. Paul doing this in a sustained way?[6] Can LGBT community centers around the country become places that preserve the story of our past by doing oral histories in ways such that younger and older connect with and learn from each other?

I returned to the practice of oral history in the 1990s, when I began working on a biography of Bayard Rustin. There was a queer element to this work, of course. Rustin was gay, and he had to navigate the intense homophobia of the 1940s, 1950s, and 1960s as he pursued his fight for peace and social justice in the pacifist, civil rights, and labor movements. Yet oral history figured in this project very differently than in my earlier one. Rustin's life was not queer centered. His public career revolved around issues—nuclear weapons, racial justice, economic inequality—that were mainstays of twentieth-century US history narratives. Thus, most of the individuals I interviewed were not in any way queer identified. I was also conducting these interviews not to get the life histories of my subjects but to have them elaborate on the life of Rustin. Finally, not only was there a wide documentary trail for the organizations and movements with which Rustin was involved, but also the archives contained rich repositories of oral histories conducted by others, particularly of the civil rights movement. In working on Rustin's life, I not only did interviews of my own but also read transcripts of interviews in the JFK and LBJ Presidential Libraries (recall the model and motivation of the Columbia Oral History Project with regard to Important Men) as well as at Howard University, with its substantial collection of interviews with grassroots civil rights activists.

Early on, I made the decision not to interview the surviving civil rights leaders with whom Rustin had worked. In the oral histories that I was reading in libraries, I noticed a significant difference between the interviews that were done in the 1960s, close to the events, and those done in the 1980s. A revision of memory appeared to be going on, not so much in terms of the facts of history—what had happened—but in terms of the evaluation of people and their roles. I was not interested in conducting a third round of interviews in which participants, in the more gay-tolerant atmosphere of the mid to late 1990s, revised their views of Rustin as an activist and a homosexual.

But the pacifist movement was another story. In certain ways one could say its history paralleled that of the homophile movement. Pacifists in the United States of the 1940s and 1950s were beyond the boundary that separated normal from deviant. Like the homophile activists, they had been largely neglected not only by historians but also by the antiwar activists who came after them. Most of them had not been interviewed endless times by journalists and historians; most of them did not have well-rehearsed versions of their history. As with homophile activists, one could make a claim for their bravery, since to be a pacifist during World War II and at the height of the Cold War was to stand way outside the definition of a good American.

I also felt toward these pacifists a certain kinship. Just as the homophile movement broke ground that I later benefited from in the 1970s, male conscientious objectors in particular had, at midcentury, pioneered an opposition to war and militarism that, later, I struggled to express as a draft-eligible young man at the height of the Vietnam War. As I delved more deeply into the history of the Fellowship of Reconciliation and the War Resisters League, the organizations for which Rustin worked, I found myself wanting to give these pacifists their due. I hoped that my interviews with them would allow me to reconstruct in as rich and nuanced a way as possible Rustin's pacifist history.

I have to admit that I approached these interviews with a trepidation that I had not experienced in my earlier project. While I carried respect, admiration, and even a bit of awe into both sets of encounters, my agenda, to the degree that I had one, was very much out there with the homophile activists. But, with most of my pacifist subjects, I carried a worry that made me strategize how I would raise the issue of Rustin's sexuality. I did not want to make them defensive; I did not want the interview to shut down. After all, Rustin had experienced in the peace movement a certain measure of censure and isolation because of his sexuality. Would my raising it, even a half century later, create a barrier between my subjects and me that would prove impossible to surmount?

I opted for an approach that seemed both sensible and ethical: waiting until we were well into the interview before I introduced the subject. It made sense to me because much of what I wanted from them was an understanding of pacifist activism and of Rustin's role in the peace movement. Talking about that had to lead eventually to a discussion of his sexuality because, at some point in the narrative, we inevitably came up against the scandals and controversies associated with Rustin's homosexuality. As it turned out, I need not have worried. To the best of my recollection, everyone was forthcoming about it. Some brought it up themselves, and others talked about it once I introduced the topic. Some said less than others, but not, I sensed, because of discomfort, hostility, or a conscious decision to withhold.

Interviewing heterosexuals about homosexuality is an interesting adventure. I suppose one could argue that these were not typical heterosexuals, if such a group even exists. As religious pacifists, these were good men and women committed to the dignity of every human life. They were devoted to building a world based on allegiance to a common humanity. I learned or perhaps had confirmed that homosexuality in that era was not something named among them, even as many also claimed to "know" about Rustin. They "knew" about Rustin in part because of assumptions made about masculinity. Rustin's dress, his way of speaking, his carriage, and his interest in the arts and high culture all marked him as not traditionally male. I learned as well that there was a divide between private and public. Rustin's difference was of no consequence until there was a public naming that almost inevitably, given the era, caused scandal. And I learned that there was a difference between religious and secular pacifist circles. The latter could have cared less about Rustin's sexual desires. Indeed, the trouble he got into and the difficulty that religious pacifists had in dealing with it almost seemed to make Rustin more heroic in the view of these secular radicals.

Interestingly, working on the Rustin biography also pointed out to me how indissolubly linked are the practice of oral history and research in print materials. More revealing than any of the oral histories I conducted were two caches of documents that I never expected to find. One was a large set of records detailing Rustin's time in federal prison during World War II. It provided correspondence to and from Rustin along with material from prison officials about Rustin's sexuality. It was a "eureka" moment unlike anything I've experienced in forty years of studying history. The other was the correspondence between Rustin and Davis Platt, his lover at the time. A generation older than me, Platt was someone who had been in my extended gay social circle in New York in the 1970s. He had been at parties at my home many times in that decade. I never knew about his relationship with Rustin, but when he learned that I was working on a biography, he contacted me and made available letters that Rustin had written while serving time in federal prison and that Platt had saved for a half century. He also consented to two interviews, which had a warmth and vitality that went beyond anything I experienced in interviewing Rustin's pacifist colleagues. In this case, the identity and the relationship of interviewer and subject deeply affected the experience. Oral history helped strengthen cross-generational connections as well as friendship. With Platt, as it had been for me with Harry Hay two decades earlier, the experience of oral history was magical.

For the past few years I have been doing research on Chicago. I hesitate to be more specific than that because, unlike my dissertation on pre-Stonewall activism or my biography of Rustin, this has not yet coalesced into a clear and well-defined book project. Instead, I am allowing myself to roam around in materials about the history of sexuality in Chicago in the twentieth century. Queer topics, in the broadest sense, naturally figure in this, but I can't claim yet that the project is queer centered.

For me, the most dramatic difference between this work that I've begun in the first decade of the twenty-first century and the research I started as a graduate student in the 1970s is that a huge mass of easily accessible material is available for me to examine without my having to search and search and search for it. The Gerber/Hart Library, a GLBT community-based library and archives, has lots of collections, as well as runs of newspapers and newsletters produced by GLBT community organizations. The Leather Archives and Museum, another community-based institution, does as well. But materials about sexuality, including things one could define as queer, are also to be found at places like the Chicago History Museum, the University of Chicago, and the University of Illinois at Chicago. I know progress narratives are out of fashion these days, but to me this is progress.

So, unlike in the 1970s, when I had to track down informants to interview, I can now go to the Gerber/Hart Library and read transcripts of dozen upon dozen of oral histories of GLBT activists and community members done by researchers who came before me. It is a privilege and a thrill to be able to do this. And, once again, it evokes in me feelings of immense gratitude. I know that, because of this prior work, I will be much better prepared when I begin to do interviews of my own for this project. I am also grateful for another reason. Some of these interviews were conducted as long ago as the early 1980s. Since then, some narrators have died, and these oral histories are the best source of information we will ever have about their lives.

The transcripts can also serve as a curriculum for the practice of oral history, a curriculum that I never took before I learned interviewing by doing it. Some of these interviews are so rich, so overflowing with information and insight, that I wish they had gone on forever. And some of them are, frankly, terrible. The difference between the valuable ones and the disasters is almost never about the narrator. Sure, sometimes one senses shyness or detachment in a narrator, a reluctance to speak or an abrasiveness of style that almost any interviewer would have difficulty penetrating. But more of the time the failure is that of the interviewer. She or he goes in there with an agenda, and the agenda simply does not mesh with the life experience of the narrator. The interviewer poses too many questions of a factual kind: Did you know so-and-so? Were you at such-and-such? Were you a member of this group? When the person says no, the conversation grinds to a halt.

Reading these weak interviews makes me cringe, and not only because of the wasted opportunity. Rather, I read them with the awareness that my interviews, too, are now accessible to others who can pass judgment on them. I wonder what they read like. I donated all my materials about Rustin to the Swarthmore College Peace Collection, the archive that has the largest number of collections that relate directly to his life. In the case of these interviews, I can just sit at home and reread the transcripts because, when I worked on this project, I had the privileges of a senior faculty member with a research assistant whose job it was to transcribe the tapes. But, as a graduate student taking forever, it seemed, to finish a dissertation on the homophile movement, all I did was take notes from the tapes of my interviews as if I were listening to a lecture in class and now and then replay short segments to copy out what sounded like "good quotes." I donated those tapes to a community-based archive in New York City that later went under. Most of them made their way to the New York Public Library, where I know they have been used by others. To me it is amazing that they survive at all since, as a graduate student living at bare subsistence, I bought the cheapest possible cassette tapes for interviewing subjects. Writing this essay makes me want to go back there and listen to them.

Reading the interviews done by others and imagining listening once again to interviews I did a generation ago put into bold relief for me something I did not think much about when I made that trip to California in 1976. The living, breathing face-to-face interview becomes, in time, another collection in the archives. For all the power and the magic of the experience, oral history requires of us critical skills of assessment and evaluation not unlike what all archival materials demand. Especially when our subjects are not the rich and the famous and the influential, for whom a well-cleared documentary trail already exists, oral history promises to make a place for them in accounts of the past—indeed, to make history read differently because of their presence. But interviews are not transparent. Like documents, they beg for analysis and interpretation. And, once that work commences, the values and life experience of the interpreter—the historian—inevitably become part of the story.

9

Finding History, Creating Community

When the writing of gay and lesbian history started in the
1970s, it occurred almost entirely outside the boundaries of
the university. Independent scholars, often rooted in a world
of activism, began doing research and, in many places in
the 1970s and 1980s, they created community-based history projects to support this work and make it accessible.
In Chicago, the Gerber/Hart Library and Archives was one
such organization. As a board member of Gerber/Hart, I
spoke at its annual dinner in 2004 and affirmed the importance of history as a resource for communities struggling to
define themselves and to stake out a place for themselves
in the larger culture.

I taught my first college history course more than thirty years ago. Occasionally I have had a real lemon of a class where nothing seemed to go right and
I would wake up in the morning with dread in my stomach. Occasionally I
have thought, "If I ever have to give another lecture on the origins of the
Cold War I will kill myself!" But, most of the time, I have loved teaching
history. It has been a great privilege, and it has proven endlessly new and
exciting. It may be true that we cannot change the past, but I have plenty
of evidence, from what has happened in my classroom, that the past can
change us. I have a wealth of good memories: of classes that sparkled, of

discussions that were filled with brilliant student comments, of moments when I could see the light bulbs flashing inside the heads of my students.

Of all these moments, here is one of my favorites. The setting is the University of North Carolina in Greensboro in the mid-1980s, where I was teaching a history of sexuality course. At that time and place, it was not your typical history class. Also, I was offering the course in the evening, because evening classes attracted a much broader and therefore more interesting range of students. One of them, Linda, was a middle-aged woman with two sons who were old enough that she was now returning to school to get certified as a high school teacher.

In this particular meeting, I had just finished lecturing on the early career of Margaret Sanger, an American radical who made the fight for birth control her life's mission. Sanger's work in this period is a wonderfully dramatic story of outrageous daring and determination. She was a woman who broke free of the constraints on women's lives and went on to change the world. I think I may even have started the lecture by saying that, in a list of the most influential Americans of the twentieth century, Sanger could be ranked in the top five!

The lecture was now over. A discussion was going on. Everything seemed fine. And then, all of a sudden, I caught a glimpse of Linda out of the corner of my eye. Something was happening in her, because she was visibly shaking in her seat. I looked at her and said, "Linda?" She almost raised herself out of her chair—she was a big woman—and in a booming voice that I cannot pretend to imitate she screamed: "*HOW* could I have reached the age of *FORTY* and *NO ONE* has *EVER* told me about Margaret *SANGER* before? *WHY* has this been *KEPT* from me?"

If you think that history is simply the story of what happened in the past, then Linda's questions do not make much sense. You might look at her and say, "Well, I don't know. I guess you never bothered to look far enough, or you just didn't take the right courses in school." But every student in that classroom knew that lurking behind these particular questions about her and Margaret Sanger was a very deep insight about history.

History is not simply the story of what happened in the past. For the most part, history has been the story that the winners tell about what happened in the past. History has consisted of stories about the privileged and the powerful, about kings and popes, generals and giant capitalists; stories about every last Founding Father and president; and commentaries on the so-called great thinkers from Plato to Nietzsche. Occasionally, and

I do mean occasionally, something else or someone else might slip through, like the storming of the Bastille or the Boston Tea Party, or the life of a Frederick Douglass or a Jane Addams or a Sojourner Truth. Even then, characters like these generally had just a brief appearance, a walk-on part only.

By the time I was teaching my history of sexuality course in Greensboro in the mid-1980s, that version of history had begun to change. It changed because of something called "the '60s." The 1960s left nothing untouched in this country. It was not something that happened only at lunch counters in the South, or at big marches on Washington, or in Haight-Ashbury in San Francisco, or in the fields of Woodstock, New York. The '60s also happened in libraries and archives as a small army, composed not of soldiers but of nerdy researchers, tried to make their own revolution by rewriting the past. With a lot of determination and imagination, they were able to uncover and write stories about the slave community in the South, the stockyard workers in Chicago, immigrants in cities all over the United States, and prostitutes in the Wild West. They were able to restore these people to history, thereby giving us a different view of the past. And with that came different angles of vision on the present and future, too.

Gay, lesbian, bisexual, and transgender people were among the later arrivals to this new version of history. At first glance, in the 1960s and early 1970s, we seemed an unlikely subject for historical study.

A generation ago, the dominant idea about GLBT people was that we didn't really exist. Oh, yes, there were some individual freaks and sexual perverts. But a people? A community? A social group with shared experiences and institutions? In this era, the pressure on queer folks to stay as far out of view as possible was immense. Hiding in the closet, wearing a mask, lurking in the shadows, and living a double life were all common metaphors used to describe queer life in this era. How do you write the history of a group of people who tried to cover their tracks? How do you write the history of people who spoke or wrote in code, who burned their letters and diaries, or who passed as the other gender so successfully that no one ever knew?

Fortunately, because the infectious power of the '60s had not quite been extinguished yet, there were a lot of Americans who still believed that anything was possible and that the unimaginable could be done. Some of them turned their energies toward uncovering and creating a queer history. It did not happen in the citadels of American higher education. For the most part, it didn't happen at Harvard or Princeton or the University of Chicago. It was not done primarily by individuals who had tenure, who got summers off for research and writing, who had access to prestigious fellowships, and who had research assistants to do their bidding. It started on the ground, in the decade after Stonewall, in the new queer communities that were taking shape around the country. History was being found and made by men and women who believed that a people without a history was a people impoverished, a people made powerless. Making history was going to be their contribution to creating a vibrant and proud community.

A key figure in this effort was Jonathan Ned Katz. A college dropout, he joined the Gay Activists Alliance in New York in the early 1970s and got all excited about the new gay militancy. He decided to make history his niche. He searched for documents, initially in the most obvious places, and began finding them: the journals and letters of Walt Whitman, sodomy prosecutions in the colonial period, articles in old medical journals, the transcripts from obscenity trials. He put these together into a play, *Coming Out*, that consisted entirely of words from historical sources. It was an underground sensation. He kept going with his research until he was able to put it all together in a several-hundred-page book that he titled *Gay American History*. Published in 1976, it suddenly made it possible to believe that we had a history, that it could be found, and that it could arouse and fire people up.

Katz's book certainly played a major role in motivating other people to begin digging into this hidden past, but some were coming to this project on their own, as well. In Washington, DC, Judith Schwarz started to comb through encyclopedias and reference books for biographical information on women. She kept coming across the phrase "close friends and devoted companions" to describe the relationship that two women had with each other. It was her "Aha!" moment. Schwarz went on to produce a book on a club of bohemian women in Greenwich Village in which women loving women were at the heart of the enterprise. Elizabeth Kennedy and Madeline Davis were living in Buffalo, New York, in the 1970s. They began doing oral histories of street-fighting, working-class women of the 1930s, 1940s, and 1950s who built a public lesbian world before Stonewall and before the revival of feminism. Eric Garber became fascinated by the lyrics of the so-called race records of the 1920s and 1930s. He uncovered a vibrant black queer world in Harlem and showed how it intersected with the Harlem Renaissance, something that most writers on the subject had ignored. Jim Steakley was living in Germany in the early 1970s. He got caught up in the German gay movement and began doing research on the history of the first German queer movement that stretched back to the 1890s. Returning to the United States, Steakley put together a two-hour slide show and lecture about German gay activism before and after World War I and how it was destroyed by the Nazis. Audiences sat there stunned at this history. There are many other examples of these activist, community-based historians embarking on this work in the 1970s and finding remarkable stories.

This work of historical discovery and excavation was not just an effort of individuals. It was also a collective enterprise. In different cities, people with a passion for history were finding one another and forming groups to guarantee that our history got researched and written and that the materials got preserved. In the 1970s and early 1980s, lesbian and gay history projects formed in Boston, Buffalo, New York, Chicago, Washington, DC, San Francisco, and probably other cities, too. New York saw the creation of the Lesbian Herstory Archives, the first organization of its kind in the country. In Chicago, activists with a passion for books and history founded the Gerber/Hart Library. All over the place, folks were looking for ways to preserve a record of our past, of our history as a people and as a community. We were driven in part by the conviction that knowing our history would contribute to making us a people and a community. In 1979, during the weekend of the first gay and lesbian national march on Washington, a group of individuals involved in these various projects met for the first time. There was a sense that, just like the 100,000 queers who were marching in the nation's capital to create a better future, we could make a better future by uncovering a history that had been hidden and by changing how we understood the past.

All of this was happening on the margins of the academic world, outside the walls of the great libraries and archives in the United States. A few of us engaged in this project had some connection to universities. Gayle Rubin, who was writing a history of the leather community, was a graduate student at the University of Michigan. I was a graduate student in history at Columbia. Estelle Freedman taught at Stanford, and Elizabeth Kennedy taught at SUNY–Buffalo. But this work was not being prepared for academic conferences, and it was not being published in academic journals. It was rooted in our communities; it was presented to community audiences; and it was published in queer newspapers and magazines. We relied on members of the community to provide us with the raw materials for our history. All of these efforts were shoestring operations, done on a dime and with a lot of love. The work brought plenty of emotional satisfaction but little financial reward or fame.

Let me jump ahead to the present. A lot has changed in the decades since that ragtag group of would-be historians met in Washington in 1979.

Some mainstream institutions have become responsive to us. The San Francisco Public Library and the New York Public Library have made a major commitment to collect queer historical materials. Universities like Cornell and Duke have developed huge collections on sexuality. There are LGBT studies programs at a growing number of universities. There are gay and lesbian studies sections in bookstores. Award-winning books on gay, lesbian, and transgender history are reviewed in major newspapers across the United States. Here in Chicago, I was actually hired to teach gay and lesbian studies courses at the University of Illinois campus. At the University of Chicago, there's a lesbian and gay studies project, and the university has hosted a major conference on queer history. The Chicago History Museum, in conjunction with the LGBT community, has mounted a series of major lectures and panels on Chicago's queer past. These are all good and important developments.

But, maybe because I remember the bad old days when there was not even the pretense or a veneer of acceptance of us by mainstream institutions or maybe because I remember how thrilling these community events were and how they made history freely available to people, I still have a fierce loyalty to community-based, community-controlled efforts to discover and preserve and share the stories of our past. There are all sorts of stories that still haven't been told.

Some of these community efforts are much better established than they were twenty years ago. The Lesbian Herstory Archives owns its three-story building in Brooklyn. The San Francisco Lesbian and Gay History Project has grown into the Gay, Lesbian, Bisexual, and Transgender Historical Society of Northern California, and it now has paid staff. Chicago's

Gerber/Hart Library occupies a space many times the size of its original location. There is also a Leather Archives and Museum in Chicago.

But in these conservative times, when a Bush administration exalts market-driven outcomes, when all not-for-profit ventures are struggling, when our national government is hostile to anything queer, and when even a proposed community center in Chicago needs business tenants in order to be viable, I worry about relinquishing control of our history to any institution that is not ours. I pray that the community will remember the value of these grassroots efforts to save our history. Gerber/Hart and the institutions like it around the country are treasures. They are gems that need protection and polishing and all our appreciation. I thank all of you for coming here tonight to support your local history project and the valuable, essential work that it does.

10

The Power of Community History

Allan Bérubé was one of the key figures in the 1970s and 1980s in the birth of the community-based LGBT history that I described in the previous essay. He and I had been intimate friends and collaborators in the shared project of researching and writing this history. His unexpected death, in 2007, provoked this essay, which is both a tribute to him and a reflection on the importance of community history as a tool for social change. Since I wrote it, Estelle Freedman and I have edited a collection of Allan's work, *My Desire for History: Essays on Gay, Community, and Labor History*.

The obituary of Allan Bérubé that appeared in the *New York Times* began with a reference to his MacArthur Fellowship and then moved on to *Coming Out under Fire*, his groundbreaking history of gay men and lesbians during World War II. Such obvious attention to these two markers as the signal achievements of his life is understandable. The MacArthur award labeled Allan a "genius," and a book about World War II planted him squarely in the mainstream of American history. As a topic, it is readily legible to almost everyone as "important."

This essay first appeared as "Allan Bérubé's Gift to History," *Gay and Lesbian Review Worldwide* 15, no. 3 (May–June 2008): 10–13.

I think of Allan differently. "Public intellectual" is a contemporary phrase that perhaps comes closer to capturing who he was and what he did, but even that distorts my picture of him. "Public intellectual" conjures images of tenured academics of high repute—my former dean, Stanley Fish, pops to mind—who, besides composing their scholarly studies, also publish op-eds in the *Times* and the *Washington Post* or essays in the *New Republic*. Or, these days, they blog and are quoted by other bloggers. That still isn't Allan.

Allan was a community historian. He believed passionately in the power of history to change the way individuals and even whole groups of people understood the world and their place in it. Except for short interludes, such as the year he held a Rockefeller Fellowship at the Center for Lesbian and Gay Studies in New York, he was always without formal—and paid—connections to the institutions that sustain intellectual and cultural work. He reported, so to speak, to the people whose history he wrote about. He most cared about how community members—LGBT folks and, later, working-class people and labor activists—responded to his talks and his writing, not in the sense of craving their approval but more as evidence that the history he uncovered was having an impact.

Allan's death has made me think about the state of LGBT community history. Much has changed in the decades since he and a random collection of folks scattered across the country began digging into a queer past. Some of that change has been for the better, some perhaps not. By most measures, there is more queer history circulating in the public sphere than ever before. But one could also argue that this history is more detached than ever before from the community it describes.

I first met Allan in the spring of 1979. I had come to San Francisco from New York for a stay of several months to research a history of the pre-Stonewall movement. My best friend, Estelle Freedman, a faculty member at Stanford who was a pioneer in the field of women's history, had just gotten to know Allan through meetings of the recently formed San Francisco Lesbian and Gay History Project. She plotted an early introduction of the two of us, suspecting as only best friends can that he and I would hit it off. We did. My calendar for that year has "Allan B" marked across Saturday, May 12. That day, we began a conversation that, by one measure, lasted well into the night but in another sense continued for decades.

That spring, queer San Francisco was experiencing a tumultuous moment in its own history. In 1978 California had faced a statewide ballot initiative, Proposition Six, that would have prohibited the employment in the schools of gay men and lesbians. San Francisco activists played a key part in the successful mobilization against it. Soon after its rejection at the polls, Harvey Milk, the first openly gay supervisor in San Francisco and a leader in the anti–Prop Six campaign, was assassinated by Dan White, a conservative former supervisor. The trial of Dan White for murder was just concluding when Allan and I met. The queer rioting at City Hall that followed the verdict—the stunning spectacle of a row of burning police cars set on fire is its central image—remains the backdrop to this period of time when, as I experienced it, a gay, lesbian, and transgender community history began to flower.

The publication, in 1976, of Jonathan Ned Katz's *Gay American History* had launched Allan's own explorations. Allan, a college dropout, took inspiration from the fact that Katz, another college dropout, had produced such a magnificent piece of historical research. So, in the hours when he was not working as an assistant manager of a neighborhood movie theater, Allan reeled through newspaper microfilms at the San Francisco Public Library and snooped through archival collections across the Bay at Berkeley's Bancroft Library. By the time I met him, he had accumulated quite a trove of material.

He was also, by 1979, not working alone. Allan and several others, almost all without academic affiliations, had recently formed the San Francisco Lesbian and Gay History Project. I'm not sure whether this was the first such group in the United States, but it certainly brought together a set of impressive intellects. Besides Allan, there was Jeff Escoffier, Estelle Freedman, Eric Garber, Amber Hollibaugh, and Gayle Rubin; today, their collected works would make for a busy season of reading. That summer, the History Project went public with two remarkable events: Allan's "Lesbian Masquerade," an illustrated talk about women who passed as men in nineteenth-century San Francisco, and "Spontaneous Combustion," a panel that provided a historical dimension to police harassment of queers in San Francisco.

Katz's *Gay American History* had a section, called "Passing Women," that provided documentary accounts of female-bodied individuals who lived and moved in the world as men. In working his way through nineteenth-century newspapers, Allan had found a substantial number of such stories, including a few that were so detailed that he could almost reconstruct a short biography with pictures. Allan premiered "Lesbian

Masquerade" at the Women's Building during Pride Month, before a crowd of several hundred. The thirst for history was so great that a man presenting this material in the days when separatism was still powerful produced barely a ripple in the audience; nor was there controversy about his labeling this history as lesbian. Instead, Allan's ability to project queer life more than a hundred years back in time produced laughter, applause, tears, and a thrill that coursed through the crowd.

A few weeks later, in early August, the History Project convened a panel, "Spontaneous Combustion," that included Jeff; Amber; Lois Helmbold, a teacher at San Jose State; and me. Again the hall was packed. Various incidents in the weeks since the City Hall rioting had added fuel to police-community tensions, and the audience was seething with anger. At this distance in time, I can't remember what the others talked about. But I know that I spoke about the late 1950s and early 1960s, when sustained police attacks on queer bars provoked rebellion within the bar world. As I put it then, the movement and the subculture had converged in San Francisco in those years, and that convergence had helped produce a pre-Stonewall movement more elaborate and powerful than any other comparable movement anywhere else.

I remember that my argument, which seems so obvious to me now, was as much a product of witnessing contemporary events as it was of pulling some inherent meaning out of the historical record. That is, having seen how gay men poured out of the bars on Castro Street the night of the Dan White verdict, marched to City Hall, and set those police cars aflame, I was more easily able to attach a significance to an earlier bar rebellion that had erupted spontaneously from beyond the boundaries of a much tamer homophile movement. And, just as witnessing contemporary events allowed me to see the past differently, an historical interpretation of the bars as a resource *for* political mobilization had contemporary implications, as well. Many gay liberationists and lesbian feminists evinced intense hostility toward the bar world; they saw bar patrons and the bars themselves as an obstacle to political consciousness. Here was an example of how past and present might speak to each other, how researching history and offering it to a community audience could create productive dialogue and debate that, in turn, might shape tomorrow's activism.

Meanwhile, as Allan continued to show "Lesbian Masquerade" in the Bay Area, his visibility as a local historian brought an unexpected reward. A friend of a friend told Allan that, for several years, a neighbor had been saving a cache of correspondence he had found when he moved into his current apartment. The letters had apparently belonged to the previous resident, Harold Clark, now deceased, and they chronicled the friendship and experiences of a group of gay men who had met while serving in the military during World War II. Allan was beside himself; his correspondence overflowed with excitement. In these pre-fax, pre-scanning days, he filled his handwritten letters to me with long extracts from those of Clark and his wartime buddies. The materials launched Allan on the ten-year project that became *Coming Out under Fire* and that, along the way, generated even more grassroots historical work. He put together a new slide talk on World War II, and, as he traveled with it around the country, veterans flocked to see the show and then made themselves available for interviews, thus adding their voices to the historical record. I can't prove the connection, but I have a strong hunch that the organizing among veterans that exploded into the open during the gays-in-the-military debate of 1993 had something to do with the way that Allan embedded his historical work in community organizations and in networks of older gay men and lesbians. His many public talks brought veterans together and out of the closet. It validated their historical experience and made the military's contemporary exclusion policy all the more bitter and enraging.

I'm emphasizing Allan in this telling of how a community-based history emerged at the end of the 1970s because he was central to how I experienced it. But, really, this tale could be relayed through the work of any number of folks. By the early 1980s, the history slide talk presented to a community audience had become something of a rage. I saw Jim Steakley mesmerize an audience of several hundred in New York with a presentation, almost two hours long, about the German gay movement in the early twentieth century. Judith Schwarz entertained folks with an account of a pre-Depression-era world of bohemian women in Greenwich Village. Members of a Boston lesbian and gay history project crafted a lecture with slides that stretched from Puritan New England in the seventeenth century to the mid-twentieth century. Roberta Yusba, a San Francisco history project member who had become fascinated with the lesbian pulp novels of the 1950s and 1960s, assembled a slide talk filled with images of the cover art that not only was informative but also often elicited gales of laughter. About this time, too, Greg Sprague, a graduate student at Loyola University, began researching Chicago's GLBT past. He scoured newspapers, found documents, and put together a slide show that helped bring folks out of the closet who, in turn, became available to be interviewed by him. Sprague's work morphed into a local history project that, a generation later, still lives on in Chicago in the form of the Gerber/Hart Library.

I also remember well the traveling history presentation put together by the women of the Lesbian Herstory Archives in New York, one that I saw Joan Nestle deliver a few times in different cities, at a point when her speaking gigs and mine seemed to overlap quite a bit. The LHA rightly prides itself on its identity as a collective, and I don't mean to single out Joan here. Still, anyone who has encountered her over the years knows that "charisma" barely does justice to the impression she leaves with audiences. Her presentations around the country inspired lots of lesbians to see their own lives and the lives of other women in their communities as having historical significance. Letters, photos, diaries, scrapbooks and other memorabilia have been saved from the dump because of the work of the Herstory Archives.

The folks I've mentioned saw themselves as primarily engaged in a project of historical reconstruction, but there were other community-based intellectuals working in the '80s who drew upon history, as well. Michael Bronski, Jeff Escoffier, Essex Hemphill, Amber Hollibaugh, Mab Segrest, and Barbara Smith all come to mind: activist intellectuals—or maybe intellectual activists—who incorporated history into their cultural and political work and who addressed their work directly to the community about whom they wrote.

As various slide talks traveled around the country and fed, intellectually and emotionally, not just their audiences but also the individuals who produced them, community-based historians also drew sustenance from an activist community press that was hungry for material and had not yet morphed into heavily commercialized enterprises. Toronto's *Body Politic*, for instance, published multiple-part series by Jim Steakley on the German movement and my work on the radical origins of the Mattachine Society. *Gay Community News* out of Boston, *Lavender Woman* from Chicago, and *Gay Sunshine* in the Bay Area, all papers that reached beyond their place of publication, carried writing about history. Marie Kuda, a community historian in Chicago, could count on the local queer papers to publish her work. Even the *Advocate*, which, under David Goodstein, was moving rapidly in the direction of a corporate model, snatched up long pieces by Bérubé and Sprague. In what I refer to as the "long" post-Stonewall decade, there was a hunger for history, and, to the degree it was satisfied, nourishment came from researchers and writers who presented their work in community contexts.

What happened to this kind of community-grounded historical work? Where did it go? Like so much else from that long post-Stonewall era, I think of it as having been swamped by and buried under the period of upheaval that stretched roughly from the March on Washington and the birth of ACT UP in 1987 to the Stonewall 25 commemorations in 1994. Someday, a smart historian will need to chart and explain the depth (and limits) of the change during those years. It far surpasses anything associated with Stonewall, and, in many respects, the legacy seems both more complex and more ambiguous to me.

Take, for example, what happened to the practice of LGBT history. I've just painted a fairly rosy picture of the work of community historians in the late 1970s and 1980s. In terms of the satisfaction and thrill that the work brought to both the practitioners and the audiences, it *was* glorious. But it was also a tale of struggle, as so much of gay and lesbian life still was in those post-Stonewall years. It was a story of working with few resources, of doing the work part time in between the jobs that paid the rent, of lacking institutional roots and stability. There were still very few published books on queer history. Folks were dependent on the traveling historians, burdened under the weight of slide trays and projector, or on the happenstance of stumbling upon the articles that appeared unpredictably in a press whose circulation was not very wide.

By the mid-1990s one could point to a host of indicators that signaled a change in how knowledge about LGBT people got produced. A series of large, dynamic queer studies conferences had taken place at major elite universities. Queer theory became for a time the academic rage. In the wake of the new visibility that AIDS militancy and the gays-in-the-military debate provoked, the mainstream press and the academy embraced new books like George Chauncey's 1994 landmark study, *Gay New York*, thus giving gay history an unprecedented scholarly legitimacy. More archives and historical societies began to collect and preserve our materials. More dissertations started to flow out of the academy. More of us had tenure-track jobs. To make the change personal: I still wake up in the morning and can't believe that the state of Illinois is paying me well to teach gay and lesbian history classes. I laugh and laugh with delight at the wonderful things that happen, with great regularity, in the undergraduate course that I teach and that I think of as "Gay 101."

This is all to the good. I do not want to turn back the clock. But something got lost along the way, and Allan's death has jolted me into noticing it. Teaching a group of undergraduates is worthwhile work, but they scatter in forty different directions at the end of each semester rather than encountering each other with regularity through a network of organizations, institutions, and businesses that sustain a collective identity. Writing academic history that will get one tenured is worthwhile work. It seeps into the professional literature and, slowly (oh so slowly), works a change in the content of historical narratives. But academic history is written differently from community history. It has to pass muster with a different audience; it has to frame its concerns in ways that speak to the professional literature; it has to impress an audience of peers with its mastery of a scholarly apparatus. It is not, for the most part, readily accessible to a community audience.

In Chicago over the past few years, the Center on Halsted (an LGBT community-based organization) and the Chicago History Museum (formerly the Chicago Historical Society) have partnered to present a series called "Out at CHM." Three times a year, the museum hosts an evening of queer history programming. Last spring, I coordinated and emceed an evening called "Gay Is the Revolution." As preparation, over a period of a few months, I worked with a few Chicago activists from the Stonewall era, interviewing them collectively and separately, drawing out the themes in their experiences, and helping shape their memories into a cohesive program. I offered a historian's take on the era, and they each presented, vividly and passionately, their reflections on what they had lived through and accomplished a generation earlier. The large auditorium was packed to overflowing; people hung on every word. Two hours passed, and still no one wanted to leave. If we could have stayed longer, if there were continuing venues available for the kind of discussion that was ready to bubble up from that audience, who knows what sort of conversations about politics, values, visions, and other matters of great consequence might ripple outward?

The evening reminded me of the slide talks of Allan and others a generation ago. I felt again, palpably, the hunger for history as a resource for self-affirmation as well as its power as a tool for constructing community. And I felt saddened that the resources for a community-based history and community-based historians have not grown at a rate commensurate with how the institutions of the LGBT community have grown in the past quarter century. Some of the community-based history organizations that formed a generation ago still exist, but none of them come anywhere near to having the resources of money, space, and staff that each could productively use.

George Orwell once wrote something to the effect that whoever controls the past commands the future. I don't know if he was right. But, just in case he was, I'd like to know that the many queer histories needing to be written and told would rise up from and out of our own queer communities.

Part III

Local Stories

Most of my historical research has had a national focus, whether in the form of a study of pre-Stonewall gay and lesbian activism, or a broad history of sexuality in the United States, or the biography of a figure like Bayard Rustin, whose activism was embedded in movements with a national and sometimes even international scope. But, after living in Chicago for a few years, seeing the breadth and scope of its LGBT activism, and recognizing the ways that this history had not been told, I found myself curious to explore it. Some of what I came upon in reading Chicago-based newspapers and organizational newsletters did not surprise me, but some of it did.

In an effort to have this local history reach a nonacademic audience, I began to write an occasional history column for the *Windy City Times*, a weekly LGBT newspaper in Chicago. Some of the stories were about social life, some about activism, some about oppression and the broader context of gay, lesbian, bisexual, and transgender lives. The following are a selection of these history columns.

11

Who Wears the Pants?

Many of my students joke about the Gender Police. Of course, they're not talking about an actual division of the Chicago Police Department or any other law enforcement agency. Instead, they're referring to all those arbiters of behavior who force people into the straitjacket of appropriate male and female behavior. The list of culprits is long: the popular boys and girls in high school, advertisers and Hollywood celebrities, school principals and sports coaches, and many others.

What they often don't realize is that, for most of Chicago's history, policing gender did fall to the police. Chicago passed its first law against cross-dressing in 1851, when it was still not much more than a frontier town. The prohibition against cross-dressing was included in a broader statute that made it a crime if anyone "shall appear in a public place in a state of nudity, or in a dress not belonging to his or her sex, or in an indecent or lewd dress, or shall make an indecent exposure of his or her person, or be guilty of an indecent or lewd act."

Chicago was not alone in passing such a law. According to Bill Eskridge, author of *Gaylaw*, in the second half of the nineteenth century "cities of every size and in every part of the country" adopted laws to enforce gender-conforming dress codes.

These laws remained on the books for over a century. Then, in the 1970s, most of them bit the dust. The challenges to enforcing gender-based

This essay first appeared in *Windy City Times*, September 9, 2009.

clothing norms became overwhelming. Male hippies were growing their hair to shoulder length. Women's liberationists were violating all sorts of gender boundaries. High school students were refusing to abide by the dress codes set by adults and were going to court to protect their right to self-expression. Even straight-as-an-arrow business executives were abandoning the male costume of suit jacket, hat, and tie.

But Chicago found itself in an uproar about its cross-dressing ban a whole generation earlier. In the middle of World War II, an independent-minded nineteen-year-old provoked front-page news stories, judicial sermons, outraged comments from government officials, and debates among the city's aldermen. When it was all over, the city's cross-dressing law had been revised in an important way.

It all began on a January night in 1943 when Evelyn "Jackie" Bross was picked up by the Chicago police. Bross was the eldest of thirteen children in a Cherokee family. Her father had moved them to Chicago from Utah in order to take advantage of wartime job opportunities. Like her father, Bross worked in a defense plant and was employed as a machinist. She worked at the Chicago Die Casting Company at 2512 West Monroe and was walking to her home at 2754 West Jackson when the police stopped her. According to the *Chicago Tribune*, Bross was "dressed in blue flannel trousers, a plaid sport shirt, a plaid mackinaw jacket and oxfords." Topping it off, she had "a mannish hair cut."

Appearing in Women's Court the next morning, Bross told Judge Jacob Braude that she wore men's clothes because they "were more comfortable than women's clothes and handy for work." She stood her ground defiantly. "I wish I was a boy," she declared. "I never did any wrong. I just like to wear men's clothes." Denying that she was trying to deceive anyone, she informed the court that "everyone knows I'm a woman." Judge Braude avoided an immediate decision by ordering Bross to see a court psychiatrist.

Coming in the middle of wartime, when millions of women were wearing pants every day in shipyards and aircraft factories and other defense jobs, the arrest of Bross hit a raw nerve. Many spoke out on her behalf. The city's leading club women supported her on feminist grounds: "Women's suffrage and slacks ought to go hand in hand," the *Tribune* reported them arguing. Harry Guilbert, head of the regional federal office for war industry employment, was enraged at the arrest. "If the girl cut her hair short, she should be awarded a medal instead of a court summons," he told reporters. "Safety directors in factories everywhere have tried to encourage women to cut their hair short."

The arrest of Bross provoked action by the Board of Aldermen. William Cowhey of the Forty-First ward spoke up at a board meeting the day after Bross was arrested. He proposed an amendment to the law in order to prohibit cross-dressing only when there was "intent to conceal his or her sex."

One can just imagine the snickers in the aldermanic chambers that day. Members were debating the city's budget in the midst of a war, and here was Cowhey asking them to take a stand on who could wear pants. But the aldermen also didn't anticipate the level of public interest. Cowhey wrapped his proposal in wartime patriotism. "We're in a war," he told the aldermen. "Today, with the war industries calling for safe dress, we should permit women to wear comfortable clothes. If slacks are comfortable, let them be worn!"

Cowhey's proposal passed. The statute against cross-dressing was amended. Now it was supposedly okay in Chicago to wear whatever clothes you wanted—as long as police couldn't claim that you were trying to deceive others or that the clothing was lewd. Milking the debate for a few laughs, the front-page story in the *Chicago Daily News* informed readers that it was now "perfectly permissible for housekeeping husbands to wear the kitchen apron out for a dash to the grocery."

But the debate about who could wear pants didn't end with law reform. Judge Braude decided to exercise some judicial discretion and used the bench as a pulpit.

The next week, when Bross returned to court, a strange drama unfolded. Also in the Women's Court that day was Theodora Fitzpatrick. No one would mistake her for a man. The papers described her as looking "a bit like a Hollywood star." With a "mass of wavy blond hair, tied with a blue ribbon," she wore "a neat tailored slacks suit." The police had picked her up on suspicion of prostitution. In fact, she was returning from a visit to New York to see her sailor husband.

The contrast with Bross couldn't have been greater. Braude made them stand side by side, the glamorous blonde and the factory worker in "rough trousers, sweater, lumberjack shirt, and muffler."

The judge could not resist sermonizing. "Miss Fitzpatrick has a right to wear slacks," he said. "Miss Fitzpatrick shows that there should be no objection to women wearing slacks if the wearer does not intend to impersonate a male." Looking sternly at Bross, he pointedly said, "There's a difference."

Given the public outrage over the arrest of Evelyn Bross, Braude was not about to find her guilty and send her to jail. But he just wouldn't let go of his gender-policing role, and he put Bross under psychiatric supervision for six months.

Bross didn't give an inch. Defiant to the end, Bross told the judge directly: "I'll put on a skirt if I have to, but I won't let my hair grow. If I dress like a girl, I'll look like a boy anyway, and I'll be picked up more often — the police will say I'm impersonating a girl."

As a historian, there's so much more about this episode that I want to know. What happened to Evelyn Bross in the succeeding decades? Did Bross stay in Chicago or return to Utah after the war? If Bross stayed, did she make a life for herself in the circles of butch-fem lesbians who patronized the bars of the 1950s and 1960s? Or did Bross, as some of the press quotes suggest, see himself as male so that today, perhaps, he might have identified as trans?

And what about Bross's Cherokee heritage? The news articles suggest that the family accepted Bross for who she — or he — was. Does this offer some insight into the traditions of many native American peoples who made space in their cultures for gender-crossing individuals? The newspaper articles that I stumbled across don't give me enough information to know.

But one thing I can say for sure. Despite the public support for Evelyn Bross and the change in Chicago's cross-dressing law, in the postwar decades the police kept making arrests — at lesbian and gay bars and on the streets of Chicago — of those who pushed against gender norms in clothing. "Who wears the pants?" remained a hot topic for another generation.

12

The Lavender Scare in Chicago

If you've ever taken a US history course, you're bound to have spent some classes on the Cold War and McCarthyism. It was a paranoid time. Having just defeated fascist powers in Europe and Asia, US leaders grew fearful of an imagined Communist threat. The very phrase "Cold War" suggested that peace was an illusion, that the country always had to be ready for war. For the first time, the United States built a large permanent military. Militarism became so powerful that even a former general like President Eisenhower told Americans to beware of "the military-industrial complex."

To many politicians and journalists, the Communist menace was much closer than the Soviet Union. Joseph McCarthy, a senator from Wisconsin, built his career around accusing government employees of being disloyal. But McCarthy was not alone in this. Lots of public figures together helped make the hunt for Communists and their sympathizers a national campaign. In the process, precious freedoms of speech and association were compromised, and lives were ruined.

What most history courses don't tell you, however, is this: during the McCarthy era, the witch hunters ousted a lot more gay men, lesbians, and bisexuals from government jobs and the military than they did political radicals.

David Johnson, a historian who studied at Northwestern and now teaches at the University of South Florida, has written a very gripping book

This essay first appeared in *Windy City Times*, November 5, 2008.

titled *The Lavender Scare*. He offers a close look at life in Washington, DC, in the 1940s, 1950s, and 1960s, when the purges of "sex perverts"—as gays, lesbians, and bisexuals were labeled—were at their height and the persecutions most intense. He paints a terrifying portrait of government investigations, secret surveillance, and police abuse. Women and men lived in fear. Coworkers and neighbors spied on one another and became informants. FBI and military investigators engaged in chilling interrogations of suspects. Thousands and thousands of folks lost jobs or were expelled from the military. Many others were cut off from prospective employment. Some packed up and left town; others took their own lives.

While Johnson naturally focused his story on Washington, DC, reading his book made me curious as to whether there was a Chicago angle to the Lavender Scare. Of course, many federal employees lived in the city, from postal workers to those who staffed various federal offices, and they were subject to the ban on the employment of lesbians, gays, and bisexuals. But I wondered how or even whether the investigations and purges were covered by the local press. Even if most of the action was in the nation's capital, did local news coverage bring the story into Chicago's homes? Did queers in Chicago know about what was happening? What impressions about gay men and lesbians did the press perpetuate?

Sure enough, the *Tribune* gave prominent coverage to the issue. The story broke early in 1950 when a State Department official mentioned in passing that a number of fired security risks were homosexuals. Over the next three years, the basic outline of the *Tribune*'s articles remained the same: a lax Truman administration allowed "moral misfits" to remain on the government payroll. Although homosexuals could be found in every agency, they especially seemed to concentrate in the State Department. Because they were desperate to escape exposure, they easily fell prey to Communists who blackmailed them into betraying government risks. Hence they were all security risks. Only when Eisenhower became president, in 1953, did the government take an aggressive stance, and the topic finally faded from view.

As I read through all these stories, a number of things stood out. Above all, the language dripped with contempt. It seemed designed to arouse outrage among straight readers and shame and terror among anyone who wasn't. Reporters routinely used words like "perverts," "degenerates," and "misfits." They wrote of "unnatural tendencies," "sordid practices," and "moral depravity." Stories described the "shocked outcries" coming from "horrified legislators" who, the paper claimed, "recoiled" at what they heard in closed committee hearings.

The *Tribune* portrayed the nation's capital as a moral cesspool. Washington was overrun by unmarried females starved for love; Communist agents then "entice women into a life of eroticism." The city, it reported, was "infested" with "nests of perverts." Investigators testified about wild parties and sex orgies for lesbians and for male homosexuals.

The *Tribune* made the dangers seem immense and the risks very great. Senate investigators, it informed its readers, found that "one homosexual can pollute an entire government office." It described how, throughout history, moral weakness had been responsible for "the death of nations." In the midst of the Korean War, it told about sex perverts found in the American foreign service in both Korea and Hong Kong. These "moral degenerates" could be found in the most sensitive places. It reported that Russia kept lists of sex perverts in enemy countries like the United States.

Then there was the matter of evidence—or, rather, the absence of it. Over and over, members of Congress like McCarthy and his allies made the claim that gay men and lesbians were susceptible to blackmail. The *Tribune* dutifully repeated this in virtually every story. But there were no examples, no instances, no hint of proof. The closest reporters came to a concrete example was a reference to a scandal in Germany fifty years earlier.

Most infuriating of all is the blatant partisanship that drove the *Tribune*'s reporting. If you read its coverage closely, you'll notice that the paper was using the story as a way to attack Truman and the Democrats. The staunchly Republican paper of Colonel McCormick, as its conservative owner was known, employed the popular dislike of gays and lesbians to mobilize opinion against Democratic control of the federal government. McCormick despised President Franklin D. Roosevelt and the New Deal. He hated the expansion of the federal government created by Depression-era programs like Social Security, unemployment compensation, and subsidies for farmers. His paper used every opportunity that came its way to attack Democrats. Consider this headline: "Move to Oust Perverts in U.S. Jobs Defeated—Democrats Vote as Unit to Reject Proposal." Or this one: "Sex Perverts' Files Vanish, Probers Told; Insured Promotion in Truman Regime."

Compare the *Tribune*'s coverage with that of the Democratic-leaning *Sun-Times* and the partisan motivations become even clearer. The *Tribune* went out of its way to exaggerate the dimensions of the problem. It used figures ranging from 4 to 8 percent to describe the size of the homosexual population; that would mean thousands of federal employees in Washington and as many as 100,000 across the country. By contrast, the *Sun-Times* wrote in terms of "two ten-thousands of one per cent," a proportion so small as to be of no concern at all.

The McCarthy era was a scary time for anyone who didn't follow the sexual straight and narrow. Even those who didn't work for the federal government had to be aware that the witch hunters were on the offensive. In the early 1950s, the *Tribune* didn't have any counterbalancing news stories about the gay and lesbian community. "Perverts" and "degenerates" were all we were during the years of the Lavender Scare.

13

Pulp Madness

Of all the topics I cover in my gay studies classes, a candidate for favorite is the lesbian pulp novel. In the 1950s and 1960s, publishers released them by the hundreds. The name stems from the low-grade paper stock on which they were printed, but "pulp" came to symbolize something else as well: the cheap and tawdry. Pulp novels carried the scent of shame and scandal. On one hand, they were very visible in this era of the closet. You could find them at drugstores and newsstands across the country. On the other hand, you wouldn't want to be seen reading one.

Part of what attracts me to the pulp novel is that it lets students see that things aren't just one thing or the other, good or bad, antigay or pro-gay. Instead, the past—like the present—is complicated and contradictory. We spend time looking at a Power Point presentation of lots of these paperback covers. The titles seem to say it all: *By Love Depraved, Degraded Women, Forbidden, The Damned One, Satan's Daughter, The Evil Friendship.* "Strange" is used as a modifier for every possible noun: *Strange Passions, Strange Seduction, Strange Lust, Strange Thirsts.* Copywriters seemed to work from a very abridged dictionary. Warped, tormented, unnatural, twisted: the words all make the same point. Lesbian is bad, bad, bad.

Of course, these novels weren't primarily meant for lesbians. The intended buyers were all those so-called one-handed readers—heterosexual men turned on by the thought of lesbians making love. Their numbers

This essay first appeared in *Windy City Times*, July 23, 2008.

were large enough to propel skyward the sales figures for many pulps. Indeed, lots of these books were written by heterosexual men who knew that the readers were likely to be other heterosexual men.

So what's to study here? Isn't the lesbian pulp craze just another example of how the 1950s were the worst time to be queer? Well, not entirely. The pulp genre also opened an opportunity for lesbian writers. Pulp publishing was like a small crack in the wall of oppression, and some lesbians found a way to slip through. Writers like Ann Bannon, Marion Zimmer Bradley (writing under the pseudonym "Miriam Gardner"), Paula Christian, and March Hastings were able to manipulate the genre and win the loyalty of lesbian readers.

Leaving behind sensationalism and refusing to pander to male sensibilities, they worked to create believable scenarios populated by characters that a female reader might identify with. Sometimes, the publisher cooperated. A novel by March Hastings, published in 1960, had the title *The Unashamed*, revealing a bit of pride and self-respect. The cover illustration showed two women in a pose and with facial expressions that suggested tenderness and love.

Still, lesbian authors couldn't entirely abandon the formulaic plots, especially in the more repressive 1950s. They worked within constraints, and, as a reader today will quickly discover, these are not tales of a lesbian-feminist utopia.

One of the most important of these lesbian writers of pulp fiction was Valerie Taylor, who lived here in Chicago for more than two decades and, in the 1960s and 1970s, was quite an "out and proud" activist. Taylor wrote almost a dozen novels in the course of her career. Two of them, published in the 1950s, are very revealing of both the limits and the possibilities of the pulp genre.

Whisper Their Love, Taylor's first novel with lesbian content, was published in 1957. It tells the story of Joyce, a working-class girl from small-town Illinois who has just arrived at a college for white women in North Carolina. Family dysfunction trails her: Joyce was illegitimate, never knew her father, and was raised by a puritanical aunt while her mother, Mimi, was a traveling saleswoman. At college, her roommate Mary Jean, who goes all the way with a boyfriend, sets Joyce up on a date, but Joyce rebuffs the young man's aggressive advances. On a visit to Chicago to attend Mimi's wedding to her boss, Joyce loses her virginity to her mother's fiancé the night before the wedding. Traumatized, she returns to school where the dean, Edith Bannister, comforts her . . . and takes her to bed.

Edith is a lesbian. She has a circle of lesbian and gay friends in town, takes Joyce to parties and clubs, and introduces her to the grim realities of gay life at the time. Secrecy is imperative, because society does bad things to queers. Tell no one, she warns, or else jobs will be lost and lives ruined. Edith herself had had an affair with a teacher when she was in high school. She told a friend about it, and the result was expulsion from school and suicide for the teacher.

Meanwhile (there are *always* "meanwhiles" in these novels), Mary Jean has gotten pregnant, and Joyce helps her procure an abortion from a kindly old doctor in town. But then Mary Jean gets pregnant again, and this time she commits suicide. Joyce breaks up with Edith and is rescued from a life of both lesbianism and mean heterosexual men by John, the nephew of the abortionist, who is a Korean War vet, intends to become a doctor, knows psychology, is understanding of Joyce's lesbian interlude, and promises not to have sex with Joyce until she wants to. Presumably they live happily ever after.

Okay, I know this plot summary is not making you rush to your computer to buy a used copy online. And lesbians at the time were probably not too thrilled at the plot's final destination either. But, really, it's a pretty absorbing read, and I was struck by the implied feminism of much of the plot. Girls on the edge of womanhood in the 1950s had it hard. Life could be treacherous. Men were not women's best friends.

Taylor's next novel was *The Girls in 3-B*. It tells the story of Annice, Pat, and Barby, three high school graduates from downstate Illinois, as they come to Chicago together to make their way in the world. Even more than *Whisper Their Love*, this book charts the path of young white women in the 1950s; one could easily assign it in a women's history or social history course. Annice, an aspiring poet, hooks up with a heartless young beatnik who gets her pregnant and abandons her; Pat has an unrequited crush on her handsome boss, who takes women to bed and then moves on; Barby, who was raped at age thirteen by the banker in her small town, is forced into bed by the superintendent of their Hyde Park apartment building.

But all turns out well for each of them. Annice is rescued by a nice young man who will marry her despite the pregnancy. Pat is courted by a Polish Catholic office boy, who respects her when she says no and takes her to Sunday mass with his parents. And Barby meets Ilene, a supervisor at work who has recently broken up with her female lover of several years. Barb doesn't know what a lesbian is, but she knows she's attracted to Ilene and curious about her. Their courtship starts with lunch dates and moves on to an affair that is sweet and tender and without emotional upheaval, and the reader knows that Barb has found a relationship that will be good for her. It's hard to imagine that there were many such portraits in the 1950s of a young woman's introduction to lesbian love.

If the truth be told, I read these two novels less because of a fascination with the pulp genre (it's the covers that grab me) and more because I started to become fascinated by Valerie Taylor. She's an extraordinarily interesting figure, a woman who deserves a biographer.

14

Valerie Taylor

A Woman for All Generations

It's hard not to think generationally. Groups of people come of age at a particular historical moment, and it marks them forever, creating a bond. I grew up in an environment where everyone spoke of "the immigrant generation." We all knew what it meant: the old folks were different from the young. African Americans of a certain age speak of growing up under Jim Crow, in the segregated South; it shaped them in profound ways. Journalists write about Baby Boomers or Generation X. Tom Brokaw pens a best-selling book called *The Greatest Generation*. A large group of aging Americans speaks of "the '60s" in a way that says "it made us who we are."

Within the LGBT world, notions of generations circulate, too. People refer to the Stonewall generation or the separatist generation to describe an experience that distinguishes them from other gays or lesbians. Whatever the label, the assumption is that our generation, however defined, makes us who we are. As we move through life, the world changes, and we don't. It's as if we're trapped forever in a bygone time.

I think what draws me to Valerie Taylor, the pulp novelist, is that she resisted this pigeonholing. Though she lived to be eighty-four, she flat-out refused to remain stuck in the box of a particular coming-of-age experience. She always remained a woman of the moment, a woman who changed with the times.

This essay first appeared in *Windy City Times*, August 6, 2008.

Velma Nacella Young (Taylor's birth name) was born in 1913 in Aurora, Illinois, when it was still a small town beyond Chicago's sprawl. Her family had little money but plenty of books, and, when Velma had the chance to attend college, she seized it. Two years at Blackburn College in Carlinville, Illinois, gave her credentials to teach at country schools. They also made her a socialist. This was in the middle of the Depression, and lots of Americans were seizing socialist ideas of economic justice.

In small-town America in the 1930s, there weren't many images of lesbian life. Nor was it common then for a woman to support herself. And so Velma Young, like who knows how many women-loving women of her generation, got married. She had three sons with her husband, William Tate. But he proved to be "an alcoholic no-good bum," and, after fourteen years of marriage, Velma took her sons and left. While much of white America was entering the "Father Knows Best" era of idealized family life, she was breaking out of the housewife box.

Writing was her way out. Velma had been composing stories and poems since childhood. In 1952, using the pseudonym Valerie Taylor, she published, in her words, a "raunchy heterosexual love story" titled *Hired Hand*. With the $500 she received for it (a solid chunk of cash in those days), Taylor—as we'll now call her—"went out and bought two dresses and a pair of shoes, got a job, and consulted a divorce lawyer. . . . That was a good little royalty check," she recalled, many years later.

Despite the huge sales of pulp novels, authors did not receive a fair share of royalties, and Taylor always needed a day job to support herself and her sons. But she wrote steadily, moving decisively into the lesbian pulp genre. She published *Whisper Their Love* and then *The Girls in 3-B*. In the 1960s Taylor wrote a series of linked novels with unambiguous titles like *Stranger on Lesbos* and *A World without Men*.

The increasingly overt subject matter of her books reflected the change in Taylor's life after leaving her husband. She was now romantically interested in women. But lesbians in Chicago in the 1950s, as Taylor reminisced, "didn't have the underground network the men had. . . . There was a lot of loneliness." Lesbians as well as gay men were cautious about revealing themselves—"In those days, you'd lose your job if you ever came out"—and a single mom raising three teenagers could not risk being out of work.

Over time, Taylor developed a circle of friends. But her first sense of lesbian "community" came through *The Ladder*, a magazine produced by the Daughters of Bilitis, a lesbian homophile organization. It began publishing in 1956, as the lesbian pulp boom was taking off. From its start, *The Ladder* paid attention to lesbian culture and literature, and it reviewed Taylor's work. Taylor came to know Barbara Grier, who wrote most of *The Ladder*'s literary columns. She also corresponded with lesbian writers like May Sarton, Elsa Gidlow, and Jeannette Foster.

Taylor's visibility as a writer meant that many small-town lesbians wrote to her and asked for advice about meeting other lesbians. She'd tell them to sit at a drugstore lunch counter with a copy of *The Well of Loneliness* or with a Beebo Brinker lesbian pulp. If a woman exhibited signs of interest, she was probably a lesbian. Such were the challenges of building community in the 1950s.

Maybe it was a yearning for community that impelled Taylor, in the mid-1960s, to do something most lesbians and gay men of her generation were unwilling to risk. She joined the small but courageous homophile movement. Since a Daughters of Bilitis chapter never sunk deep roots in Chicago, she participated in Mattachine Midwest, helping to edit its newsletter. Her columns reveal a feisty personality who didn't mince words. When *Time* printed a particularly ugly antigay article, Taylor opined, "The pages are too stiff to wrap garbage in and the magazine is no good for anything else." Writing about the many syndicate-run gay bars in Chicago, she said that "they prey on gay people."

When lesbian feminism and gay liberation exploded into life in the early 1970s, most of Taylor's generation kept a distance and remained discreetly in the closet. Not Taylor. She jumped in with both feet. In 1973 she was one of the featured speakers at the noon rally at Civic Plaza during Pride Week. Acknowledging that she was older than almost everyone else there, Taylor introduced herself as a representative of "the gay grandmothers of America." The next year, she helped Marie Kuda organize the first of several annual Lesbian Writers Conferences, which brought together women from around the country. Taylor gave keynotes at more than one of them.

Her message to the younger generation was powerful, visionary, and sometimes unsettling. "The whole world should be our subject matter," she told those at the conference of writers. "All of life belongs to us." For Taylor, feminism and gay liberation weren't for the fainthearted. "Revolution is never a straight-line process . . . a great many people get hurt." She wanted folks to think big: "We need not choose between the struggle for world peace and the fight for women's liberation. . . . The entire world is our battlefield."

Taylor spent the last decade and a half of her life in the warmer climate of Tucson. Sometime in the 1980s, she wrote an essay in which she asked, "Have you ever wondered what happened to old Amazons?" The question grew out of experience. In 1980 Taylor learned that Jeannette Foster, the pioneering lesbian scholar, was incapacitated and in need of financial help. Taylor established a Sisterhood Fund and raised money from lesbians around the country to support Foster in the last year of her life. In 1993 Lee Lynch, a younger lesbian writer, did the same for Taylor. "I knew my sisters wouldn't let me down," an eighty-one-year-old Taylor told an interviewer. "There really is a lesbian community all over the place."

She might have added that she had helped to build it.

15

In the News

These days, we take for granted the newsworthiness of LGBT topics. Gender identity gets left out of the latest draft of the Employment Non-discrimination Act, and the ensuing battle for transgender inclusion becomes a mainstream news story. Same-sex marriage, don't-ask-don't-tell, the use of the "F" word as a slur by a television star: these all get splashed across the pages of print media or become fodder for nighttime television commentary.

It wasn't always so. In 1951, when Donald Webster Cory (a pseudonym) published *The Homosexual in America,* he identified what he called a "conspiracy of silence" that blanketed the nation's press. Gay and lesbian life wasn't considered a fit subject matter for the "family newspaper" that millions of Americans picked up on their way to work in the morning or had delivered to their homes each day.

Of course, editors selectively enforced this silence, honoring it only in the breach. The *Chicago Tribune* had no compunction about writing about the dangers posed by "men of perverted sex tendencies." The *Chicago Defender* felt free to claim that lesbians controlled the city's prostitution trade. But articles that simply described life as it was experienced by gay men and lesbians? That allowed them to speak in their own words and set the terms of the coverage? Not on your life.

This essay first appeared in *Windy City Times,* July 9, 2008.

When did this journalistic state of affairs begin to change? Historians love the concreteness of dates, and in this case we have a precise one—December 17, 1963. On that day, the *New York Times*, whose motto is "All the news that's fit to print," carried this headline: "Growth of Overt Homosexuality in City Provokes Wide Concern." The accompanying article described a flourishing male homosexual underground as the city's "most sensitive open secret."

Perhaps because the *Times* presents itself as the "newspaper of record" in the United States, this article provided journalistic permission for other papers to follow suit. Over the next couple of years, copycat articles appeared in city newspapers around the country. Atlanta, Denver, Washington, DC, and Seattle were just some of the cities where reporters decided to expose the gay world to their readership. Chicago's turn came on June 20, 1966, when the now-defunct *Daily News* began a four-part series.

To our contemporary sensibilities, the content of the series would be enough to make thousands of angry queers spontaneously storm the headquarters of the publisher and then sit in until apologies were issued and the evil deed rectified by providing space for rebuttal. In the series, a judge described homosexuals as "sick people." James O'Grady, the police lieutenant in charge of the antiprostitution detail (and who was to become police chief briefly in 1978), talked about "fag bars" and "queers." The doctor who directed the municipal court's psychiatric unit referred to homosexuality as "socially distasteful." The reporter described gay men as "disturbed" and as "deviates."

The headlines and section headers that the *Daily News* employed were just as bad: "Twilight World That's Tormented"; "Cops Keep Watch on Deviate Hangouts"; "Homosexuality a Sickness? 'No' Say the Deviates"; "His Bizarre Double Life."

But our contemporary eyes are not the best ones for judging how these articles were viewed at the time. In the context of 1966, they represented progress, a journalistic opening wedge of sorts. Why? Because "tormented" and "deviate" and "disturbed" and "affliction" were not the only descriptions expressed in the series. I wouldn't go as far as to say the articles displayed balance—if by balance we mean equal weight to antigay and progay sentiments. But it is definitely true that the reporter, Lois Wille (who had already won a Pulitzer Prize for a 1963 series on the refusal of government agencies in Chicago and Cook county to provide contraceptive services to poor women), allowed dissenting opinions to be heard. She found ways to insinuate that there was more than one viewpoint about homosexuality. She thus gave legitimacy to a *debate* about homosexuality where, before, there was nothing but a negative consensus.

She did this in different ways. Sometimes she posed questions, like these in the opening article: "Can and should deviates be 'contained' to keep them from spreading further? . . . Or are these disturbed, misunderstood men needing help, understanding and the freedom to live in their way?" She suggested that the gay world was made up of all kinds of people. Yes, there were "the dregs of the invert world," but there were also those who led "happy lives" and who made "good neighbors."

Wille held public policy up for criticism, too. A major topic in the series was police behavior. She wrote at length about the crackdown against gay bars, the raids and the closings, and the mass arrests. But Lieutenant O'Grady's defense of police activity did not go unchallenged. Wille interviewed Pearl Hart, whom she described as a lawyer with fifty-two years of practice in civil liberties law. Hart called police conduct unethical and said the raids and arrests were a waste of time and taxpayers' money. "It just doesn't make sense to go after homosexuals," she told Wille.

The series also let it be known that some homosexuals were challenging the way things were. Sometimes this took the form of organizations, like Mattachine Midwest, whose president Wille approvingly described as "a tall rugged-looking businessman"—no stereotype he! But sometimes more spontaneous forms of resistance showed up. She described a wonderful scene in court where a well-dressed defendant began shouting at the judge: "I'm happy. Are you happy? Well I am. . . . Don't tell me I'm sick." According to Wille, this kind of response was becoming typical as gay men no longer listened meekly to what prosecutors and judges had to say.

The *Daily News* articles were as revealing for what they left out as for what they contained. There was not a single mention of lesbians. This was a series about male homosexuals, and lesbians never entered the discussion. There was no mention of their bars, no mention of their social circles, and no mention of any difficulties they faced. The articles also had no racial descriptors. This effectively coded the discussion as one about white men, implying that gays are all white. By and large, the locations Wille identified for gay bars and cruising areas were North Side locations; the South Side was absent, reinforcing the sense that this was a white social phenomenon.

These silences were not surprising, but they were especially unfortunate. At a time when silence in the press was more the rule than not, a series like this one was something of a road map. For the very closeted, these articles offered information. It named bars. It named locations. In other words, it provided hope to the very isolated that they might find others. But that hope, alas, didn't extend to everyone.

16

Gay Power!

"Mattachine" is not exactly a household word. To the degree that the name has come down to us, it most often registers as "Oh, yeah, those are the people who tried to do something in the years before the Stonewall riots started the *real* gay liberation movement." The name itself has the ring of another era, another planet even. In those days, even the activists couldn't say "gay" or "lesbian." They came up with names like Mattachine Society or Daughters of Bilitis, and they called themselves the "homophile movement." What the hell, you may ask, is a "homophile"?

Imagine my surprise, then, when I came upon the phrase "gay power" in a 1966 newsletter of Mattachine Midwest. Sitting in one of the carrels at the Gerber/Hart Library, I was startled. Almost three years before Stonewall, this band of supposedly cautious activists in Chicago was using a phrase I associated with the most militant and radical queer activists. What was going on here?

Some of what was going on was the times: "the '60s." A spirit of rebellion was all around. In June 1966 Stokely Carmichael, a civil rights activist working in Mississippi, had used the phrase "black power!" in a protest march across the state. The words captured the anger, frustration, and determination of many African Americans who had experienced too much white violence and too many denials of basic human rights for way too long. "Black power" came to symbolize an unwillingness to go slow. It

This essay first appeared in *Windy City Times*, June 4, 2008.

stood for a belief that abuses of power had to be met with at least an equal and opposite force.

These sentiments and experiences weren't confined to Mississippi. In the summer of 1966, the Reverend Martin Luther King Jr. came to Chicago to assist in efforts to open up the housing market in the city's segregated neighborhoods. Marchers, who included many priests and nuns, were met by the ugly violence of white mobs. It drove home the message that peaceful protest and efforts to negotiate reasonably weren't going to do the trick.

That year, 1966, was a particularly bad one for the city's gay men. Issue after issue of the Mattachine Midwest newsletter reported on the latest police outrage. Chicago's police force seemed out of control. "Enticement, Entrapment, and Harassment face the homosexual every time he steps into the street," the newsletter declared.

Illinois had repealed its sodomy law in 1961, becoming the first state to decriminalize sexual behavior between consenting adults in private. But, almost as a response, police stepped up their tactics against "public" sexual activity. Reports came to Mattachine of all sorts of aggressive police practices. Cops were exposing themselves in public rest rooms in their effort to make lewd-conduct arrests. Plainclothes officers in "obviously seductive attire" walked the streets that gay men cruised. They'd strike up a conversation and then, when the unsuspecting target invited the officer home, arrest him for solicitation. Or, police would hang out in gay bars and listen to the conversations around them. When they heard a pickup line, it was all they needed to arrest bartenders for running "a disorderly house" and cart off patrons for being "inmates" of the house.

Early in 1966, newspapers in Chicago revealed that the police had a "stop-and-quiz" policy. If cops didn't like the look of someone, if they suspected a person even in the absence of evidence of any crime, they could stop him or her; demand name, address, and place of employment; require identification; and grill the person for an explanation of his or her presence on the street. Black men in white neighborhoods, women alone at night wearing clothes that seemed too sexy, and queeny-looking guys: all faced stop-and-quiz procedures.

These were police-state tactics. But refusing to cooperate was a tricky matter. It could lead to an arrest for disorderly conduct or loitering. At least one gay man who didn't provide information on his place of employment was arrested on charges of "no visible means of support." The list of potential dangers was a long one.

Mattachine Midwest tried, again and again, to set up meetings with police to discuss the department's policies. Every time, the police declined the invitation. Meanwhile, as spring and summer wore on, Mattachine's newsletter reported a continuing series of raids on gay bars and bath houses. It also reported the "sadistic" public exposure in the *Chicago Tribune* of the names of those arrested.

The anger of Mattachine members came through in the newsletter. "As children, we were told that the policeman was there to protect and help us," the editor wrote. "To the homosexual citizen such thoughts are pure nonsense." As the year wore on, Mattachine's rhetoric grew more and more heated: "'Lawless police' is a phrase which still aptly describes Chicago's cops . . . the entrapments, shakedowns, brutality, and corruption continue . . . no one is immune." "Quit buying the right-wing line about crime in the streets and wake up to YOUR rights. Crime is as much rampant inside the police department as elsewhere."

An unmistakable sense that folks were fed up, that they'd had enough, jumps from the newsletter's pages each month. "It's time things were changed," the newsletter told its readers. "It's time to stop running." Mattachine urged gay men to fight back: "Hold your heads up high. Be proud of your individuality. Spend your energy fighting for equality." Finally, as the year ended, almost in exasperation Mattachine's president, Jim Bradford, burst out: "Maybe we need to form a 'Gay Power' bloc!"

Bradford's declaration is a good reminder that rebellion was in the air here in Chicago fifty years ago. It was percolating from the ground up, on the streets and in the bars and in the parks, wherever queers found themselves in confrontation with the law. Stonewall was one expression of that, but it didn't need to be imported to Chicago from New York to rile people up. There were more than enough home-grown grievances to start the talk about "gay power."

17

Risky Business

In 1963, as a high-school sophomore, I saw my first Broadway play. Afterward, strolling through Manhattan's theater district with my friends, I also saw my first homosexuals: three young men, thin as toothpicks, with long, teased hair, their fingers fluttering, mascara, rouge, and powder on their faces. I couldn't take my eyes off them. Their appearance thrilled and terrified me.

In the 1960s, before rainbow flags and equal signs on SUV bumpers, gay and lesbian visibility came primarily through gender bending. Occasionally, queerness might attach to an individual in the public eye. Bayard Rustin's arrest on sex charges was widely publicized. Allen Ginsberg's sexually explicit poetry provoked outrage. Marlene Dietrich and Greta Garbo played roles that suggested lesbianism, but that's because they wore men's clothes. Lesbian moviegoers might hope that, maybe, they were lesbians in real life. I'll never know whether the young men I saw that day in 1963 were gay. But crossing gender boundaries—especially through dress and hairstyle—was so closely tied to homosexuality that it didn't matter. I saw them and I knew: they were what I felt I was. I came back to Times Square many times, hoping to find someone else who was queer. Eventually, I did. Those street fairies, as they were widely termed in those days, helped me discover gay life.

My experience was not unique. Recalling her days in New York in the 1950s, Joan Nestle, a founder of the Lesbian Herstory Archives, has written

This essay first appeared in *Windy City Times*, September 10, 2008.

that butch-femme couples "made lesbians culturally visible." She describes these couples, who "often provoked rage" when they appeared on the streets, as models of courage. Histories of lesbian life in San Francisco, Detroit, and Buffalo all make the same point.

We don't have a book-length account of lesbian life in Chicago in the decades before Stonewall. But we are blessed with a richly detailed study of the culture of drag performance and street fairy life. Esther Newton, who is one of the great figures in contemporary queer studies, was a graduate student in anthropology at the University of Chicago when she decided to do her dissertation on a gay topic. *Mother Camp*, the book she produced more than forty years ago, was based on fieldwork in Chicago and Kansas City in 1965 and 1966.

"Drag," Newton wrote then, "symbolizes gayness." She described drag as "an open declaration, even celebration, of homosexuality." Those who cross-dressed, she argued, were effectively saying, "I'm gay, and I don't care who knows it; the straight world be damned."

When Newton made her observations, drag was a big part of gay bar life in Chicago. In 1966 seven gay nightspots had full-time drag shows, employing roughly thirty performers. At a time when much of Chicago life was racially segregated and Martin Luther King Jr. was planning massive protests, many of these performers were African Americans. Drag shows packed in patrons on weekends; two hundred or more might press into the space. Some bars with drag shows were located near one another, and the crowds moved back and forth during an evening in order to catch all the shows. The experience helped create a sense of community.

Most of the time drag shows were pure fun. Performers did hilarious impersonations of older showbiz figures like Mae West and Sophie Tucker. They bantered with the audience, using the people in front of them as material for their jokes. But sometimes a political message surfaced. Newton described impersonators who referred to the fact that Illinois, alone among the fifty states, had repealed its sodomy law. One spoke to the audience about the Mattachine Society. "If you think we're not gonna march," he said, "you're out of your mind." This was before Stonewall and gay liberation.

Gender crossing in these bars was confined to the stage. At night's end, the performer removed jewelry, makeup, and gowns and returned to male clothing. Among bar patrons, any gender crossing was risky business. It was against the law, and police were eager for arrests. Bar managers kept customers in line.

But outside was another matter. There, Newton reported, young gender crossers made the streets the site of their performance. Like the street fairies I saw in Times Square, they presented themselves for anyone to see. They were most visible in those neighborhoods with a reputation as gay; in fact, their presence helped mark a neighborhood as queer. They could also be found in areas that attracted johns looking for prostitutes.

Life for a street fairy was difficult and dangerous. Challenging gender boundaries openly made it hard to get a job. Many had to support themselves through prostitution. Add this to their violation of the laws against cross-dressing, and one could say, as Esther Newton did, that they lived "outside the law . . . in continuous interaction with the local police." Police harassment often meant long arrest records.

Fragments of evidence about James Clay highlight just how vulnerable street fairies were. A twenty-four-year-old African American who lived on the West Side, Clay already had twelve arrests by 1970. Charges included impersonating the opposite sex, solicitation to commit prostitution, battery, resisting arrest, aggravated assault, and attempted murder. A hardened criminal, right? Wrong! All of these are charges that easily stem from the efforts of a transperson of color to make a living on the streets. Clay likely made the mistake of soliciting plainclothesmen; he likely tried to escape, which translates into resisting arrest. And, to make sure of a conviction, police officers could define physical resistance to them as aggravated assault or attempted murder, which then got plea-bargained down. Clay's twelve arrests resulted in three convictions between 1965 and 1969. One of his arresting officers was James Finnelly.

In the wee hours of the morning the day before Thanksgiving 1970, Finnelly and his partner, Thomas Bolling, spotted Clay, who was wearing women's clothing, flagging motorists. They gave pursuit and chased Clay into a building. Clay managed to shake them off and escape. In an unmarked car, the two officers kept cruising the neighborhood near Madison and Francisco. They found Clay, who had changed into men's clothes, and tried to arrest him. Clay got free again, but this time Finnelly and Bolling fired eight shots into his back.

The *Sun-Times* and the *Defender* carried stories about Clay's killing, and both papers wrote in ways that suggested doubt about police veracity. But no witnesses came forward. The recently formed Chicago Gay Alliance called for an FBI investigation into the slaying, arguing that Clay's civil rights had been violated. But the FBI refused. CGA wrote that "street transvestites are the most up front part of our community. . . . Cops use transvestites to take out their hatred for those of us they can't reach so easily. . . . James Clay was a Gay martyr." Clay's killing helped provoke the formation, in 1971, of the Transvestites Legal Committee, which may have been the first transgender political group in Chicago.

Postscript: Thirty-five years after the killing of James Clay, Amnesty International released a report, *Stonewalled*, that looked at police practices in Chicago. "Transgender people of color," it concluded, "are especially at risk of police abuse." Much has changed since 1970. And much hasn't.

18

Let's Dance!

"If I can't dance, I don't want your revolution." At some point in the 1970s, it seemed like every third person I knew had a poster emblazoned with these words. Attributed to the early twentieth-century anarchist, Emma Goldman, the sentiments captured the exuberance of some of that era's lesbians and gay men. (As it turned out, Goldman never said this, but that's a whole other history tale.) In discos, at women's music festivals, on college campuses, and at street fairs, queer folk looked as if we were dancing our way to freedom. Unlike the dour images of men storming the citadels of power, the gay revolution was going to be fun.

I suspect that for some politicos—straight or queer—the association of dancing and revolution is evidence of just how trivial gay liberation is. But, if so, they don't know much history.

In Chicago in the 1950s and 1960s, the prohibition on public same-sex dancing was pretty nearly complete. The Chicago Police Department *might* make an exception for a Halloween or New Year's masquerade ball—though even here, most of the dancing couples looked to be of the opposite sex. But the bars did their own serious policing not just of dancing but of any form of touching. An arm around someone's shoulder or a playful squeeze of someone's butt could be enough to send lurking plainclothes officers into action, and arrests for public indecency would follow. Same-sex dancing in this kind of climate? Not likely.

This essay first appeared in *Windy City Times*, June 18, 2008.

Folks from that era who went regularly to the bars loved them and were loyal to them, but it was a bittersweet love. "The bars are the only place for Gay people to go to get together outside of home," one of them wrote. And then, in the next line: "There is no question that they were for shit." No wonder that, when gay liberation groups started forming at the end of 1969, the creation of new gay and lesbian spaces—and the opening of those spaces to same-sex dancing—would be high on the list of priorities.

The first group in Chicago to take on the name of "gay liberation" was on the South Side, in the Hyde Park neighborhood, and included a number of University of Chicago students. At first they met mostly to talk, but talking soon led to action. One of the first actions, in January 1970, was to attend a campus mixer (a "mixer" was a dance in the lingo of the '50s and '60s) and dance together. Fewer than a dozen gay men and lesbians showed up for the action, and, according to Step May, one of the participants, "we were all scared to death." But nothing bad happened, and so, emboldened, they decided to hold the first out-of-the-closet same-sex dance on campus.

Because some of the Chicago Gay Liberation members were University of Chicago students, they had access to campus facilities. They reserved the dining hall in Pierce Tower, a dormitory, for a weekend night in February. But who would come? Was it too big a space? Would they feel foolish if only two dozen campus queers showed up? So they did a "real leafleting blitz," as May recalled, going to gay bars on both the South and the North Sides. Vernita Gray, who was there, remembered that folks came from all over the city, not just from the campus.

"Black, white, brown, straight, gay, male, female—600 liberated people danced freely to live music," one of the attendees reported. "Even the security guards seemed to enjoy the scene." The crowd was mostly "young" and "hip." One can just imagine the long hair on the men, the women with granny glasses, and bell-bottom jeans on everyone.

This was too much fun not to do again. In April, there was a second dance, this time in Woodward Commons, a women's dorm. More than a thousand showed up. Not to be outdone, lesbian and gay students at Northwestern and at Circle Campus (today's University of Illinois at Chicago) scheduled dances, too, for later that spring. The dancing bug was proving contagious.

Bold as all this was, these actions were still, in one sense, cautious. After all, campuses by the late 1960s had come to seem like another world; wholly different standards of morality, politics, and values held sway. Of course these radical environments would embrace these queer celebrations. I can almost hear the stoned hippie saying, "Grooooovy!" at the sight of all those same-sex couples swaying to the music. But, could same-sex dancing happen off campus, in Chicago proper?

Chicago Gay Liberation decided to find out. The group rented the Coliseum, a structure near 16th and Wabash that, in bygone days, had hosted professional hockey and basketball games, roller derby, and major political conventions. It was a huge space. And, most important, it was a *public* space in every sense of the word. This was pushing the boundaries and taking a big risk.

Folks were scared. Might the police invade the place? Was there the danger of a "giant bust"? Renee Hanover, the lawyer for the gay groups, pressed hard on the police to make sure nothing would happen. The police did show up to patrol the area on April 18, but there were no arrests and no interference.

The dancing crowds didn't quite fill the place, but two thousand people came, making this perhaps the biggest openly acknowledged queer gathering in Chicago history. "The dance floor was filled with laughing faces," reported Mattachine Midwest's newsletter. Its writer waxed eloquent about the dance. It "introduced freedom as the remedy that will end the closet as a way of life. The faggots came out for their public, the band was great, the vibes were beautiful. . . . The revolution has just begun, and the dances are part of it."

One thing leads to another, as my mother often warned me. In this case, the heady pleasures of a few dances led straight to the door of a popular local bar. The weekend after the Coliseum dance, gay and lesbian liberationists showed up with picket signs outside the Normandy Inn, near Chicago and Rush Streets. The flyers they distributed listed their demands: "Gay people can dance both fast and slow . . . no arbitrary dress regulations . . . no discrimination against women."

The Seed, a local alternative radical newspaper, reported that the Normandy was "nearly empty" that weekend, as protesters kept patrons away and "convinced the owners they would have to take the wishes of Gay people seriously." The owners caved in, and other bars quickly responded, as well. For queer Chicagoans, dancing had come to stay.

19

Writing for Freedom

If I think back on the steps that brought me to embrace being gay, I see that they follow a path littered with books. First was *Advise and Consent*, a wildly popular novel from the late 1950s that I read before starting high school. The main character, a senator who had a gay affair while in the army, commits suicide when he's threatened with exposure. From there I moved on to *Another Country*, by James Baldwin. One gay character kills himself. Another finds happiness, but only by moving to France. My life prospects had now improved to 50–50, but how would I get to France?

In college, I read Oscar Wilde's *De Profundis*. It's an eloquent, passionate, and strong-willed defense of love between men, but Wilde wrote it while in jail, which is where, apparently, you end up if you're gay. Books were letting me imagine that there were other homosexuals in the world. They were even giving me the words to defend my feelings and attractions. But jolly and hopeful they weren't.

Then, in 1973, Mimi, a friend who identified as bisexual and lived in a group household, gave me a brand-new novel that, Mimi said, she had read in a single sitting. It was published by something called Daughters Press, a feminist collective in Vermont; the author was a lesbian activist named Rita Mae Brown; and the intriguing title was *Rubyfruit Jungle*.

Sure enough, it was an irresistible page turner. Brown seized upon core American themes and shaped them into a completely lovable lesbian

This essay first appeared in *Windy City Times*, October 22, 2008.

coming-of-age story. Molly Bolt, the narrator, perfectly fit the mold of a rugged individualist; she was determined to clear her own path in life. Just like the heroes of nineteenth-century Horatio Alger novels, with luck and pluck Molly was going to rise from her dirt-poor origins until success was hers. She did all this with a side-splitting, sassy humor that made me laugh out loud. Sure, as a woman and a dyke she faced trials and tribulations. But you knew—*I knew*—that nothing would stop her. I had never before read anything like this, and I, too, stayed up all night to finish.

I don't think it was an accident that the author of *Rubyfruit Jungle* had already cut her teeth in the lesbian, gay, and women's liberation movements. Rita Mae Brown created a ruckus in the National Organization for Women when she raised lesbian issues. She helped write "The Woman-Identified Woman," one of the classic radical lesbian manifestos of the time (its opening line: "What is a lesbian? A lesbian is the rage of all women condensed to the point of explosion."). As part of the "Lavender Menace" contingent, she disrupted a feminist conference in 1970 in order to make lesbian issues visible. Brown was also in the collective that published *The Furies*, an influential lesbian-feminist journal of that period.

Rubyfruit Jungle was a new kind of queer writing. It was writing designed to set its readers free. Now that kind of political writing, I know, can lead to some pretty dreadful books. But, in this case, it produced a novel that, four decades later, still thrills readers of every sexual persuasion. Reading it in 1973 alerted me to something that was going on among lesbian activists that I didn't yet see happening much in my gay male circles. Lesbian feminists seemed to believe in the power of culture to help remake the world.

One way of grasping this difference is to look at two of Chicago's early queer newspapers: *Lavender Woman*, which ran from 1971 to 1976, and *Gay Crusader*, published between 1973 and 1976. At the risk of a generalization that I know won't hold true for every page, the *Crusader* tended to report on news and events. It was about the activities of a movement—demonstrations, organizations, political happenings. *Lavender Woman* was about culture, consciousness, and ideas. It covered at length the new world of women's music. It explored lesbian literary history. It was as likely to have a centerfold of poems as it was to include photos of a rally.

This emphasis on culture as a force for liberation shines through in the annual lesbian writers conferences held in Chicago between 1974 and 1978. The conferences were the inspiration of Marie Kuda, whose own history of community activism stretched back before Stonewall. Valerie Taylor, who keynoted the first conference, remembered getting a telephone call near the end of Chicago's winter. She heard Kuda saying, "What we need here is a lesbian writers conference!" So Taylor said, "Fine," and a few women gathered at her North Side apartment to begin planning. According to Taylor, Kuda was "the energy and the brain power" behind all five conferences.

The conferences took place on the South Side, initially at the First Unitarian Church in Hyde Park and later at the Blue Gargoyle. Women came from as far away as Boston, Florida, and Colorado. Even though some notable figures attended—Paula Christian, who, like Taylor, was an icon of the lesbian pulp era, spoke at one—Kuda meant the conferences as "a meeting of equals."

Saturdays consisted of a series of workshops that, according to one participant, filled "every nook and cranny of the First Unitarian Church, from the loft to the crypts." Workshops ran the gamut from the practical to the creative to the slightly ridiculous. Given the strong homophobic bias among mainstream publishers, lesbian writers worked hard to master the technicalities of self-publishing. Independent lesbian presses were springing up around the country in the 1970s, and these Chicago conferences helped lesbians teach one another the mechanics of publication and distribution. Representatives of women's presses and magazines came each year and generously shared their mailing lists. By the third gathering, in 1976, one attendee commented that "slowly and methodically lesbians are beginning to chip away at barriers that seemed impenetrable."

Many of the sessions focused on the creative process. There were workshops on fiction, poetry, journalism, and theater. Women risked the vulnerability of sharing their work with strangers. At one workshop, lesbian feminist beliefs in collectivity led to the writing of a short story together, with each participant contributing a sentence at a time. This drove at least one of the women there to the edge of distraction. But more often, women left workshops filled, as one wrote, with "an intense and exhilarating energy."

The conferences also paid respect to lesbian literary history. "All of us build on the lives of those who have gone before," Valerie Taylor told those at the first conference. Keynote speakers described the work of writers from Sappho through Virginia Woolf. Others presented slide shows with images of writers and their books. Tee Corinne gave a presentation on the visual history of lesbian sexuality with a sampling of the five thousand slides she had amassed in the course of her research. These conferences were about the creative process, for sure. But they also attempted to teach history at a time when there weren't many queer courses in colleges and universities.

And there were moments of fun. I wish I could have been at the Saturday night party in 1978 when many of the attendees came in costume, dressed as their favorite lesbian literary hero.

Putting on these conferences was a massive amount of work. In 1978 Kuda announced that the fifth was likely to be the last. But she shared with those who were there her utopian fantasy of the future: "My greatest dream is for a weeklong festival of lesbian arts with music at one end, literature at the other. In between, all the visual arts. Wouldn't it be great at McCormick Place—right after Illinois passes the ERA?"

20

Dade County, USA

It's a winter evening in 1977, and I'm clad only in a towel. I'm prowling the corridors of the Everard Baths in New York. The Everard is not one of those new bathhouses in tune with the spirit of gay liberation. It has no amenities. There are no pleasant lounges for sitting around and socializing; there's no entertainment to bring men together in easy camaraderie. The place is grungy, and its patrons get right to the point, which, of course, is sex.

The Everard does have an old portable television. It's plopped on a table in a corner of the large basement space, where there's also a swimming pool so uninviting that, in all my visits to the Everard, I've never seen someone take a dip in it. Tonight, when I wander through, I notice a crowd standing around the TV, raptly attentive to, of all things, a news report. As I walk over to see what the attraction is, I overhear a series of sharp, angry comments. These guys are pissed. A reporter is describing events in Dade County, Florida, where someone named Anita Bryant is waging a campaign against a gay rights ordinance. Whenever her smiling face and coiffed hair flash across the screen, a new round of curses spews from the mouths of these towel-wrapped men.

The scene arouses my activist sensibilities. I remember thinking, "If politics has entered the basement of the Everard, gay liberation has reached much farther than I thought!"

This essay first appeared in *Windy City Times*, November 26, 2008.

No event in queer history enjoys a higher reputation than Stonewall. The 1969 riots are celebrated every year with scores of parades and marches in dozens of nations across the globe. "Stonewall" has become shorthand for militancy, resistance, and pride. Yet, its power has been as a symbol. We commemorate Stonewall after the fact. Not many people experienced it directly, and not many more read about it as news.

By contrast, the 1977 campaign to repeal the gay rights statute in Dade County, Florida, involved huge numbers of people. It was a local event with a national reach, a story with legs. Newspapers and television covered it for months, the first time this was true for a "gay rights" story. The battle in Dade County, home to the city of Miami, did more to build a national lesbian and gay movement than any other single event. It reached deep into cities and towns around the United States, leaving local communities stronger and better organized. It created a vibrant sense of participating in a common project, a feeling of shared danger.

The Dade County saga began simply enough. In January 1977 the county's board of commissioners voted to add sexual orientation to its civil rights statutes. The story might have ended there, as it had in a couple of dozen other cities that had passed nondiscrimination ordinances, except for one resident of the county who attended the final hearing. Anita Bryant, a popular singer who had once been a runner-up in the Miss America pageant, was outraged by the county board's action. A born-again Christian, she testified with Bible in hand, and afterward she vowed to fight the ordinance. She and her husband, Bob Green, founded an organization, Save Our Children, to lead a campaign for a ballot initiative to repeal the gay rights law.

Bryant's celebrity status—she'd had gold records; she toured with Bob Hope and performed at military bases; she was under contract with the Florida Citrus Commission to promote the sale of the state's orange juice—guaranteed media attention for this county commotion. She gave journalists plenty of good quotes. The sentiments that poured from her mouth were inflammatory. At the county commission hearing on the anti-discrimination statute, Bryant declared, "I'm on fire. . . . Homosexuality is an abomination. . . . Homosexuals will recruit our children. . . . They will use money, drugs, alcohol, any means to get what they want."

Bryant sounded this theme of recruitment again and again. On a trip to Chicago to appear on the nationally televised *Phil Donahue Show*, she told the *Tribune*, "Children are very easily persuaded . . . a homosexual is not born, they are made. So there has to be some recruitment."

By the time voters in South Florida headed to the polls in June, Bryant's statements had become apocalyptic. "We will prevail," she informed a roomful of supporters and journalists, "against a life style that is both perverse and dangerous to the sanctity of the family, dangerous to our children, dangerous to our freedom of religion and freedom of choice, dangerous to our survival as one nation, under God."

Rhetoric like this—at one point she referred to gays and lesbians as "garbage"—did more than mobilize people to vote for repeal. It provoked homophobic violence. In Miami, the Roman Catholic archdiocese was also campaigning against the gay rights ordinance. Priests delivered Sunday sermons on the topic and read to their parishioners letters from the archbishop instructing them to vote for repeal.

This message of intolerance saturated the heavily Catholic Cuban population of Miami. When Ovidio Ramos, a spokesperson for the Latin Committee for the Human Rights of Gays, took part in a call-in program on Spanish-language radio, the calls were so hateful and threatening that a depressed Ramos committed suicide a few days later. When another activist, Manuel Gomez, appeared on a Spanish-language television show, his car was firebombed. Later, after Gomez addressed a rally in the heart of the Cuban community, he was assaulted and left for dead in an alley. So many angry calls came into the Dade County gay coalition that police began to provide its offices with round-the-clock protection.

But the campaign didn't just mobilize the homophobes. It galvanized gay men and lesbians around the country. After gay bars in Miami posted signs announcing, "We do not serve Florida orange juice," the *Advocate*, a national gay news magazine, issued a call for a national boycott of Florida citrus products. By March, the boycott had spread not only to big cities like Boston and Dallas but also to Idaho's only gay bar. Just as I'd observed at the Everard that winter night, politics was becoming part of the evening conversation in gay and lesbian bars across America.

The growing network of lesbian and gay organizations also took up the cause. The national council of the Metropolitan Community Church passed a resolution encouraging its congregants to support the fight for gay rights in south Florida. Contributions from almost every state arrived at the office of the Dade County gay coalition. Activists traveled to Florida to help in voter education campaigns. Assessing the work that was being done, Jean O'Leary of the National Gay Task Force contended that "the national debate provoked by the Dade County referendum has united and strengthened us as a national movement."

The Dade County campaign energized the Chicago queer community, too. *Gay Life*, the main community paper in 1977, carried articles about it in every issue that winter and spring. A local coalition formed to support Florida's gays. Community leaders planned a major fund-raiser, the "Orange Ball," for Uptown's Aragon Ballroom in May.

Just a few days before the fund-raiser took place, the antigay onslaught struck close to home. "EXTRA! EXTRA! EXTRA!" a special edition of *Gay Life* announced. "Anita Bryant invited to Chicago." The *Chicago Tribune* had just run a four-part series on child pornography, and the series pointed its finger straight at gay men. The series sparked a panic in the city. A Chicago alderman, Edward Burke, hastily scheduled City Council hearings on the problem and asked Bryant to testify. Waves from the Save Our Children crusade were crashing against the Windy City's shores.

21

Every Kick Is a Boost

As the campaign to repeal Dade County's gay rights law headed into its final weeks, Chicago unexpectedly faced its own Save Our Children campaign. In mid-May, the *Tribune* began a four-part, front-page series on child pornography. The headlines seemed designed to agitate readers. "Child Pornography: Sickness for Sale," the Sunday paper announced to homes and families across Chicagoland. "Chicago is center of national child porno ring," it told readers heading to work on Monday morning.

The reporters, Michael Sneed and George Bliss, painted a terrifying picture of the dangers facing children. Up to 100,000 people were involved, they claimed. The industry not only photographed and filmed children but also sold their sexual services to adult men. The menace was near at hand. "Chicago is the headquarters of a nationwide ring trafficking in young boys," they wrote. "A nationwide homosexual ring with headquarters in Chicago has been trafficking in young boys, sending them across the nation to serve clients willing to pay hundreds of dollars for their services."

Law enforcement officials used extreme language to portray the danger. The Cook County state attorney called the industry "one of the most sordid rackets I've ever encountered." A detective compared it to "spider webs strung out all over the nation." Another described what happened to the boys as "a crime worse than murder."

This essay first appeared in *Windy City Times*, December 3, 2008.

The series put the gay community in a difficult spot. To attack the *Tribune* risked sounding like a defender of child sex abuse. Yet the reporting was irresponsible and unbalanced, and the claims stretched credibility. The paper purported to expose the sexual exploitation of children, yet in the whole series only five short paragraphs mentioned young girls. The writers claimed to have spent three months investigating an industry that exploited tens of thousands; they said Chicago was a major center of it; and they cooperated closely with police. Why, then, could the police only find two fourteen-year-old "victims"?

Over and over, the series fingered the city's gay men as the source of the danger. Major evidence for the existence of the ring of child abusers came from "an informant in the area of Clark and Diversey," which was then identified as "a center of homosexual activities in Chicago." The commander of the youth division of the Chicago Police charged that the North Side office of Children and Family Services was "a center of homosexuality," colluding with the sexual abuse of its young clients.

Some details were downright bizarre. A detective claimed he had seized from a national ringleader thirty thousand index cards with the names of clients, but the State Department was said to have destroyed all the cards! The mastermind of the biggest network of child porn lovers was supposed to be a convict in an Illinois state prison. How did he manage all this, one wondered?

But sex panics don't require believability. The *Tribune* had set hysteria in motion. Alderman Ed Burke conducted public hearings. Governor Thompson appointed a state task force on child pornography. The US attorney opened an investigation, and the Cook County state attorney convened a grand jury. Police and building inspectors descended on thirty-four adult bookstores and shut them down. Legislators in Springfield introduced eight bills to control the menace. Police stepped up their harassment of gay male cruising areas. And the *Tribune* editorialized about "the plague" that was thriving right here in Chicago.

The exposé provoked a rapid response from gay and lesbian activists. Even before the series ended, representatives from several organizations held a press conference to denounce the reporting as an "indictment by insinuation of the entire gay community." Demonstrators chanted, "Stop the witch hunt now!" as they picketed City Hall. Bill Kelley and Paul Goldman spoke at Alderman Burke's City Council hearings. At a march in

New Town, according to one report, "the gay community's anger at the *Tribune* series boiled over."

A week after the series began, more than four thousand men and women arrived at Uptown's Aragon for the Orange Ball, a fund-raiser to help fight the referendum in Dade County, Florida. The one-two punch of antigay crusades in Florida and Chicago made the event the largest queer benefit in the city's history. Businesses displayed posters, bars contributed door prizes, and organizations provided volunteers.

Even the harassing presence of police failed to dampen the crowd's enthusiasm. Chuck Renslow, who produced the event, told the audience they were living through "a time of war"; he called for "unity of purpose . . . as one family." Bob Basker, from the Dade County gay coalition, worked the crowd up by reading from ads that Save Our Children had placed in the *Miami Herald*. Bryant had allegedly recently declared that "God hates homosexuals because they eat sperm."

On June 7, as nearly everyone predicted, an overwhelming majority of voters in Dade County cast ballots to repeal the antidiscrimination statute. Anita Bryant danced a jig when she heard the news and announced that she was preparing to transform Save Our Children into a national campaign to repeal similar ordinances in other cities. Chicago's editorial pages added to the pain of the vote. "Miami sends a message," said the *Daily News*. "The people simply aren't ready to accept homosexuality as a constitutional or human 'right,'" in defiance of "moral codes in effect for millennia." The *Tribune* editorial board told readers that "we share the concern of parents . . . who see [homosexuality] as a latent threat to society." It advised gays and lesbians to practice "discretion."

For Chicagoans, however, the story wasn't over. Bryant was coming to Chicago the following week to perform at a Flag Day benefit concert for the Shriner's Children's Hospital. Gay men and lesbians descended on the Medinah Temple, located at Wabash and Ohio, to protest the singer's appearance. Marchers six abreast circled the building, as a large contingent of police looked on. "Anita is McCarthy in drag," one placard proclaimed. "God drinks wine, not orange juice," said another. Afterward, a large contingent marched over to Pioneer Court and the *Tribune* building, to chants of "Boycott the *Tribune*."

Claims about the size of the demonstration varied, from a conservative police count of two thousand to one participant's estimate of ten to fifteen thousand. But no one disputed that it was a unique event in the city's queer history. "Exhilarating," recalled Linda Rodgers, a bartender who was there. "One of the biggest things that ever hit Chicago for the gay community," Grant Ford, the publisher of *Gay Life*, remembered. "There was just this feeling in the air that we could accomplish something," said Rich Pfeiffer, who organized Chicago's annual Pride parade. "It was an incredible feeling . . . a feeling of empowerment."

Gays and lesbians in Dade County in 1977 lost an antidiscrimination law, but the months of headlines, fund-raisers, rallies, and demonstrations—across the nation and in Chicago—had accomplished something profound. Renee Hanover, an activist lawyer in Chicago who had participated in movements for social justice for decades, expressed it well. Bryant and Dade County had "unified and strengthened us as a national movement. Never before has one fight stirred the national gay and lesbian community to such fervor." Or, as one anonymous demonstrator told a *Tribune* reporter after the Dade County votes were tallied, "I don't think people should be disheartened. . . . Every kick is a boost."

Part IV

History's Lessons

22

Remembering Bayard Rustin

In spring 2006 the *Magazine of History* devoted a special issue to the topic of sexuality. It was an important moment in the development of the history of sexuality as a recognized field of study, since this was a publication of the Organization of American Historians, the main professional association for those whose field is US history. In this piece on Rustin, I argue that his relative neglect in many accounts of the black freedom struggle inevitably distorts the lessons we draw from history. Instead, if we "remembered" Rustin and inserted him into the heart of the story, we might come away with some more unsettling and radical lessons.

In her 2004 presidential address to the Organization of American Historians, Jacquelyn Dowd Hall described history, the stories about the past that we remember, as "always a form of forgetting." Scrutinizing what she called the "dominant narrative" of the civil rights movement—a triumphal story that begins with the *Brown v. Board of Education* decision and the Montgomery bus boycott in the mid-1950s and ends with the Civil Rights and Voting Rights Acts a decade later—Hall argued that it "distorts and suppresses as much as it reveals."[1]

This essay first appeared in *OAH Magazine of History* 20, no. 2 (March 2006): 12–14.

If one had to choose a single event to illustrate both the standard interpretation of the civil rights movement and Hall's caution about it, it would be the March on Washington. Several decades later, the March has come down to us as a moment of hope, unity, inspiration, and vision. Standing in front of the Lincoln Memorial before a peaceful crowd of 250,000 Americans, black and white, young and old, male and female, the Reverend Martin Luther King Jr. delivered an oration that high school students now memorize for speech contests. Its central recurring line—"I have a dream"—has become as well recognized and as thoroughly American as "We hold these truths to be self-evident."

Standing in the background as King intoned these words was Bayard Rustin, another civil rights activist. Barely known today beyond the circles of professional historians, Rustin was the man who, more than anyone else, made the March on Washington happen. When the *Washington Post* profiled Rustin two weeks before the demonstration, it closed its article with the comment "He's Mr. March himself." After the event, *Life*, one of the most popular mass circulation weeklies of that era, featured Rustin on its cover.[2] How could he have figured so prominently at the time and yet be so peripheral to historical memory today? Why have we forgotten Bayard Rustin? And what do we suppress when we forget him?

Of Rustin's importance to the African American freedom struggle there can be no doubt. He was one of the moving forces behind the Congress of Racial Equality (CORE), a key organization of the civil rights movement. Founded in 1942, CORE pioneered the use of Gandhian nonviolence to challenge racial injustice. Throughout the 1940s Rustin trained and led groups of nonviolent protesters in actions against segregated restaurants, movie theaters, barber shops, amusement parks, and department stores. In 1947 he spearheaded an interracial team of activists who traveled into the South to test continuing segregation in interstate bus travel despite a Supreme Court decision against the practice. A year later, Rustin led a campaign of nonviolent resistance against racial segregation in the armed forces. Throughout these years, he traveled incessantly, lecturing to audiences across the country and inspiring countless numbers of young men and women to take action on behalf of social justice. "I was transformed listening to him," one young pacifist recalled. "I was absolutely hypnotized."[3]

In February 1956, in the early stages of the Montgomery bus boycott, Rustin traveled to that city to offer his services to the boycott leaders. He made contact with the young Martin Luther King Jr., and the two men quickly formed a deep bond of trust and respect. Rustin offered to the in-experienced King a wealth of practical knowledge about how to use non-violence effectively. Over the next few years Rustin functioned as a key adviser and mentor to King. He put him in touch with men like A. Philip Randolph, perhaps the senior statesman among African American activists at the time. He mobilized support among progressive union leaders for King and the Southern freedom movement. He persuaded King of the need to form an organization to carry on the struggle beyond Montgomery, and he drew up the outline of what became the Southern Christian Leader-ship Conference. In the late 1950s, Rustin proposed, planned, and organized demonstrations in Washington that gave King a national platform from which to project his message of resistance to racial injustice. Together with A. Philip Randolph, in 1963 Rustin pushed and prodded other civil rights leaders to support a national March on Washington. No wonder that, when the time came, Rustin was the man who organized it.

And organize it he did! In just seven short weeks, he set up an office and put together a skilled and energetic staff. He negotiated with federal officials to secure legal permission for the March and rally, fashioned a set of demands around which all civil rights organizations could unite, and drew national religious and labor organizations into the coalition. John Lewis, a militant young activist who had gained fame as a Freedom Rider in 1961, visited the office that summer and saw Rustin at work. "This was Bayard at his best," he later reminisced.[4]

With a résumé like this, how can we all *not* know who Bayard Rustin is? What stands between his profound contributions to the African American civil rights movement and our historical memory? Rustin had three liabilities—three strikes against him, if you will—that have made it difficult to incorporate him into a simple narrative of progress toward equality and justice that most Americans can applaud.

First of all, Rustin had been a Communist. He joined the Young Com-munist League in the 1930s, attracted by its militant approach to fighting against the suffering caused by the Great Depression and the violence that African Americans faced in the South. Tens of thousands of other Ameri-cans of conscience made the same decision that he did during those years. Communists seemed to have answers to problems that neither Democrats nor Republicans could solve. Although Rustin did not remain a Commu-nist for long (he broke decisively with the Communist Party in 1941), he never disavowed the value of the experience for him. "I'm happy I had it," he once reminisced. "It taught me a great deal, and I presume that if I had to do it over again, I'd do the same thing."[5] Though no longer connected to the party, for the rest of his days Rustin remained critical of the inequalities that capitalism produced and embraced a political philosophy of democratic socialism.

During the long decades of the Cold War, nothing marked someone as so beyond the boundaries of Americanism as did involvement with the Communist movement. Communists were dangerous and menacing; they were disloyal and subversive. In the eyes of J. Edgar Hoover, the long-time director of the Federal Bureau of Investigation, once someone had been a Communist, that person would always be considered a threat. Rustin's Communist past justified government surveillance of his activities. For many years the FBI tapped his home telephone, and agents of the bureau secretly disrupted his work. How could a Communist be a civil rights hero? How could someone so critical of American free enterprise be central to the struggle for black freedom in the United States?

Rustin was also a pacifist, another identity difficult to incorporate into notions of American heroism. The Revolutionary War created the nation, and the Civil War saved and improved it. For more than two centuries, American men conducted war against the native peoples of the continent, allowing the United States to spread from the Atlantic to the Pacific. In the 1940s the nation fought—and won—a world war, and in the 1950s and 1960s it waged a global cold war against the Soviet Union and Communism.

Rustin said no to this history of patriotic violence. The same moral values that made him adapt Gandhian nonviolence to the struggle for racial equality in the United States made him refuse induction into the armed forces during World War II. While millions of Americans were fighting overseas, Rustin was serving a term in federal prison. The same moral values that allowed him to face down segregationist mobs nonviolently made him protest against the Korean War and demonstrate against the nuclear arms race. Rustin's moral economy led him to reject the rabid Cold War rhetoric that justified the militarization of American society during these years. "We are living in 'an iron lung of militarism,'" he wrote during the Korean War.[6]

Rustin was true to his word. He was arrested for protesting outside draft boards after the federal government instituted peacetime conscription. In 1955, the same year that the Montgomery bus boycott started, he was part of a band of pacifists who disrupted tests of a civilian defense system in the United States. Rustin took his protests against war and nuclear weapons to Western and Eastern Europe and to Africa, as well.

In Rustin's view, war would never bring peace, and violence would never bring justice. To him, nationalism and imperialism were destructive forces in the world. He saw the African's struggle for independence from European colonialism and the Southern Negro's struggle for full citizenship in the United States as two sides of the same coin. In Rustin's eyes, racial justice would never come to a world in which one nation fought to dominate another.

Finally, Rustin was a gay man. Today, in the second decade of the twenty-first century, gay things often seem everywhere. We see gay characters on network television and in Hollywood movies. Issues like same-sex marriage and the rights of gay men and lesbians to serve openly in the armed forces are discussed in our daily newspapers and television newscasts. Legislators debate whether to protect gay people from job discrimination, and all over the country teenagers form gay/straight alliances in their high schools. Though same-sex love and relationships remain hotly contested subjects, the presence of gay men and lesbians in American society is an acknowledged fact of life.

This was not so in Rustin's day. Between the 1930s, when he came into adulthood, and the early 1960s, when he was most influential in the black freedom movement, homosexuality was roundly condemned, harshly punished, and pushed out of sight. Every state had sodomy laws that criminalized homosexual behavior. Every religious faith damned it as sinful. The medical profession classified a homosexual orientation as a form of mental illness. In the 1950s the federal government prohibited the employment of gay men and lesbians, and the military even excluded those with homosexual tendencies. Local police forces felt free to raid gay and lesbian bars and other meeting places, and they routinely arrested people en masse for holding hands, for dancing together, or for inviting someone to come home with them for the evening. The morning newspaper often printed the names and addresses of those arrested, and men and women lost jobs as a result.

To be gay in these decades meant living with an almost constant awareness of vulnerability. Most men and women responded by staying deep in the closet and leading secretive double lives. Many married. Many others told no one but their closest friends. They dissembled with their family and at work, creating a façade of heterosexuality to protect themselves from exposure and trouble.

Rustin was not "out of the closet" in the way that phrase has meaning today, but neither did he attempt to deny his attractions to men. Davis Platt, one of his intimates from the 1940s, recalled that "I never had any sense at all that Bayard felt any shame or guilt about his homosexuality. That was rare in those days. Rare."[7] Yet his openness only made him more vulnerable. His willingness to go in search of sexual partners put him in the path of police officers looking to make arrests, and more than once Rustin found himself hauled into court on gay-related charges. In 1953 he was convicted in Los Angeles County under California's lewd-vagrancy law, and he served a sixty-day sentence.

Rustin's homosexuality and the trouble it brought him created an endless series of difficulties for him. In the Christian pacifist world in which he worked, it made him appear morally suspect. He worked as if on probation, always in danger of losing his place in the movement. In the South, where white segregationists seized any opportunity to discredit the black freedom struggle, Rustin's sexuality was potentially a liability of great consequence. It meant that he had to work one step removed from Martin Luther King so that neither King nor the Southern Christian Leadership Conference could be tainted by Rustin's identity.

Throughout the 1950s and 1960s, concerns about Rustin's sexuality rippled through the movement for racial justice. Sometimes the concerns came from friends and allies, as when activists in 1956 urged him to leave Montgomery as quickly as possible in order not to give enemies of the bus boycott a weapon with which to attack it. Sometimes rivals within the movement used it to limit Rustin's influence. In 1960 Adam Clayton Powell, a member of Congress from Harlem, threatened to spread scurrilous rumors about Rustin unless he was removed from a political project. Enemies of everything Rustin fought for often broadcast his homosexuality as a way of discrediting him and his causes. In 1958 an American Legion chapter in Montana publicized his conviction in Pasadena in an effort to have his lectures in the state cancelled. The most dramatic example of these attacks came in August 1963, in the weeks before the March on Washington. Strom Thurmond, a white supremacist senator from South Carolina, inserted into the Congressional Record information not only about Rustin's left-wing past but also about his homosexuality.

Put all of these liabilities together—a Communist past in Cold War America, a pacifist in an armed-to-the-teeth national security state, and a homosexual during the years that one historian has labeled "the Lavender Scare"[8]—and one can understand why Rustin would have developed a style of leadership that tended to keep him out of the public eye. But historians have an obligation to look beyond the surface of things, beyond the strategies that historical actors devise to disguise their role in events. We are expected to dig through the sources until we can piece together as truthful a reconstruction of the past as possible.

So let me rephrase slightly the questions I posed at the beginning: What would happen if we inserted Rustin fully into the popular narrative of the civil rights movement? We might have to acknowledge that the vision and the energy and the skills of radicals were essential to its success, that agitation for racial justice was often most likely to come from those who stood far outside mainstream assumptions in the United States. We might have to acknowledge that the fight for civil rights drew strength and resources from other movements of dissent and that a belief in racial equality often lived alongside a commitment to peace and to the redistribution of wealth in America. We might also have to acknowledge that the distinction Americans like to draw between the private sphere and the public, between matters like sex and matters like politics, is a fragile one. We might have to acknowledge the complicated intersections between race and sexuality and recognize how love and intimacy become excuses for oppression that crushes human lives no less than other forms of injustice. We might, in short, find ourselves with a more truthful version of a vital part of America's past.

23

The 1979 March on Washington

Its Place in History

Ever since the 1963 March on Washington, protest marches in the nation's capital have held an almost magical allure. Whatever the issue that provokes the event—racial justice, reproductive freedom, opposition to war—participants tend to remember the events fondly and make big claims for them. Nineteen seventy-nine was the year of the first of several national marches for gay and lesbian (later expanded to include bisexual and transgender) rights. In 2004, on the occasion of its twenty-fifth anniversary, I presented these remarks at a panel discussion at the Gerber/Hart Library and Archives in Chicago. My goal was to move beyond the nostalgia and the hyperbole in order to grasp what the march had actually accomplished.

How we all seem to love anniversaries! Think about the masses of folks who show up each year for Pride Marches in June, for St. Patrick's Day parades, for Cinco de Mayo celebrations. Anniversaries provide moments for civic reflection. In May 2004, newspapers were filled with stories

This essay first appeared in *The Gay and Lesbian Review* 10, no. 2 (March–April 2005): 33–34.

assessing the meaning of *Brown v. Board of Education* on its fiftieth anniversary. Audiences sat in university lecture halls, community meeting spaces, and houses of worship to think about the struggle for racial justice. Commemorations like this can propel change in the present, as individuals draw lessons from the victories and struggles of the past. So it is important that we are taking time today to recall the 1979 March on Washington on its twenty-fifth anniversary.

However, the more I have thought about what I want to say, the more I have found myself skeptical that the march is anything more than a footnote in history. This is perhaps a heretical comment to make on a panel like this, but maybe I can illustrate my doubts by comparing the 1979 event with two other famous marches:

- In August 1963 approximately 250,000 people from every part of the country assembled in Washington for an event that has become so iconic that we often simply refer to it as "the March on Washington." The march was a major story in every news outlet of consequence in the United States. Large national organizations with membership in the hundreds of thousands—indeed, in the millions—backed the venture. In the months before the march, local demonstrations erupted in hundreds upon hundreds of communities around the country. President Kennedy sent national civil rights legislation to Congress. Agitation for racial equality was at such a high level that it took only seven weeks for organizers to pull such a large crowd to Washington. In other words, continuing agitation for black freedom, a national infrastructure of organizations, and a realizable national goal together made it a strategic time to march on Washington.
- In November 1969 more than 400,000 Americans gathered in Washington to protest the Vietnam War. Just a month before, antiwar activists had organized coordinated events in cities and towns from coast to coast; more than a million individuals participated in these local protests. The war was a front-page story every day. Antiwar agitation was roiling Congress. The key slogan of the march—"Bring the troops home"—was something that could be implemented only by the president. Thus, as in 1963, lots of people were already in motion, there was a focused demand very much related to the government in Washington, and the eyes of the country were on the issue.

Now look at the 1979 March. At that point in time, there were no national gay and lesbian organizations of any consequence. The gay and lesbian movement had no significant national goal that had any chance of being achieved. There had not been much in the way of gay demonstrations in the months preceding the march. The mainstream news media paid almost no attention to the event or to queer issues more generally. Finally, despite the movement's claim that "we are everywhere," the crowd barely approached 100,000, significantly smaller than the standards for an impressive national mobilization.

Judged by the standards of history, the 1979 March was not a success. But can it tell us anything about that era? Why is it worth thinking about? Why wasn't the gay and lesbian movement, ten years after Stonewall, more visible on the national stage?

A Look Back at the 1970s

The 1970s were a vitally important decade in gay and lesbian history. The changes that occurred were huge. But those changes were also unevenly distributed. Their benefits were not experienced equally by everyone across the country.

Change in the 1970s can be measured in a number of ways. In 1969, on the eve of Stonewall, there were perhaps fifty organizations in the United States that identified themselves as gay or lesbian. By the end of the 1970s there were thousands. Some were overtly activist organizations, some religious, some cultural, and some social or recreational. These organizations were most densely concentrated in urban centers and university towns. A thriving print culture had arisen, consisting of newspapers, journals, and magazines. These were especially important in projecting outward into this emergent visible community a language of pride and a stance of militancy, something not found in mainstream media reportage. In many larger cities and radicalized university towns, this militancy had succeeded in containing police harassment. Law enforcement practices had changed enough in the decade so that, combined with the new openness and militancy, a much expanded and more secure commercial gay world existed.

What kind of activism provoked these changes, and what kind of activism did these changes sustain? In a nutshell, the answer is "local." Police practices were a local matter. The passage of civil rights statutes that included sexual orientation, an innovation of the 1970s, happened only locally, at the municipal and county level of government. Even the few achievements that seemed national in scope, like the end of the federal ban on civil service employment of gays, lesbians, and bisexuals, materialized through the work of local DC activists.

Effective activism required coming out. The imperative to come out was probably the central message associated with the Stonewall generation. Just about everything the movement achieved in these years depended on the work of individuals who had discarded the protective secrecy of the closet and who stopped leading their queer lives in secret. Although it seemed to activists in the 1970s that our numbers were legion, this was true only in comparison to the pre-Stonewall era. The overwhelming majority of people who identified as gay, lesbian, bisexual, or transgender remained in the closet. A closeted majority doesn't translate into a powerful political movement with a national presence.

Even the few gay stories that reached a national audience confirm how local the movement was. In 1975 Sergeant Leonard Matlovich appeared on the cover of *Time*. Matlovich's high-profile coming out happened at a time when, because of the Vietnam War, the military's authority was at a low point and it was vulnerable to outside pressure to change. This was an ideal moment to launch a campaign against the military's exclusion policy. But who would have coordinated this campaign? Which organization? Which activist networks? Which media contacts would have been utilized? Where was the mass of out-of-the-closet service personnel to move it beyond one man's experience? Instead of spawning a national mobilization, the Matlovich story faded away.

Two years later, another queer story made headlines. In Dade County, Florida, a fierce political battle erupted over a gay rights ordinance. Anita Bryant, a former Miss America runner-up and a spokeswoman for the citrus industry, emerged as the public face of the antigay forces. The national media seized on the drama of the confrontation. But the event that provoked it all was quintessentially local, and Dade County spawned other local repeal campaigns.

So why was there a 1979 March on Washington? What could it possibly have achieved? Can it teach us anything now?

I went to Washington for the event and was one of those who marched that Sunday. Having been to some huge antiwar demonstrations, I was disappointed by the relatively small size of the crowd. I can barely remember either the march or the rally afterward. But I do have three vivid memories from that long weekend:

- On Friday, friends and I wandered around Washington as tourists. Wherever we went, we found packs of lesbians and gay men swarming through the city. The heart of the District of Columbia seemed transformed into an enormous version of San Francisco's Castro neighborhood. The sense of occupying the nation's capital was thrilling.

- Several of us who were pioneering in the research and writing of queer history used the weekend in Washington as an opportunity to convene activists involved in local community-based gay and lesbian history projects. These projects had popped up in several cities and were generating a lot of interest. It was the first time that many of us met one another. We each talked a bit about the research we were doing and what we were finding—nuggets of historical information about working-class butch lesbians in Buffalo, about lesbian bohemians and radicals in early twentieth-century Greenwich Village, about the first generation of homophile activists in the 1950s, and about the experiences of gays and lesbians during World War II. Ideas flew around the room faster than I could write them down, and the whole event was exhilarating.

- On Saturday night (but maybe I am mistaken as to when this happened), there was a pre-march outdoor entertainment on the Mall. A gay marching band from Los Angeles performed, the first time I had ever encountered such a phenomenon. One of its members was decked out in full regalia, twirling batons in both hands, flinging them seemingly higher than the top of the Washington Monument, and having the time of his life. Everyone went wild with delight. His performance was not going to lead to a gay rights bill in Congress, but it made all of us happy and all of us feel connected in some deep emotional way.

These events suggest for me the shape of the March's limited importance. Many groups with common interests used the convergence in Washington as an opportunity to meet, learn from one another, and strengthen our ties to one another. Exuberance characterized our weekend together, and we came away with a heightened sense of possibility. All weekend long, we performed our respective versions of queer pride, and we saw graphically the geographic breadth of our local activism. The March helped us *imagine* a movement that might someday be national but that by no stretch of the imagination yet existed.

In 1987 a crowd that dwarfed anything in Washington's history proved that a nationwide queer constituency had come into being. Many of the organizers of this massive march were involved in the 1979 event. Did the 1979 march plant the seeds of what flowered eight years later? Not really. The 1987 March was sandwiched in between the display of The Names Project quilt on the Mall and an unprecedented mass civil disobedience outside the Supreme Court building. These two events tell us what crystallized a national movement: the immense tragedy of the AIDS epidemic and, partly because of that tragedy, the rage provoked by the Supreme Court's 1986 *Bowers v. Hardwick* decision upholding sodomy laws.

If the 1979 March has anything to tell us, it is that the process of building a national movement with any kind of power is long and often frustratingly slow. It comes when grievances that are connected to the national government, mobilizations that are related to achievable goals, and organizations that have a broad and motivated constituency converge. It does not arise by wishing it into existence with a call to march on Washington.

24

Some Lessons from *Lawrence*

The 2003 Supreme Court decision *Lawrence v. Texas* was heralded as one of the most important events in US LGBT history. By declaring state sodomy statutes unconstitutional, the decision put an end to centuries of criminalizing same-sex love and affection. Yet, at the same time, it created barely a ripple in the daily life of most men who love men and women who love women. In what sense, then, can it be considered important? What can we learn from the decision? This essay, which originated as remarks for a panel discussion at the University of Illinois at Chicago in the fall of 2003, is my attempt at answering such questions.

Any right-thinking person ought to be thrilled by *Lawrence v. Texas*, the 2003 Supreme Court decision that declared unconstitutional state laws criminalizing sodomy. In June 2003 the highest court of a nation that claims to have been conceived in liberty and sees itself as the birthplace of freedom in the modern world declared that sodomy laws have no place in a free society. According to Justice Anthony Kennedy, author of the majority

An earlier version of this essay appeared in H. N. Hirsch, ed., *The Future of Gay Rights in America* (New York: Routledge, 2005), 3–14.

opinion, the case of John Lawrence and Tyrone Garner, arrested for having sex together in the privacy of Lawrence's home, involved "transcendent dimensions" of personal liberty. Criminalizing same-sex acts, Kennedy declared, "demeans the lives of homosexual persons."[1] This bracing judicial rhetoric was inspiring to the gay men and lesbians sitting in the courtroom that morning. Linda Greenhouse, the constitutional law reporter for the *New York Times*, observed that "several were weeping, silently but openly," as Kennedy read the opinion.[2] But anyone who values personal freedom and the right of individuals to control their own body ought to have cheered as well. As William Brown, a Londoner, put it when he was arrested almost three hundred years ago on the charge of sodomy, "I think there is no crime in making what use I please of my own body."[3] Who would argue with that?

A wide range of commentators have made bold claims about the decision's significance. David Garrow, a Pulitzer Prize–winning historian who writes about both civil rights and sexuality, called it "one of the two most important opinions of the last 100 years."[4] Carolyn Lochhead, the Washington-based reporter for the *San Francisco Chronicle*, described it as "a watershed" in the history of the gay rights movement.[5] The opinion "sent shock waves around the country," according to the *Advocate*, a national gay magazine.[6] Lawyers involved in the gay rights movement were especially effusive in their praise. Ruth Harlow, legal director of Lambda Legal, the largest litigation group of its kind, characterized *Lawrence* as "a historic, transformative decision."[7] Jon Davidson, another Lambda lawyer, said it was "monumental . . . a day of liberation."[8] Across the country, queer activists hailed it as the gay community's equivalent of *Brown v. Board of Education of Topeka, Kansas*, the 1954 Supreme Court case that ruled racially segregated public schools to be inherently unequal and hence unconstitutional.

Nor were detractors any less restrained in their views. Cultural conservatives predicted all sorts of dire consequences. Scott Lively, director of the American Family Association of California, declared that *Lawrence* "puts a stamp of approval on anything-goes sexuality."[9] The case opened up "a complete Pandora's box," according to Sandy Rios, president of Concerned Women for America. Americans were facing a "moral Armageddon," she proclaimed.[10] The country was now on "a slippery slope" of moral decline, said the president of one Christian evangelical seminary.[11] Employing the imagery of the war on terrorism, the Reverend Lou Sheldon of the Traditional Values Coalition referred to Kennedy's opinion as "a 9/11 major wake-up call that the enemy is at our doorsteps."[12] In a passionately worded dissent, Justice Antonin Scalia predicted "a massive disruption of the current social order." Judicial approval of bigamy, incest, and bestiality was next, he predicted.[13]

Most striking, both sides in America's much-hyped "culture war" saw *Lawrence* as clearing the path to same-sex marriage. *Newsweek*'s cover about the case ignored sodomy laws altogether and simply asked, "Is Gay Marriage Next?"[14] Evan Wolfson, a lawyer who has made same-sex marriage his life's work, claimed that prohibitions against it were now on "very shaky grounds."[15] Lawrence Tribe, a Harvard University legal scholar, called laws against same-sex marriage "constitutionally suspect."[16] Patricia Logue, one of Lambda's attorneys, forecast that gay marriage was "inevitable now," while Chai Feldblum, a Georgetown law professor active in lesbian and gay rights efforts, saw it happening "in the next decade."[17] Despite the fact that Justice Kennedy stated that the case "does not involve" same-sex marriage, Justice Scalia, in his dissent, countered: "Do not believe it. . . . Today's opinion dismantles the structure of constitutional law that has permitted a distinction to be made between heterosexual and homosexual unions." In the wake of *Lawrence*, Scalia asserted, "what justification could there possibly be for denying the benefits of marriage to homosexual couples?"[18]

Most of these pronouncements miss the mark badly. As I will argue in this essay, the *Lawrence* case is important, and it does have much to teach us. The lessons it offers are especially vital to grasp if one is interested in understanding how to make change in the United States. But its significance, though great, is both more modest and more sobering than some of the viewpoints quoted seem to suggest.

In the rest of this essay, I will elaborate three lessons that we can extract from *Lawrence*:

- Intellectual work can be a force for change in society.
- Despite how little same-sex sodomy laws touched the lives of gay men and lesbians in the early twenty-first century, declaring them unconstitutional will make a difference. But precisely what kind of difference remains an open question, and it is a difference that will grow in importance as time passes.
- Significant as Supreme Court decisions have been in American history, the nation's highest court is not generally at the cutting

edge of progressive social change. Rather than lead, the Supreme Court most often follows. In other words, its decisions matter, but not in the inflated way that contemporary spin—from activists, the media, or disgruntled justices—would have us believe.

At first blush, these lessons may seem contradictory. For instance, if the Court follows rather than leads, how much can its decisions actually matter? Yet I believe these points to be consistent with one another. Nor am I claiming that these are the only lessons one can extract from the case. But understanding these three allows us to absorb *Lawrence* in ways that can help us make sense both of history and of events since the decision.

I. Intellectual Work Can Be a Force for Change

In *Lawrence*, the Supreme Court did something highly unusual: it overturned one of its previous decisions. Just seventeen years earlier, in *Bowers v. Hardwick*, a divided Court had let stand a Georgia sodomy statute. *Lawrence* was not the first instance in which the Court had done this. Perhaps the most famous example was the school desegregation case of *Brown*. There the Court reversed a position it had taken in 1896 in *Plessy v. Ferguson*, when it affirmed the constitutionality of segregation laws. But the principle of stare decisis—to stand by what has already been decided—has by and large characterized the history of the federal courts.

The reasons should be obvious. A common practice of reversing itself would subject the Court to a charge of capriciousness. In what sense are we governed by the Constitution if a high court can rule first this way and then that way, according to the views of its changing membership? In what sense does the Constitution matter if a court can change its mind in response to shifts in public opinion? Wouldn't this bring us the judge-made law against which conservatives so frequently rail? Isn't it the responsibility of the legislative, not the judicial, branch of government to remain accountable to the popular will? As Justice Kennedy put it in his opinion in the *Lawrence* case, "The doctrine of stare decisis is essential to the respect accorded to the judgments of the Court and to the stability of the law."[19]

Notwithstanding this principle, Kennedy also unambiguously declared, "*Bowers* was not correct when it was decided, and it is not correct today."[20] What would allow him to reject so forthrightly the opinion of a previous

Court, especially when two of his colleagues had participated in the earlier decision? The concise answer is "History."

As is generally true in important cases, interested parties on both sides of the question submitted amicus curiae ["friend of the court"] briefs. One of these came from a group of historians, of whom I was one. Since sodomy statutes have a long history, it made sense for scholars who study the past to express their views. Indeed, in two earlier challenges to state sodomy laws, I had been asked to submit an affidavit.

In *Lawrence*, the need to bring historical perspective to bear was especially relevant because the 1986 *Bowers* decision had been so heavily laden with references to history. Writing for the majority, Justice Byron White declared in *Bowers* that "proscriptions against that conduct have ancient roots."[21] In a concurring opinion, Chief Justice Warren Burger was more expansive. "Decisions of individuals relating to homosexual conduct," he proclaimed, "have been subject to state intervention throughout the history of Western civilization. Condemnation of those practices is firmly rooted in Judaeo-Christian moral and ethical standards. . . . To hold that the act of homosexual sodomy is somehow protected as a fundamental right would be to cast aside millennia of moral teaching."[22]

We historians offered a different view of the past. Our brief put forward two propositions: "no consistent historical practice singles out same-sex behavior as 'sodomy' subject to proscription" and "the governmental policy of classifying and discriminating against certain citizens on the basis of their homosexual status is an unprecedented project of the twentieth century."[23] In other words, we took a point of view defying the conventional wisdom that, until recently, homosexuality was soundly proscribed and vilified.

In arguing the first proposition, the brief was not claiming that the prohibition of same-sex acts was new. Rather, it asserted that the prohibitions "have varied enormously," that the laws covered a wide range of acts, and that, for the most part, the state has only haphazardly enforced these laws. Drawing on the contrast between acts and identities, a distinction common in the historical literature, the brief pointedly stated that "the phrase 'homosexual sodomy' would have been literally incomprehensible to the Framers of the Constitution, for the very concept of homosexuality as a discrete psychological condition and source of personal identity was not available until the late 1800s."[24]

Building on this first point, the brief then went on to argue that specifically antigay policies and laws were very much products of the relatively recent past, that they had a short half life rather than a long pedigree. The document charted the surge of police activity against gays in the middle decades of the twentieth century, the codifying of discriminatory policies by the federal government, and the rise of "new demonic stereotypes of homosexuals."[25] In the end, rather than the ancient roots or the millennia of moral teaching that *Bowers* called forth, the historians transformed same-sex sodomy laws into a method invented in the twentieth century by a powerful state to target a class of its citizens for cruel, blatant oppression.

In his opinion for the majority in *Lawrence*, Justice Anthony Kennedy leaned heavily on the argument presented by the historians. *Bowers*, he effectively said, got its history wrong. "There is no longstanding history in this country of laws directed at homosexual conduct as a distinct matter," he wrote.[26] Kennedy's opinion went on to discuss history at some length, not only incorporating the argument in the historians' brief but also citing and independently quoting a number of the works of historical scholarship noted in the brief. Kennedy offered a history of sexuality that one might reasonably label a "social construction" perspective. This viewpoint, that the meaning of human sexual behavior varies profoundly over time and across cultures, allowed him to propound a view at odds with the majority's presumptions in *Bowers*. Sodomy laws may go back centuries, but criminal-izing a group of citizens because of their intimate lives and then denying them basic rights in the public sphere because of their sexual identity were not deeply rooted in the nation's past.

Why was Justice Kennedy able to argue this so confidently in 2003 whereas his predecessors, seventeen years earlier, were equally assured that the record of the past was unambiguously hostile to homosexual expres-sion? Was Kennedy simply wiser than they? The key reason is that the historical scholarship from which he drew did not exist when the opinion in *Bowers* was written. Check the references in both the historians' brief and Kennedy's opinion. The overwhelming majority of the works of history cited were published from the mid-1980s on. Whatever Kennedy's views of the Fourteenth Amendment and the Due Process Clause might be, he needed "backup" to discard such a recent contrary decision. This is what the historians offered.

The academic inquiry that both feminism and gay liberation have opened up since the 1970s, their belief that sexuality is historical and cultural and that it helps structure social inequality, made the rewriting of constitu-tional jurisprudence in *Lawrence* possible. History has never simply been the unadorned story of what happened in the past. For the most part, history is composed of the stories that the winners tell about the past. Contesting this version of the past, as historians of race, gender, and sexuality have done in the last generation, is an important part of the work of creating a more egalitarian society, grounded in principles of social justice. *Lawrence* shows us that intellectual work does matter, that ideas can be a force for change.

II. *Lawrence* Will Make a Difference—But Later, Not Now

From a certain angle, one could reasonably argue that the *Lawrence* case hardly makes a difference at all. Compare it, for instance, to two earlier cases that are widely recognized as historic: *Brown v. Board of Education* and *Roe v. Wade*, the 1973 decision that declared unconstitutional most laws criminalizing abortion.

In 1954, when the Court decided *Brown*, the law in seventeen states mandated racially segregated public schools. A majority of African Americans lived in these states. Jim Crow laws separated blacks and whites in everyday life—in restaurants, movie theaters, public parks, highway rest stops, swimming pools, beaches, and countless other places. *Brown* was an invaluable asset that led, over the next decade or so, to the dismantling of the legal structure of racial segregation.

In 1973, when the Court's decision in *Roe v. Wade* overturned state anti-abortion laws, abortion was a crime in almost every state. Each year, several hundred thousand women and many medical practitioners braved arrest, conviction, and imprisonment as they went in search of or performed abortions. With *Roe*, abortion almost immediately became widely available, and the impact was dramatically and quickly felt by large numbers of women and men.

In 2003 the Court issued *Lawrence* and—almost nothing changed. The number of states with sodomy laws had been steadily declining since 1960, when all fifty states still had these laws, to the time of *Bowers*, in 1986, when only twenty-four states retained them, to 2003, when the number had dwindled to thirteen. Even in these thirteen, sodomy laws were rarely enforced. Hardly any gay men and virtually no lesbians were being arrested for same-sex acts in private with a consenting adult. In Harris County, Texas, where John Lawrence and Tyrone Garner were arrested, there hadn't been a sodomy prosecution in the previous twenty-two years. More to the point, the laws under which police did make arrests—ordinances against public lewdness, vagrancy, and disorderly conduct—remained on the books, still available for use by law enforcement officials with homophobic inclinations. It is safe to say that, a month or even a year after *Lawrence*, it would have been hard to fill a modest-sized living room with gay men, lesbians, or bisexuals who could point to changes in their everyday lives because of the case.

Nonetheless, the case will make a difference, even if that difference needs to be measured in ways other than by its immediate impact. Let me put it this way: if new interpretations of history played a role in making the *Lawrence* decision possible, *Lawrence* in turn matters because of how it will change even further the history of same-sex relations.

One way in which *Lawrence* is important is that it closes a very long chapter in the history of sexuality. Even though the impact of sodomy laws was different in seventeenth-century British North America than it was in Texas in 2003, the laws that *Lawrence* invalidated were nonetheless part of a history of criminalizing same-sex acts that stretched back uninterruptedly for centuries. This continuity has now been broken. As years pass by, the shadow cast by sodomy laws will recede farther and farther away. Criminality will no longer shape how gay men, lesbians, and bisexuals live now and instead will become part of a past untethered to daily life now. Over time, this will make a difference.

The effects of criminal status over the past few generations have been profound. Even if rarely enforced, sodomy statutes rationalized the imposition of a broad range of other penalties. How can persons whose deepest emotional yearnings make them prone to criminal activity be allowed to occupy a position of public trust? Sodomy laws served as a self-evident reason to bar gay men, lesbians, and bisexuals from government employment. They justified exclusion from professions such as law, medicine, and teaching in which moral character figured prominently. A propensity to commit crime served as grounds for denying to lesbian and gay parents custody of their children or visitation rights. For decades, sodomy laws were the unanswerable response as to why gay bars should be raided and shut down: they were sites that existed only to facilitate illegal sexual activities. While most of these practices have been fading in recent decades, the continuing existence of sodomy laws was a link to this past. These statutes kept the stigma alive, making it available for deployment by the family court judge, the vice cop, or the school principal in charge of hiring. This history is now over. *Lawrence* detached homosexuality from a criminalized past.

A second way *Lawrence* is important is that it has now attached same-sex relations to quite a different history, one that situates sexual expression within the realm of expanding personal liberty. In the eighteenth century, when the Constitution was written and ratified, sexuality in the United States was normatively contained for whites within a marital reproductive framework. Over the past two centuries, more and more Americans have voted with their desire and transformed sexual expression into something intended to bring intimacy, happiness, and pleasure. Two hundred years ago, the average number of children to which a white American woman gave birth was seven. Today the fertility of American women hovers around two. Although the timing and the rate of decline have varied, this reproductive revolution has cut across all groups of women born in the United States. Race, religion, region, ethnicity, educational level, and economic status: these characteristics have affected when the decline in fertility set in and how quickly it happened but not whether it has occurred. Sexuality has increasingly entered the realm of personal choice, the sphere of individual liberty.

Over the past half century, the Supreme Court finally began to recognize this de facto revolution in the sexual lives of Americans. It has brought this new meaning of sex into the sphere of constitutional jurisprudence. One set of decisions did not involve sexual behavior directly but rather concerned the cultural representation of sexuality. Beginning in 1957 with the *Roth* case, a long series of challenges to federal and state obscenity statutes came before the Supreme Court. Enforcement of these laws placed powerful constraints on the depiction of human sexuality in the public sphere, whether in news media, film, television, the performing arts, or literature. The Supreme Court never went as far as to declare these statutes unconstitutional. But, by narrowing considerably the operation of these laws, it opened up to view not only a world of pornography but also more mundane forms of sexual expression. Much of the gay and lesbian literature and a good deal of the queer press of the post-Stonewall decades would not have passed muster under the obscenity standards of the pre-*Roth* era. It would be impossible to overstate how important these rulings on obscenity were.

Although these decisions fell under the rubric of free speech and the First Amendment, underlying the Court's approach was a view of sexuality that was distinctively modern. Delivering the majority opinion in *Roth*, Justice William Brennan described sex as "a great and mysterious motive force in human life . . . one of the vital problems of human interest."[27] Can one imagine a major public official in the United States a century or more earlier speaking about sex with those phrases?

A second set of cases addressed sexuality in the context of reproduction. In *Griswold v. Connecticut*, the Court struck down a Connecticut law that restricted access by married couples to contraceptives; in *Eisenstadt v. Baird*, it overturned a Massachusetts law that restricted access by the unmarried to contraceptives; and in *Roe v. Wade*, it eliminated state laws that prohibited abortions in the first two trimesters of a pregnancy. Through these, the Court constructed what it termed a "zone of privacy" rooted in constitutional notions of liberty. In *Griswold* the justices applied to the marriage relationship language that invested it with great power: "a right of privacy older than the Bill of Rights . . . intimate to the degree of being sacred . . . as old and as fundamental as our entire civilization."[28] In *Eisenstadt* the Court notably extended this right to privacy beyond the framework of the couple. "The marital couple is not an independent entity with a mind and heart of its own," Justice Brennan wrote, "but an association of two individuals. . . . If the right to privacy means anything, it is the right of the individual, married or single, to be free from unwarranted governmental intrusion."[29]

On the surface, these decisions, including *Roe*, appear to be about reproduction, not sexuality. Yet, in sustaining the right of individuals to choose not to have a child, the Court was simultaneously affirming their right to have sex without procreative intent. These decisions elevated sexual expression—or, more precisely, nonprocreative heterosexual acts in private between consenting adults—to the status of a protected liberty that the US Constitution guaranteed.

The importance of *Lawrence* lies in the way it explicitly drew homosexual acts between consenting adults in private into this framework of constitutional rights. "Liberty presumes an autonomy of self," Kennedy declared near the beginning of his opinion. Calling *Griswold* "the most pertinent beginning point in our decision," he described "an emerging awareness" over the past half century that "liberty gives substantial protection to adult persons in deciding how to conduct their private lives in matters pertaining to sex." This right, he wrote, "extends beyond the marital relationship."[30] Unlike any other Supreme Court case in history, *Lawrence* placed the intimate lives of homosexuals within the realm of human rights. This certainly deserves to be called important.

Still, it is worth reiterating that the importance of *Lawrence* does not lie in what it offers now. Closing the door on a long history of criminality simply confirms what was almost universal practice in the United States already. Placing the expression of same-sex desire within the context of human rights and personal liberty implies a promise, though it leaves unspecified the content of the promise or a timetable for delivering on it. But, while *Lawrence* barely matters at all today, the difference it makes will grow in significance with the passage of time. As the stigma of criminality fades into the more distant past, the notion that sexual expression is a human right will ineluctably get incorporated into our understanding of what freedom entails. Over a generation or two, this shift in perspective will have an impact whose force no one can yet measure.

III. The Supreme Court Follows Rather Than Leads

What about marriage? Isn't a constitutional ruling in favor of same-sex marriage the promise that *Lawrence* tantalizingly extends? And won't this promise be delivered sooner rather than later? From Justice Scalia and religious conservatives to gay and lesbian activists to the editorial writers of many newspapers, commentators across the political and social spectrum drew the same conclusion. *Lawrence* paves the way for the Supreme Court's endorsement of gay marriage.

In one sense, this viewpoint is accurate. When the day comes on which the Supreme Court declares marriage a constitutional right regardless of the gender of one's partner, it undoubtedly will cite *Lawrence* as one of the key cases that led the Court to such a decision. But, in the short run, if one is looking for predictors of what the Court will do soon, there is very little reason to take this claim seriously. If *Lawrence* teaches us anything, it is that the Supreme Court follows rather than leads. Rather than chart brand new directions for society, it tends instead to confirm change that has already occurred. Its rulings bring law into alignment with shifting values and social norms. The Court consolidates an emerging consensus; it does not launch novel social experiments.

The *Lawrence* opinion itself substantiates the claim that the Supreme Court follows along paths that have already been laid out instead of leading society into unexplored territory. Justice Kennedy repeatedly emphasized how uncontroversial the elimination of sodomy laws was. As early as 1955, he wrote, the model penal code of the American Law Institute called for the decriminalization of all sexual acts between consenting adults in private. He cited the British Wolfenden Report of 1957, which recommended the same thing. Kennedy called attention to the many states that had already eliminated sodomy statutes. He highlighted the 1981 decision of the European Court of Human Rights that sodomy laws were a violation of basic human rights. He pointed to the "substantial and continuing" criticism that the *Bowers* decision elicited for upholding these laws.[31] All of these references serve a single rhetorical purpose. They emphasize that the judicial elimination of sodomy laws is not a big deal. Striking down a few remaining sodomy laws, Kennedy was trying to tell his audience, simply flows with the stream of history. It does not impose an untested social policy upon Americans.

Viewed in this light, the content and structure of Kennedy's opinion in *Lawrence* can be seen as evidence that striking down the state laws against marriage by same-gender couples will not be emanating from the Court in the immediate future. There are a number of reasons for adducing this. First, Justice Kennedy tells us so. Near the end of his opinion, he goes out of his way to comment that extending notions of personal liberty to the intimate lives of homosexual persons has no implications for the issue of same-sex marriage. "The present case," he wrote, "does not involve whether the government must give formal recognition to any relationship that homosexual persons seek to enter."[32]

Second, whereas Kennedy used a historical rationale to support his constitutional judgment about sodomy laws, no such rationale is available on behalf of same-sex marriage. Historians were able to construct a powerful case about sodomy statutes that allowed Kennedy to claim that history was on his side. By contrast, despite a huge historical literature on marriage produced by feminist historians, it would be implausible to argue that anything other than the union of a man and a woman was ever understood in the United States to constitute a marriage. Yes, there have been significant restrictions on the right to marry, most notably involving race. Yes, a few groups—like nineteenth-century Mormons and some small utopian communities—practiced plural marriage. And, yes, the law of marriage has significantly changed in the past century, particularly in terms of abolishing a gender hierarchy within marital law. But nowhere in the current historical literature is there any substantial support for a right to marry a person of the same sex.

Third, Kennedy justified his decision through reference to an "emerging awareness" in the recent past that individuals should be free to conduct their private sexual lives as they see fit. Where is this emerging awareness around same-sex marriage? Between 1993 and 2003, only four courts, in Hawaii, Alaska, Vermont, and Massachusetts, found state constitutional grounds to support recognition of same-sex unions; of these, only the court in Massachusetts was uncompromising in declaring that same-sex couples must be given access to marriage. By contrast, overwhelming majorities in the US Senate and House of Representatives supported the Defense of Marriage Act, legislation declaring that, for the purpose of federal law, marriage shall be understood to be only the union of a man and a woman. By 2004 the legislatures of almost forty states had similarly passed legislation affirming that marriage is the union of a man and a woman. In almost thirty states, a substantial majority of voters have approved referenda declaring the same thing and amending their state constitutions accordingly. This is not evidence of an emerging consensus in support of same-sex marriage. Yes, public opinion, especially among the young, is changing, and that promises more substantial progress further down the road. But a preponderance of evidence from our democratically constituted political system suggests powerful tendencies still against it.

The argument that *Lawrence* sets the stage for same-sex marriage has been a self-serving one. It serves the interests of religious opponents of marriage in that the claim works as a call to arms to mobilize the troops against this new social experiment. It serves the interests of political conservatives within the Republican Party in that it gives credence to their charge that a liberal activist judiciary is creating judge-made law. And it serves the interests of those within the gay and lesbian movement who have most strongly pushed to make marriage a movement priority in that it gives credence to their claim that this goal should be at the top of the queer agenda.

If *Lawrence* tells us anything about the marriage battle, it is that the last thing proponents of same-sex marriage should be hoping for is a Supreme Court case soon. The Court eliminated sodomy laws when there were almost no sodomy laws left and almost no support for those laws and their enforcement. When same-sex marriage is on the road to becoming as commonplace as sodomy laws were rare, then we will see the Supreme Court offering its constitutional blessing. It will take a lot of on-the-ground activist organizing and public education before we get to that place.

25

Rethinking Queer History

Or, "Richard Nixon, Gay Liberationist"?

The amount of history that has been written in the past generation about sexual and gender identity is extraordinary. At the time of the Stonewall uprising, in 1969, gay, lesbian, bisexual, or transgender history was virtually unimaginable. Now there is a large and growing body of historical writing on a wide range of topics. Yet, for the most part, it remains separate from and not integrated with general accounts of US history.

On the basis of research I began doing in 2007 about Chicago LGBT history, I developed a talk, with the attention-grabbing title used for this chapter, that I gave a number of times in the context of the fortieth anniversary, in 2009, of Stonewall and gay liberation. It is an effort to see queer history as thoroughly enmeshed in what often gets described as "mainstream" history.

On Friday night of the last weekend in June 1969, police from Manhattan's Sixth Precinct set out to raid the Stonewall Inn, a gay bar on Christopher

An earlier, abbreviated version of this essay appeared in Jill Austin and Jennifer Brier, eds., *Out in Chicago: LGBT History at the Crossroads* (Chicago: Chicago History Museum, 2011), 95–107.

Street in Greenwich Village. There were issues with the Stonewall. It served liquor without an appropriate state license. It had ties to organized crime. It brought an unruly and disreputable element to the neighborhood: too young, too countercultural, too flamboyant in its dress, too dark skinned. But, even without those issues, the police might easily have targeted Stonewall. Raids of gay and lesbian bars, with or without a pretext, and the arrest of managers, employees, and patrons as well, were unremarkable occurrences in American cities in the 1960s.[1]

Something else that was unremarkable in the United States in 1969 was the occurrence of mass demonstrations and public disorder. In New York, for instance, the 1968–69 school year saw the American Federation of Teachers, whose members were predominantly white, go on strike in protest against the actions of a community school board whose district served a mostly black and Hispanic student population. The community, for its part, had been holding rallies and protests to build support for its goal of local control of schools.[2]

In April and May of 1969, the months preceding the Stonewall raid, a coalition of African American and Puerto Rican students at the City College of New York had shut down the campus for weeks. Their demands included not only the establishment of black and ethnic studies programs but also an open admissions policy to allow every high school graduate in New York City access to a free college education in a public university. White students and students of color engaged in pitched battles on campus but then joined forces to fight the police when college administrators invited them on campus to restore order.[3]

Gay bar raids and urban uprisings: both of them everyday events in the United States in the late 1960s.

What was not typical was putting those two phenomena together. Yet that is exactly what happened on Christopher Street on June 28, 1969. When the police raided the bar and expelled most of the patrons, instead of fleeing they remained crowded together on the street outside. On a weekend summer night, foot traffic in the Village was heavy, and the crowd quickly grew larger. When a lesbian in the bar resisted police efforts to arrest her and drag her into a police van, the crowd grew agitated. People started throwing coins and pebbles and then hurled rocks from the neighborhood park just across the street. After police retreated into the bar, the crowd grew more aggressive. A few folks ripped a parking meter out of the ground and used it as a battering ram to smash through the Stonewall Inn's doors. Someone used lighter fluid to start a fire and shoved some burning garbage through a broken window into the Stonewall, where the police were now trapped. Before long, reinforcements of helmeted tactical police arrived on the scene. For the next few hours there were battles galore as police chased raucous collections of angry queens through the narrow streets of the Village. Rioting and demonstrations recurred in the Village for several more nights. Urban rebellion had come to the semi-underground queer world.[4]

In 2009 the fortieth anniversary of Stonewall was commemorated with marches, parades, rallies, and other community events in hundreds of cities around the globe and in dozens of countries across six continents. Millions of people—tens of millions—participated in these commemorative events in one way or another. New York City, whose police department provoked the rioting by raiding the Stonewall Inn, promoted the anniversary celebrations as a major attraction in the hope that they would draw free-spending tourists to New York to boost the city's sagging economy.[5]

In historical memory, the Stonewall uprising obviously matters. And yet, though Pride Parades around the globe commemorate it each June, its significance rests less in what happened on those nights in Greenwich Village and more in what happened afterward. Because the rioting occurred when and where it did—at a time when collective rebellion against established power and authority was an everyday fact of life in the United States; when adolescents and young adults were breaking with social and cultural norms; when a militant politics of racial and ethnic identity was spreading rapidly; and when notions of gender were being sharply contested—Stonewall provoked an explosion of gay and lesbian activism. It sparked the creation of a dynamic nationwide movement.[6] The activism Stonewall spawned in the early to mid-1970s was often rowdy and unruly.

An important part of the activism of the 1970s was the effort to produce new knowledge. Before the 1970s much of the public naming and defining of homosexuality came from the outside. It came from a medical profession that wrote and spoke in terms of sickness. It came from religious discourses that presented homosexual desire as sinful. It came from legal codes that defined the behavior as criminal. Newspapers commonly labeled gays and lesbians and gender-crossing individuals as degenerates and perverts. The words journalists routinely employed were a vocabulary of opprobrium, imposed on a group from the outside.[7]

One form that this effort to produce new knowledge took was researching and writing history. To appreciate the motivation that drove this early historical research, it is worth pausing to notice how different the present is from this past of only four or five decades ago. The visibility of queer folks in contemporary popular culture is commonplace: Ellen DeGeneres on daytime and evening television; Adam Lambert and Ricky Martin in the world of music; RuPaul on cable television; and network series like *Glee* and *Modern Family*. By contrast, the polemical writing of gay liberationists from the early 1970s is saturated with certain themes. Activists declaimed against the silence—"a conspiracy of silence"—that in its turn fostered their invisibility in the culture at large and then isolated them from one another. Silence, invisibility, and isolation were the key motifs against which this rebellious gay liberation sensibility constructed itself. Among those swept into this new gay and lesbian movement were small numbers of women and men committed to uncovering the stories of those "hidden from history," to borrow the title of a key anthology of historical writing.[8]

Put aside the thorny problem that if, in the past, there really had been a conspiracy of silence and lovers of the same sex had been invisible and isolated from one another, then there would not be much history that could be written. Instead, let's just start from the proposition that, in an environment where this rhetoric flourished, some people started researching histories that had not been written before.

In the rest of this essay, I want to sketch a picture of what this first generation of researchers discovered in their labors, specifically into twentieth-century US lesbian, gay, and transgender history. What topics did they write about, and what are some of the common themes to be found in this scholarship? Then I will describe a bit about my own research, which focuses on Chicago in the twentieth century, and relate some of Chicago's history in ways that seem to illustrate these common themes. Finally, I will point to ways that the Chicago experience does not fit into the older plot line that this first generation of historians sketched out, and I will suggest some implications for future research.

In looking at this earlier body of historical writing, which I will be lovingly critiquing, I will start with my own work. I was an activist in the 1970s who happened also to be a graduate student in history. As someone deeply interested in social movements and collective mobilizations in the past, I thought, "It couldn't have all started with Stonewall in 1969. There must be earlier roots to the gay liberation movement of today." And so I went looking for these roots and, through oral histories and the use of privately held archives, reconstructed its history.

I found a story, reaching back to the late 1940s, of gay men and lesbians, mostly in larger cities, banding together to try to do something about their mistreatment and the oppressiveness of daily life in the early years of the Cold War. They formed organizations like the Mattachine Society and the Daughters of Bilitis, both of which started in California. In the course of the 1950s and 1960s, these organizations spawned chapters in large cities like New York, Boston, Chicago, Detroit, Philadelphia, and Washington, DC. Caution admittedly suffused much of their work. Courageous enough to join an organization, yet fearful of the effects of public exposure of their identity, many members used pseudonyms. But they published magazines that circulated beyond the networks of organizational membership and spread a counter-discourse about homosexuality. They sought to win allies in the worlds of religion, medicine, and law. By the 1960s, in the context of an expanding culture of protest spawned by the civil rights movement, they began mounting small demonstrations in Washington, DC, against the federal government's discriminatory policies. They began to reach out to the press and television, doing interviews that provided a new kind of visibility, even if only sporadic and occasional. Before the Stonewall riots, they deployed slogans like "Gay Is Good" and "Gay Power."[9]

The work of these activists was not earthshaking. It was not as dramatic and far-reaching as what happened in the 1970s after Stonewall and the birth of a "gay liberation" perspective. But this homophile movement, as participants labeled it, laid some groundwork. It floated new ideas. It was a form of organized, self-conscious resistance.[10]

This was one approach to uncovering a hidden past. Elizabeth Kennedy and Madeline Davis took a different path. In *Boots of Leather, Slippers of Gold*, they exposed another pre-Stonewall queer world.[11] Rather than study one of the largest cities, they focused on Buffalo, New York. They looked at the worlds that working-class lesbians, both white and black, created there from the 1930s through the 1960s. Primarily through oral histories, they were able to reconstruct elaborate social networks, encompassing both friendship and romantic relationships, centered in private house parties as well as in commercialized venues like bars. As with the homophile activists I studied, these women created visibility in Buffalo but achieved it largely through the courage of butch "dykes" whose gender-crossing clothing and carriage acted like magnets, drawing others to them and creating social concentrations of public lesbianism and gender transgression. These women also engaged in resistance, though not by forming organizations and publishing magazines. Instead, they fought—literally—for the right to claim public space, to hold their girlfriend's hand, and to dance in a bar. They fought heterosexual men who invaded their spaces, and they fought police who tried to arrest them. Kennedy and Davis argued persuasively that, between the 1930s and the 1960s, a more stable, extensive, and visible lesbian world coalesced in Buffalo and that over time it developed a stronger self-consciousness about oppression and identity. The Buffalo story, you might say, was a different route to Stonewall from the one I described in *Sexual Politics, Sexual Communities.*[12]

Meanwhile, Allan Bérubé was adding another significant and dramatic piece to what we were learning about a gay and lesbian past. Bérubé was a community activist in San Francisco. Inspired by Jonathan Ned Katz's 1976 documentary collection, *Gay American History,* he trained himself in historical methods and undertook the task of researching San Francisco's queer past. His slide lectures at community venues in the Bay Area gave him enough visibility that, when someone moved into a San Francisco apartment and discovered a cache of hundreds of letters apparently written by a group of gay GIs to one another during World War II, the letters found their way to Bérubé. It launched him on the path of writing a book, *Coming Out under Fire,* that recounted the history of gay men and lesbians in the military during the war years and of the military's response to them.[13]

Bérubé constructed his story through information obtained from oral histories, private collections of letters and other memorabilia, government documents, and military records released after Freedom of Information Act requests. He came to the conclusion that the war years proved decisive in forging a collective lesbian and gay identity; this, in turn, helped to build more extensive and robust urban communities in the postwar decades. As Bérubé explained, the war years took millions of young men and women out of their small-town and family-centered environments. It put them in essentially same-sex environments: millions of men and hundreds of thousands of women in the military; millions of women in civilian jobs, living in boardinghouses in cities depopulated of single men. The war gave many young adults the freedom to experience same-sex love and romance away from the usual constraints. And it produced some surprises, such as the *Myrtle Beach Bitch,* a campy, gay-inflected newsletter produced and circulated by a number of GIs stationed in South Carolina. At the end of the war, these men and women did not all return to the communities in which they had been raised. Many stayed in the cities to which they had migrated for work or to the cities where they spent their leave, and in the postwar decade they helped create a new gay and lesbian urban world.

The final example I'll use to illustrate this early historical work is a piece produced by Eric Garber, who, like Bérubé, was a community-based historian living in San Francisco. Garber explored Harlem in the 1920s and 1930s. He looked at the literary and cultural circles of the Harlem Renaissance and the world of commercialized entertainment that grew exponentially in the wake of the Great Migration. Among the writers, artists, and performers of the Harlem Renaissance he found ample, though often coded, evidence of men-loving men and women-loving women. Through songs like "Sissy Man," for instance, the blues music of the 1920s and early 1930s openly addressed homosexual themes. Moreover, male and female impersonators were an important feature of Harlem nightlife in these years. Individuals like Gladys Bentley, who performed in tuxedo and top hat, were popular entertainers.[14]

Each of the studies I have mentioned is certainly different from the others. They move across several decades of the twentieth century, examining periods variously characterized by economic depression, full-scale mobilization for war, massive suburbanization, and anticommunist crusades. They look at white and black, at men and women, and at working-class and middle-class social worlds. They examine social life and cultural production as well as public advocacy and political organizing. They locate their subjects in institutions like the military and in the living rooms of apartments.

But they, as well as other works I have not mentioned, also have some things in common. Most obviously, all of them self-consciously work against the themes of silence, invisibility, and isolation. From the blues songs of the 1920s to the lesbian and gay newsletters of the 1950s, people were breaking silence and making their voices heard. By coming together in urban communities, staking out public spaces for themselves, and engaging in gender-crossing behavior, these men and women were both making themselves visible and breaking isolation.

There are two other themes running through the founding texts of US gay and lesbian history that are so pervasive, so deep in the narratives, that they almost go unremarked. One is that all of this work prides itself on being stories of resistance. Whether they describe individuals who were singing songs on stage, strutting their stuff on the streets, risking arrest by going to a bar on Saturday night, joining an organization, or refusing to return to small-town life after a discharge from the military, all of these studies are histories of resistance. They do not deny the intensity of oppression. Bérubé, for instance, points out that, over the course of the war years, the military defined more expansively the grounds for discharge. Many gay and lesbian GIs faced time in the stockade as well as courts martial, and those discharged lived with the continuing effects of stigma attached to expulsion from the military. All of the studies that cover the postwar decades agree that these years were particularly harsh in their open attacks on homosexual expression, whether in the guise of formal barriers to employment, mass arrests by the police, or inflammatory journalism about sex degenerates and moral perversion. But, oppression is the backdrop for a much more elaborate explication of resistance.

A second core feature of this scholarship is what I would describe as its "queer-centric" structure. Gay men, lesbians, and gender crossers are the movers and shakers in these narratives. It is their initiative, their decisions, and their choices that drive the history forward. All of us who were writing these books and articles were certainly aware of and sensitive to historical context. We paid attention to things like urbanization, Prohibition, war, McCarthyism, and the political protests of the 1960s. But, ultimately, all of these contextual elements served as backdrop. The heart of these stories from the past was an account of how gays and lesbians attempted to shape their own worlds and their own destinies. To borrow the title of a book on women's history, they were "heroes of their own lives."[15]

Interestingly, even when historians claim to embrace a different approach, the power of this model prevails. Take, for instance, the work of two revisionist scholars. Nan Boyd has produced a wonderfully rich community study of San Francisco from the 1930s to the 1960s.[16] She tells us right at the start that the history of queer San Francisco is intimately bound together with the city's history as a "wide open town" (the phrase is the title of her book). But, after an opening that sets the stage, she then offers us a story of gay men, lesbians, and transgender people who, in the course of fighting oppression, find one another and build a vibrant community rooted in their fierce resistance to oppression. In another fine book, John Howard offers a historical study, set in Mississippi, of men who have sex with men.[17] The title of his book, *Men Like That*, immediately alerts readers to his contention that this will not be just another account of gay men in an urban environment coming into self-consciousness as a group apart. Instead, he starts us off in rural and small-town Mississippi, in automobiles and highway rest stops, among men who seek out other men for sexual pleasure or sexual release but who do not construct for themselves lives that pivot on that desire. Yet, as Howard moves us forward in time, his narrative shifts, and by the end we find ourselves in Jackson in the 1980s among gay men and lesbians who have found each other, formed organizations, built community, and are speaking out and taking action against oppression.

The power of this narrative appears irresistible. It has swept historians along almost despite the intentions of some of us. And yet it is not surprising. Most of these works, certainly the ones that have come to be considered foundational, were researched, written, and published between the mid-1970s and the mid-1990s. Those of us who worked on them came of age in the 1960s and 1970s. It was a time of massive social movements for justice, where resistance was the order of the day and where resistance was often led by people—African Americans, Chicanos, women—who saw their activism as inclusive of an effort to build and strengthen a group identity.

I am not suggesting that we crassly or dishonestly found what we were looking for. But the truthfulness and the plausibility of the history we wrote emerged from what we knew and saw. Our interpretations and narrative structures were enabled by the world of social movements and community resistance that gave birth to our work. We looked around us and saw ordinary people making their own history and shaping their own destiny. We did our historical research, and that's what we found, too.

Let me jump forward now from this previous generation of historical writing to the present. I want to describe work that I have done more recently: what brought me to it; what I am finding; and how it is leading me to rethink what I once confidently knew. I have been working on "queer" Chicago, mostly in the second half of the twentieth century but with some forays into earlier decades as well.

The project, which keeps changing its shape, began almost accidentally. On a sabbatical semester a while back, one in which I intended to write a short, synthetic survey of the gay and lesbian movement from the 1960s to the early twenty-first century, I began dipping into Chicago materials. I thought it would give the narrative greater continuity and immediacy if I could keep returning to the same locale for key illustrative examples. Chicago seemed to be the perfect city for achieving this, and not primarily because I live here and have easy access to research materials. In US historical writing, Chicago often functions as the representative or paradigmatic city. Historians writing about topics as diverse as labor radicalism, urban political machines, American Catholicism, prostitution, the making of racial ghettoes, social settlement houses, immigration, and many other topics as well study Chicago.[18] To write about Chicago, apparently, is to write about the nation. At the same time, Chicago's gay, lesbian, and transgender history is, surprisingly, less explored than that for cities like New York, San Francisco, and Los Angeles. At the point that I began this research, I was able to find only two scholarly articles of substance on queer Chicago.[19]

At first glance, much of the material I explored appeared thoroughly consistent with the broad outline of gay, lesbian, and transgender history that I sketched out earlier in this essay. For instance, the experience of Chicago's South Side in the 1920s and 1930s paralleled or, arguably, even surpassed the Harlem experience described by Eric Garber. Blues women like Ethel Waters, Alberta Hunter, Bessie Smith, and, especially, Ma Rainey, had a strong presence in Chicago. The *Chicago Defender* promoted their careers and celebrated their achievements. In part because of housing segregation, in part because of economic discrimination, African American entertainers of this era did not maintain a huge social distance from their audiences. Hunter lived on East 36th Place, and Rainey had an apartment at 35th and Wabash. Waters, Hunter, Smith, and Rainey all had romantic or sexual relationships with women in this period; Rainey was arrested and spent a night in jail after police busted a late-night party of women in various states of undress.[20]

Angela Davis has written persuasively about these blues singers, arguing forcefully that one of the key distinguishing features of female performers of the 1920s and 1930s is the "pervasive sexual imagery" in their music. Sexuality, Davis has written, was "a tangible expression of freedom" for them and the working-class women in their audiences.[21] "Barrel House Blues," a song recorded by Rainey, had these lines:

Papa likes his sherry / Mama likes her port
Papa likes to shimmy / Mama likes to sport
Papa likes his bourbon / Mama likes her gin
Papa likes his outside women / Mama likes her outside men[22]

Another one of Rainey's popular songs, "Black Bottom," is full of sexually suggestive double entendre. An ad for it in the *Defender* shows Rainey dancing exuberantly, wearing a low-cut sleeveless dress that, with one hand, she has lifted provocatively above her knee.[23]

The sexuality expressed in the music was not just about what, in our time, we describe as heterosexual. "Prove It on Me Blues," a song composed by Rainey and recorded in 1928, contains the following lyrics:

> Went out last night with a crowd of my friends
> They must've been women, 'cause I don't like no men . . .
> Wear my clothes just like any old man
> 'Cause they say I do it, ain't nobody caught me
> Sure got to prove it on me.

The ad that ran in the *Defender* to promote sales of the recording made the meaning clear. There was Ma Rainey, a burly figure in shirt and tie and a tailored men's jacket, picking up two dolled-up femmes.[24]

The male analogue of these female blues singers was the female impersonator. The *Defender* promoted female impersonators with great enthusiasm. It followed the careers of some of them, like Walter Winston and Dick Barrow, who had strong Chicago ties. While there were a number of clubs that featured female impersonator revues, the Cabin Inn was the most heralded. It had a lead impresario, "Miss Valda Gray," who staged a new show every few months. The *Defender* heaped compliments on Gray's efforts and praised the performers at the Cabin Inn as "America's most outstanding female impersonators."[25]

The paper also commonly marked the Cabin Inn as different. It variously described the club as "Chicago's oddest nitery" or "the oddest night club in Chicago" or "Chicago's oddest night spot."[26] Yet "odd" and "different" did not imply that impersonators were cordoned off in a separate queer space. For instance, during the Christmas holiday season in 1936, the *Defender* sponsored a major midnight benefit to help needy families. Seven thousand South Siders attended, and thousands more had to be turned away. The show brought together a galaxy of stars, including such luminaries as Louis Armstrong. Valda Gray, along with the rest of her troupe of impersonators, was there. When the *Defender* reported on the benefit the day after Christmas, it featured a page of photographs of "Doris" and "Peaches" and "Dixie" and "Petite," all dressed in their glamorous best.[27]

Like other big cities, and confirming the interpretation of Allan Bérubé, post–World War II Chicago had a dense concentration of bars and clubs that catered to gay men, lesbians, and gender crossers and that helped build community and solidarity. From the 1940s through the 1960s, a variety of popular nightspots—among them the Windup, the Fun Lounge, the Front Page, the Hollywood Bowl, the Carousel, the Annex, Sam's, the Baton, the Trip, and the Chesterfield—drew large crowds.

Chicago's experience also confirms a picture of the 1950s and 1960s as intensely and uniquely oppressive decades. For instance, over the three-year period from 1950 to 1953, the *Chicago Tribune* printed scores of articles, including a number on the front page, about the presence of gay men, lesbians, and bisexuals in the federal work force as well as about the efforts of congressional investigators to expose the problem and to purge the government of these employees. *Tribune* reporters commonly used phrases like "moral degenerates" and "sordid practices" and "unmentionables" and "nests of perverts" and "men of depraved tendencies" to describe male homosexuals.[28] It conjured up a federal government that, in the midst of a war in Korea and a global Cold War against Communism, was saturated with men and women whose sexual tendencies allegedly made them security risks and hence put the nation in danger.

In such a climate of openly expressed public hostility, police felt very free to harass anyone who seemed to be gay or lesbian. Gender crossers of either sex were especially vulnerable. City law prohibited wearing clothing for the purpose of concealing one's sex.[29] Women with short hair who wore pants with the zipper in the front could be—and were—arrested. One November, two police detectives fired multiple shots into the back of James Clay, a black drag queen who was trying to escape arrest.[30] Police arrested for loitering men who were sitting in parks known to be cruising areas if they did not live in the neighborhood. Handsome young cops dressed in street clothes; they staked out parks and alleys and public toilets; they came on to the men they encountered there and then arrested them for solicitation when they responded.

Above all, Chicago's police targeted gay and lesbian bars with impunity. These were the one public place where gay men and lesbians came together in groups. Police felt free to harass these businesses at will. They might, for instance, park their cars outside a gay bar and simply sit there, an effective way of keeping customers from entering the premises. Or they might enter casually and look around. If they did, business for the evening evaporated because, in the words of one manager, "if any police officer would walk in, everybody would walk out."[31] More ominously, plainclothes officers might enter unannounced and unseen. If they noticed any physical contact—an arm around the waist or shoulder, a couple holding hands, any kissing or hugging—they could arrest the manager and employees for maintaining a disorderly house, charge the offending patrons with public lewdness, and cart off the other customers for patronizing a disorderly house.

The largest part of this harassment escaped broader public notice. Most of the time, word of a raid traveled informally as gossip, as warnings passed along from one to another, through networks of friends and acquaintances and sexual partners. But, sometimes, newspapers reported on a police raid and the accompanying arrests. The article then served as a labeling device, alerting readers to the deviants in their midst and the efforts of the police to contain them and alerting those so labeled of the dangers that awaited them if they patronized such places. Early in 1949, for instance, police on the Near North side arrested ninety-one men at the Windup Lounge; stories about the arrests and trials continued for a month.[32] Late in 1951 police arrested sixty at Cyrano's Tavern at Division and State Streets.[33] In March 1962 the *Tribune* reported on the arrests of thirty-nine at the Front Page Lounge, after detectives saw two men kissing and several dancing.[34] In community memory, no event compares with the 1964 action against the Fun Lounge. Playing upon fears of the corruption of youth, the front-page headline in the Sunday *Chicago Sun-Times* announced, "Area Teachers among 109 Seized in Raid on Vice Den." There was a photograph of some of the arrested lined up against the wall in Felony Court. The page-wide headline in the Sunday *Chicago American* was "Probe Teachers' Vice Arrest." Over the next days, newspapers in the city carried the names and addresses of all public employees picked up in the raid and tracked the termination of their employment.[35]

Under these circumstances, bar owners quickly learned that they needed to make payoffs to the police in order to stay open. Yet even payoffs did not guarantee that police would leave a particular establishment alone. One tavern owner from this period described his relationship to law enforcement this way: "I felt like I had a sword of Damocles over my head." Such conditions meant that few legitimate entrepreneurs opened or invested in gay or lesbian bars. More often than not, the bars were owned and operated by organized crime, the "syndicate" or the "outfit" as it was called in Chicago. Since bars expected to close down after a certain amount of time, they were run in ways that secured a quick profit. Watered-down drinks, high prices, and a dingy atmosphere were the norm. One Chicago patron perfectly captured the paradox of bar life in this era. "The bars are the only place for gay people to go to get together outside of home," he said. "There is no question that they were for shit."[36]

Chicago also resembled other large cities in that, by the second half of the 1960s, signs of organized political resistance by lesbians and gay men were growing. By the mid-1960s the city had chapters of the two main national homophile organizations, the Daughters of Bilitis and the Mattachine Society. Mattachine especially directed its attention to police misbehavior. Its newsletter regularly railed against Chicago's police, accusing them of "entrapment, shakedowns, brutality, and corruption."[37] The newsletter identified streets known to be staked out by plainclothes police officers; it began naming them and providing readers with a physical description of the officers. Mattachine worked closely with the ACLU to document police behavior; it urged bar owners to form a protective association; and it tried, without much success, to get meetings high up on the police chain of command. By the end of 1966, homophile activists in Chicago were so angry that they picked up the rhetoric of the black power movement and raised a call for "gay power," the first such use of the term, as far as I have been able to determine.[38]

The gay liberation movement that the Stonewall rebellion helped provoke came to Chicago very early. A group that named itself Chicago Gay Liberation started meeting on the South Side, in Hyde Park, before the end of 1969. The next year, Chicago was only of only three cities to hold a rally and march commemorating the first anniversary of Stonewall. One of the earliest lesbian feminist newspapers, *Lavender Woman*, began publishing in Chicago in 1971. A group of African American and Latino activists formed an organization that they named "Third World Gay Revolution." Over the next years, lesbian, gay, and transgender activists staged a number of public actions. They demonstrated against businesses that harassed or discriminated against queer clientele. They picketed the corporate offices of newspapers that published derogatory articles. They demonstrated outside police district offices to protest harassment. They held rallies in places known to be cruising areas as if daring the police to arrest them.[39]

By the mid-1970s, after just a few years of public high-spirited militancy by these groups, police harassment, especially of bars, plummeted. It did not stop entirely, but it became sporadic and occasional, the result of an individual officer's impulses, rather than systemic and pervasive, the result of department-wide policies and assumptions. The implications of this shift were huge. The decline in police harassment brought immediate, dramatic, and visible changes. By the second half of the 1970s, one could point not merely to an increase in the number of bars owned by individual entrepreneurs but also to greater longevity for these businesses, greater geographic concentration, a relaxed queer presence on the streets, and the coalescence of a neighborhood that was, increasingly, described as gay.

What I have just described about Chicago sounds very much like the old plot line of gay and lesbian history that I sketched out earlier: a queer-centric story of resistance where lesbians, gay men, and gender crossers band together to resist oppression while building community in the process. As we move into and through the 1970s, silence, invisibility, and isolation dramatically fade as appropriate descriptors. And yet the resistance of queer Chicagoans, whether through organizations and formal mobilizations or through spontaneous protest actions, carries virtually no power to explain a vital, indispensable part of this story—the end of systematic police harassment and the opportunity it provided for a flourishing and open gay neighborhood to emerge.

The harassment of bars was just one tiny element in a much larger story of bribery and corruption, of police and organized crime, and of the day-to-day operations of the political machine of Mayor Richard J. Daley and the Cook County Democratic Party. Journalists, political scientists, and historians have produced a huge literature on Daley and on the Democratic machine that he presided over for more than two decades, and I will not pretend to have absorbed all of it. But certain characterizations recur. The journalist Mike Royko, no friend of the mayor, called Daley, in the 1960s, "with the single exception of the president, the most powerful politician in the country." The coauthors of the most prominent biography of Daley characterized him as "the most powerful local politician America has ever produced."[40]

At the heart of the mayor's power was the political machine over which he presided. Daley reputedly knew many of the Democratic precinct captains by name. In the 1960s, according to biographers Adam Cohen and Elizabeth Taylor, he had close to forty thousand patronage jobs to dispense. City employment demanded support for the machine and its candidates, from mobilizing voters at election time to acting with favor toward important supporters, whether corporate or individual, of the political machine. In return for this, city employees could expect a certain amount of freedom in the performance of their duties, the freedom, for instance, to obtain "supplements" to their income or other gratuities. Whether they were building inspectors or property assessors, machine loyalists who worked for the city could get away with a lot.

For police officers working in the precincts that housed the city's nightclub and entertainment district, including the main concentration of gay bars, this meant the expectation of payoffs from tavern owners. The *Tribune* described the system as "a police extortion racket." It was "so deeply entrenched as to be considered a way of life—a license to steal, graft a part of the emoluments of the job." Police "preyed on tavern owners . . . extracting monthly tribute from them."[41] The web of corruption was so tight that some of the city officials whose job it was to investigate corruption surrounding liquor licenses—an assistant state attorney and an assistant corporate counsel who handled liquor license revocations, for instance— were themselves either owners of gay bars or lawyers for gay bars.[42]

In a system like this, a few hundred ragtag hippie-style gay liberationists and lesbian feminists demonstrating outside a police district office had no capacity to modify police practices toward gay bars. To stop the extortion involved piercing the power of the political machine. To end the raids on gay bars and the arrests of patrons meant challenging the ability of city employees who were loyal to the machine to reap one of the expected benefits of their job.

So what did break the back of police harassment and, consequently, open the way for a public and visible urban gay neighborhood to take shape? To put it directly: the election of Richard Nixon in 1968.

As long as a Democrat was in the White House, there was unlikely to be any serious investigation of corruption in Chicago. Daley had received credit in the press for delivering the presidency to John Kennedy in 1960. Lyndon Johnson consulted with Daley before shaping legislative proposals, such as the War on Poverty, that might impact urban politics. In 1967 Johnson and the Democrats in Congress honored Daley as the "Democrat of the Year."[43] The power of the political machine meant that protégés of Daley got elected to the post of state attorney in Illinois and hence were unlikely to pursue indictments for corruption. Daley's influence with Democratic presidents meant that a machine loyalist was likely to be appointed US attorney for northern Illinois, thus closing that route to exposing malfeasance. By contrast, a Republican in the White House, and especially a Republican who attributed his earlier defeat in a presidential election to Richard Daley's machine, would be not only willing but eager to do what no Democratic president would have done: investigate corruption in Richard Daley's Chicago.

A sign of what this shift in investigatory power meant came early in 1970 when the US attorney called a grand jury to investigate the possibility of prosecutorial and police malfeasance in the killings of Fred Hampton and Mark Clark, two Chicago Black Panther Party leaders, in December 1969. If the idea of Richard Nixon and John Mitchell, his attorney general, supporting justice for black power militants seems to stretch credibility, then one can appreciate how intent the new administration was on discrediting Richard Daley and undermining his political power. In the spring of 1970, the grand jury completed its investigation into the killings and issued a scathing 243-page report that laid the groundwork for the later indictment of Edward Hanrahan, a Daley protégé who had been elected as the machine's candidate for Cook County state attorney, and thirteen police officers. The US attorney's office released the grand jury report on Mayor Daley's birthday.[44] In September 1972 James Thompson, the US attorney for northern Illinois who later became the Republican governor, handed down indictments of more than six dozen Democratic party workers for voter fraud in the primaries held earlier in the year.[45]

In 1969, the year that Nixon took office, a seemingly random case of a tavern shakedown by the police surfaced. Bob Weidrich, a columnist for the *Tribune*, began to write about it, and his coverage provided the trigger for an investigation by the FBI. In February 1971 the US attorney's office impaneled another grand jury to investigate the extortion of bar owners. It gathered evidence for twenty-two months, including from the owners of gay bars who were promised immunity in return for their testimony. The grand jury uncovered "a police extortion racket" that "preyed on tavern owners in the Rush Street and Old Town nightlife strips, extracting monthly tribute from them."[46] Between 1972 and 1974, fifty-six police officers, including the captain of the Chicago Avenue district, which contained the largest concentration of gay bars in the city, were indicted on corruption charges. The investigation, indictments, and trials generated many hundreds of news stories in the daily press, mostly between late 1972 and early 1974. Headlines that stretched across the front page—"U.S. Acts to Indict Police

Exec and 20"—recall the sensationalism of earlier ones about raids on gay bars, and the language of the exposé—"sordid spectacle"—mimics that of the "Lavender Scare" coverage of the 1950s.[47]

The main trial of officers from the Chicago Avenue police district began in August 1973 and lasted six weeks. It generated a trial transcript that was almost 7,700 pages long. Fifty-five bar owners and managers, including those from many of the city's gay bars, testified.[48] When it was all over, thirty-four officers were found guilty, and hundreds more in the department were transferred. The scandal also forced the resignation of James Conlisk, Chicago's police superintendent, whose father was a close friend of Mayor Daley.[49]

After almost two years of unrelenting publicity exposing police malfeasance, it was no longer possible for the police to harass and intimidate gay and lesbian bars—their owners, employees, and patrons—at will. After the early 1970s, a particularly homophobic police officer might target an individual or a particular business, or a district commander might go after a bar because of rumors about drug dealing or other irregularities. But the investigations, indictments, trials, and convictions in these years of police officers and commanders broke the back forever of systematic and pervasive harassment of bars. That shift in turn allowed for the flowering of a new kind of gay entrepreneurship and the growth of a new kind of openly queer neighborhood. This may be the single most profound change of the post-Stonewall era, yet queer activism, queer mobilization, and queer resistance had little to do with its happening.

What are the implications of a finding like this? Does it mean that the earlier work that some of us did—work that placed lesbians, gay men, and transgender people at the center of their own history and that saw self-conscious acts of resistance as the engine of this history—is no longer true, no longer sustainable? Does it mean that I am about to start writing a new history from the top down, in which big forces beyond the control of ordinary people, rather than social movements built from the bottom up, are what drive events and shape change?

I don't think so. But, there is no question in my mind that part of what is allowing me to see Chicago's queer history in this way is the experience—different from that of the 1960s and 1970s—of having lived through more than a quarter century of the Reagan/Bush world, an era when decision making from the top down, whether about tax policy and banking regulation or about abstinence-only sex education, has seemed to be driving events. I would like to think that, if we embed queer stories in a larger political economy, a larger national political history, they will become less separated and less self-contained, less ghettoized, and instead become seen as integral to, more connected to, and more essential for understanding broader narratives of US history.

26

The Campaign for Marriage Equality
A Dissenting View

In the twenty-first century, the exclusion of same-sex couples from the legal right to marry has eclipsed all other gay and lesbian issues. It makes headlines regularly, figures in major ways in electoral politics, and calls forth emotional appeals for equality. More than any other LGBT issue, it has elicited the enthusiastic support of liberal and progressive heterosexuals and of younger adults across the political spectrum.

From the beginning of the campaign for marriage equality, I have had deep reservations about it. It is not that I am against marriage equality, that I think the right to legal marriage should be denied. But the way the campaign has evolved, the rhetoric and arguments that supporters often employ, and the impact that prioritizing marriage has had on other pressing issues have all deeply disturbed me. This essay, which grows out of a number of talks and two earlier shorter pieces, attempts to pull all my concerns together.

This essay expands upon two earlier essays: "The Marriage Fight Is Setting Us Back," *Gay and Lesbian Review Worldwide* 13, no. 6 (November–December 2006): 10–11, and "Will the Courts Set Us Free?: Reflections on the Campaign for Same-Sex Marriage," in *The Politics of Same-Sex Marriage*, ed. Craig Rimmerman and Clyde Wilcox (Chicago: University of Chicago Press, 2007), 39–64.

May 1993. The Hawaii State Supreme Court instructed one of its trial judges to reconsider a case involving same-sex marriage. Calling marriage "a basic civil right," the justices suggested that the prohibition against issuing licenses to same-sex couples violated state constitutional bans against gender-based discrimination. William Rubinstein, at that time the director of the American Civil Liberties Union's gay rights project, called the ruling "a major breakthrough."[1] This was the first time in US history that a court came even remotely close to approving "gay marriages," and it cracked open a nationwide debate that, two decades later, in 2013, continues. Despite many twists, turns, and reversals, one can reasonably draw a line connecting this judicial instruction in Hawaii to the first same-sex marriages in Massachusetts, in May 2004, the raft of prohibitionist measures that graced many state ballots that November, the battle over Proposition 8 in California in 2008, President Barack Obama's endorsement of marriage for same-sex couples in 2012, and, most recent, two Supreme Court decisions that supported marriage equality.

By any logic, the Hawaii decision ought to have thrilled me. I study social movements. I think daily about collective efforts to achieve justice and about how disenfranchised groups act to redress their grievances. In particular, I have studied the gay and lesbian movement for almost four decades and at many points along the way have been not merely an observer but an active participant in the cause. What could be more exhilarating than to witness history being made, to watch a campaign develop for something as fundamental as marriage?

Instead, from the moment that the Hawaii courts put the marriage issue squarely on the political agenda, the unfolding of the campaign for equal access to marriage has left me distinctly uneasy. For the past two decades, most new developments in the campaign, including many of the victories, have made a gnawing discontent grow ever more insistent.

Some might attribute this response to my own particular queer history. I am a member of what is often referred to as "the Stonewall generation." I belong to an exuberant radical subset of my age cohort. We were permanently influenced by the rebellious counterculture of the 1960s and the provocative writings of pioneering radical feminists.[2] Coming out publicly during the early and mid-1970s meant that we experienced being gay or lesbian as a worldview, a political orientation, a form of rebellion against social and cultural norms. To borrow the description of John Waters, the director of such camp films as *Pink Flamingo* and *Hairspray*, I was of the generation of gay men for whom "one privilege of being gay was that we didn't have to get married."[3]

Rather than a lifestyle, being gay seemed an entry point to remaking society. By definition, we thought, queer life was subversive of marriage and the family. In a nation that was led by Richard Nixon and that was bombing Southeast Asia back to the Stone Age, any kind of subversion seemed a very good thing indeed. We imagined a world in which bonds of friendship, companionship, and sexual intimacy were knitting communities together with ties more durable than those that no-fault divorce could dissolve with a signature and a small fee.

But, no, my grumpiness about the campaign for the right to marry is not solely or even primarily caused by a philosophical opposition to marriage. It is not a sign that I am stuck in the sexual ethics of the Stonewall era, unable to reach gay maturity.

Let's jump forward in time, a decade after the Hawaii case. A deeper source of my discontent emerged in the weeks after *Lawrence v. Texas*. On June 26, 2003, the Supreme Court issued a 6–3 decision in which it declared the remaining state sodomy laws unconstitutional.[4] These laws, as much as the often-quoted biblical passages from Leviticus and the Epistles of Paul, had been the grounding for the inferior status of gay men and lesbians. The criminalization of our sexual activities was the excuse for the thousands upon thousands of yearly arrests by local police forces. The criminal behavior that might erupt at any moment was an underlying rationale for why gay men, lesbians, bisexuals, and transpeople should be excluded from government employment and other jobs that demanded moral probity. Our inherent criminality justified the denial of child custody and visitation rights after a divorce and a host of other restrictions on our rights and our lives. Even though most states had already repealed these statutes by 2003, their survival anywhere linked the present to a long history of oppression. In that sense, *Lawrence* was profoundly important. It firmly closed a chapter in US history that stretched back to the earliest years of English colonization of North America.[5]

Barely had Justice Anthony Kennedy finished reading the majority opinion when attention shifted away from sodomy laws and the story became, as *Newsweek* suggested, "Is Same-Sex Marriage Next?"[6] Print media, television journalists, and online commentators all seemed to converge around the assumption reflected in a *Los Angeles Times* headline: "Ruling Seen as Precursor to Same-Sex Marriage."[7]

Since the connection between sodomy laws and the right to marry is not immediately evident, why did it prove so easy to make this leap? One reason was coincidence. Earlier that month, the Court of Appeal in Ontario, Canada, had issued a decision clearing the way for same-sex marriage. Moreover, the national government in Ottawa quickly announced that it would support the ruling.[8] There it was, just across the border. For many same-sex couples in the United States, marriage now seemed, metaphorically and literally, within reach, a short drive or a quick plane ride away.

Another reason for the easy leap from sodomy laws to same-sex marriage was that Justice Antonin Scalia, in his scathing dissent from the majority in *Lawrence*, said it was so. Justice Kennedy's reasoning, he claimed, "leaves on pretty shaky grounds state laws limiting marriage to opposite-sex couples." In case a reader missed his point, Scalia repeated it four paragraphs later: "Today's opinion dismantles the structure of constitutional law that has permitted a distinction to be made between heterosexual and homosexual unions, insofar as formal recognition in marriage is concerned."[9]

It did not surprise me that Scalia leveled these accusations. The man is an unabashed ideologue. Scalia certainly was not speaking to his peers on the bench or even to a community of constitutional law experts outside the courtroom. He wrote those passages for a much larger constituency. He meant to sound an alarm, to mobilize the armies of the Christian right, to alert conservatives to a danger in its midst and to call them to action. How else to explain the ridiculous claim in his dissent that the Court "has largely signed on to the so-called homosexual agenda"? A phrase like that resonates not in the world of legal scholars but in the ranks of conservative Christian activists.

But it did surprise me when so many voices within the queer community and among its allies echoed that perspective. In the weeks and months that followed, lawyers, organizational leaders, journalists, and others all seemed intent on proffering the same queer spin: in the wake of *Lawrence*, same-sex marriage was now within reach and close to a sure thing. The chorus of voices grew only more insistent when, in November 2003, the Supreme Judicial Court of Massachusetts swept away the legal barriers to same-sex marriage in the state. The prohibitions were "constitutionally suspect," said one prominent legal scholar. Same-sex marriage was "inevitable," said an activist lawyer. "It's not going to happen this year or next, but in the next decade," said another. Evan Wolfson, who perhaps more than any other lawyer has pressed for a court-based assault on the laws against same-sex marriage, even appropriated Scalia's language. The restrictions on the right to marry, he said, were on "very shaky grounds."[10] It is not often that one finds gay advocates and right-wing radicals in such close agreement.

Reading all this commentary crystallized another reason the marriage campaign has provoked such queasiness within me. The source of my discontent went deeper than my personal history. It also grew from my understanding of social movements and how permanent and significant change happens. As I encountered all these pronouncements about how *Lawrence* had put same-sex marriage within our grasp, I found myself thinking, "Oh, no. You misapprehend the central lesson of *Lawrence*. If Justice Kennedy's opinion teaches us anything, it is this: the Supreme Court follows rather than leads. The Court does not boldly chart new directions. Rather, it tends to consolidate change that has already occurred." In the case of sodomy laws, the Supreme Court declared them unconstitutional forty-two years after the first state voluntarily repealed its law and at a point when a large majority of the states had done the same thing. If *Lawrence* told us anything, it was more likely that same-sex marriage throughout the United States was still a good way off. A strategy of fighting for marriage through the courts, which was the primary strategy for fifteen years after the Hawaii decision, had proved to be a disaster. It gave us not marriage but a whole new body of antigay law.

Let's jump ahead another decade, to 2013. At first glance, the picture does not appear as bleak. The president and the vice president have now both spoken out in favor of equality for same-sex couples. No longer just an issue taken up by legal advocates, the marriage campaign in some states has become a focus of LGBT activists who have mobilized voters and lobbied legislators with success. Public opinion seems to have turned, as well. Has my mood improved with this shift in strategy and tactics and an improved scorecard?

Alas, no. These victories have come at a great price. At a time when the life cycle and family patterns of Americans have grown tremendously diverse, marriage activists have aligned themselves with the most conventional form of living arrangement. When I consider the broad sweep of history, when I think of the long-term incontrovertible trends in population, in the structure of the economy, and in the organization of personal lives, I look at the elevation of marriage rights to the top of the mainstream LGBT movement's agenda and I think that, instead of flowing with the stream of history, as the movement often has, we are actually moving against history. Proponents of marriage have associated the LGBT movement, which once spoke the language of liberation, with privilege pure and simple. They have made claims for marriage that, if taken seriously, threaten to leave the needs of large numbers of LGBT people unmet and ignored.

In the rest of this essay, I would like to elaborate on these many layers of objection to the prioritizing of marriage as a goal and to the way the issue has been pursued. First, I want to offer something of a primer on how the issue has developed and where it stands now. Second, I will make some observations about strategy and tactics. How has the campaign been fought, and what has it led to? Third, I will explore how the fight for marriage equality fits—or doesn't fit—into the broad stream of historical change. Then, I will make some comments about the values that the issue and the campaign expose. Finally, I will speculate about why I think the marriage issue has proven so appealing despite all these problems.

The Movement Context: Historicizing the Issue of Same-Sex Marriage

The history of the gay and lesbian movement since its beginnings in the 1950s has been one of change so rapid and so extraordinary that it can justifiably be described as progress. Sixty years ago, when the first gay and lesbian organizations in the United States were taking shape in California, every state had sodomy laws that criminalized homosexual behavior. Local police forces used them as warrant for making thousands and thousands of arrests every year. The military's exclusion policy was unbending and absolute, and its implementation led to the discharge of thousands every year. The federal government enforced a blanket ban against its employment of lesbians, gay men, and bisexuals, and state governments and professional licensing agencies did likewise. Cold War rhetoric about perversion and sexual menace saturated the public domain. Christian religious teaching utterly condemned same-sex desires. The medical profession categorized homosexuality as disease, and many states allowed judges to send gays to asylums with indeterminate sentences and permitted parents to institutionalize their queer teenagers.[11]

The first cohort of pioneering activists had little room to agitate for justice. They tried, successfully, to secure de facto recognition of their right to assemble, a not insubstantial victory since police could argue that, when gays met together, it was prelude to criminal activity. They also won from the courts acknowledgment that their publications were not obscene. Influenced by the nonviolent demonstrations of civil rights activists, a few of them in the 1960s braved public exposure by mounting picket lines outside government buildings and carrying signs that demanded fair treatment. The most militant among them coined slogans such as "Gay Power" and "Gay Is Good" as ways of encapsulating just how far they wished to travel from mainstream beliefs and practices. Still, for all their effort, by the late 1960s there were fewer gay and lesbian organizations in the entire United States than exist today just in the state of New Jersey. And oppression was still intense and pervasive.[12]

Then "the '60s" intervened. I use this as shorthand for the few years when the United States experienced at home a broad-based challenge to authority. Core institutions found themselves under assault. At least temporarily, spheres as diverse as the presidency, the medical profession, the military, the university, national political parties, and local police saw their legitimacy questioned and their exercise of power challenged.[13]

Gay liberation and lesbian feminism rushed into this vacuum. Like those who launched the sit-in movement in the South a decade earlier, activists were relatively young. Many of them were college students or not far removed. They were deeply influenced by the message of self-assertion that came from the black power movement; by the challenge to white middle-class values that came from the counterculture; and especially by the rethinking of gender norms, sexual ideology, and family structure that women's liberation put forward. Their radicalism impelled them to violate one of the central principles of gay life in the generation that preceded them. They refused to stay hidden and keep their identity secret. Instead, they made "coming out" a new imperative. Men and women who came out more easily became activists in a movement.[14]

In the course of the 1970s, the movement achieved a host of victories. The American Psychiatric Association removed homosexuality from its catalogue of mental illnesses. The Civil Service Commission dropped its blanket exclusion of gay men, lesbians, and bisexuals from federal employment. A number of states eliminated their sodomy statutes. The Democratic Party's national conventions began to see the participation of openly gay and lesbian delegates. Almost three dozen cities enacted statutes banning discrimination on the basis of sexual orientation. Federal courts repeatedly affirmed the First Amendment speech and assembly rights of homosexuals. Of greatest significance, perhaps, activists in many cities succeeded in sharply curtailing the police harassment that had been endemic to queer life.

Measured by the expectations of the early twenty-first century, the gains provoked by gay liberation seem like just a few faltering steps on a very long road to the still unreached destination of equality. But measured by what had preceded them, they seemed huge to activists at the time. The constraints on police behavior had especially profound consequences. In the 1970s a queer public life became far more visible than ever before. It was different from the queer worlds that had existed earlier, less contingent on the whims of law enforcement, less contained and restricted. It was visible and accessible in a sustained and continuing way. Among men, it was highly commercialized, consisting primarily of bars, bathhouses, discos, and sex clubs. Among women, it was more overtly oppositional, consisting of coffeehouses, music festivals, small presses and bookstores, and art and theater collectives.[15]

Stop for a moment and reflect upon what I've described in the preceding few paragraphs. Where does "family" fit in this story? What kind of a policy agenda around family will a movement produce when the primary influences on this movement have been the hippie counterculture (think "Communes, Free Love, Woodstock Nation") and radical feminism (think "Down with the Patriarchy!")?

There was a bit of a family agenda in the 1970s. The primary plank in it was "Defend the rights of lesbian mothers," though even here the meaning of that exhortation was far different from what it might connote today. Defending the rights of lesbian mothers signified fighting to allow those lesbians who had become mothers when they were still living in heterosexual marriages to keep their children. It did not mean campaigning for the right of lesbians to choose to become mothers.[16]

To the extent that family figured in the queer politics of the 1970s, it did so in slogans, like "Smash Monogamy" and "Smash the Nuclear Family," that helped mark these activists as oppositional, as radical. Listen to what some of them had to say about the family and marriage. In "Gay Is Good," one of the earliest pieces of gay liberation literature, Martha Shelley described lesbians and gays as "women and men who, from the time of our earliest memories, have been in revolt against the sex-role structure and nuclear family structure." In "A Gay Manifesto," a widely circulated document of the gay liberation era, Carl Wittman called marriage "a prime example of a straight institution fraught with role playing. Traditional marriage is a rotten, oppressive institution." In New York City, an organization of radical queers of color asserted that "all oppressions originate within the nuclear family structure." Meanwhile, gay liberation groups in Chicago defined one of the key virtues of being gay as its contribution to breaking down the nuclear family.[17]

These were not the only sentiments in the gay and lesbian community, of course. Even in the decades of grimmest oppression, same-sex couples staged weddings to celebrate their love and commitment (someday, someone needs to research and write this history.) During the '70s, while radicals excoriated both the family and monogamy, the Metropolitan Community Church, a Christian organization created by Troy Perry to provide a safe place of worship for gays, lesbians, and their allies, performed union ceremonies—weddings, in other words—for members in committed relationships. Indeed, almost everywhere that gay folk came together through religious affiliation, a yearning for marriage would surface. In West Virginia in the mid-1970s, Jim Lewis, an Episcopal minister, gained a reputation for being sympathetic to gays. Soon couples began approaching him and begging him to marry them, even though the ceremonies would not have the force of law.[18] In the early 1970s, moreover, a few gay and lesbian couples—in Minnesota, Kentucky, Washington, Colorado, Illinois and, perhaps, elsewhere—made efforts, all unsuccessful, to have their unions recognized as legally sanctioned marriages. Even in these cases, however, appearances could be deceiving. In Washington, the application for a marriage license was made by a radical fairy intent on making screw of the institution. In Illinois, the effort was made by members of a Trotskyist group hoping that the refusal by the county clerk would lead the gay community to rise up in a revolutionary rage.[19]

But, if a consensus in the gay community was absent, the radical voice was certainly the loudest and most evident. In this era, family and homosexual seemed mutually antagonistic. Here was a place where homophobe and homosexual seemed to unite. If straight America could not imagine queers in the family photo album, neither could lesbians and gay men imagine themselves within the family's bosom. In novels as different as *Another Country*, by James Baldwin, and *Rubyfruit Jungle*, by Rita Mae Brown, queer life took shape—indeed, could only take shape—through escape from the confines of family. Queers lived in exile from home and hearth, rejected by their families and rejecting family, as well.

This, then, is where things stood in the early 1980s. Yet, a mere decade later, not only had same-sex marriage emerged in Hawaii as a viable issue, but also the gay and lesbian community had fashioned a full-fledged multi-plank platform of family issues. Matters such as partnership recognition, spousal benefits in the workplace, parenting by same-sex couples, the safety of queer youth, and gay-supportive public school policies had all become rallying points for activists.

What provoked this profound shift in the gay and lesbian community's relationship to family in so short a time? A number of developments in the 1980s contributed to this reorientation.

One factor was the impact of the Sharon Kowalski case. In 1983 Kowalski was involved in an automobile accident that left her ability to communicate seriously impaired. The courts awarded guardianship to Kowalski's father rather than to her partner, Karen Thompson, who for years was denied access to Kowalski. Across the United States, lesbian communities hosted forums, organized fund-raisers, and worked to raise public awareness about the case. After an eight-year battle, the courts eventually made Thompson the legal guardian, but in the meantime "Free Sharon Kowalski" became a rallying cry among lesbians concerned about the lack of legal recognition for their relationships.[20]

If the one case of Sharon Kowalski could so powerfully affect so many lesbians, multiply this by the thousands to begin to grasp the force of the AIDS epidemic in redefining the significance of family for gay men. In the course of the 1980s, sickness and death became part of the everyday experience of young and middle-aged gay men. Many of them faced situations where the phrase "next of kin" came into play: hospital visitation rights; decision making about medical care; choices about funeral arrangements and burials; the access of survivors to homes, possessions, and inheritance. The ugly dramas that in some situations played themselves out between gay partners and their friendship circles on the one hand and families of origin on the other exposed the legal nonexistence of same-sex relationships.[21]

A third factor inducing a shifting family politics was the emergence of newly organized constituencies, both nationally and locally, among gays and lesbians. AIDS provoked some but not all of this. From the beginning, the epidemic disproportionately affected African Americans and Latinos. Gays and lesbians of color took the lead in battling the disease in their home communities, and the infrastructure generated by AIDS funding helped build organizations—like the National Latino/a Lesbian and Gay

Organization (LLEGO), founded in 1985, and the National Black Lesbian and Gay Leadership Forum, founded in 1987—that served as their platform in the movement. AIDS also spurred the proliferation of queer organizing beyond metropolitan centers so that, by the late 1980s, the movement had an unprecedented national spread. One result was a subtle shift in the rhetoric of family away from tropes of exile and exclusion and toward themes of dialogue, engagement, and belonging. For gays and lesbians of color, family was a needed resource, a means of survival. For those living in smaller cities and towns, life often existed within a dense web of kinship ties and neighborliness.[22]

The lesbian (and, to a lesser extent, the gay) baby boom was a fourth reason family issues came to the fore. Unbeknownst to a culture that had thoroughly associated gay life with sexual abandon and deadly disease (lesbians were largely erased from mainstream discourses), more and more individuals within the community were now choosing to become parents. The means varied, from the "turkey baster" babies conceived through the cooperation of gay men with the procreative desires of lesbian friends, to the use of sperm banks, adoption agencies, surrogacy, and sex among friends. But the growing visible presence of children in the community made family less metaphorical and more descriptive of the contours of queer life.[23]

Generational change also played a role in the shifting priorities of the gay and lesbian movement. As members of the Stonewall generation advanced into middle age, more of them were likely to be settled in long-term relationships. In every way except the legal, these partnerships had the texture of marriages. At the same time, a younger generation came of age, and it had never known anything but the era of pride and visibility. Having come out to family and friends early, many had seamlessly integrated their sexual identities into every sphere of their lives. Why shouldn't they be able to get married, just like all their straight friends?

Finally, never underestimate the power of sheer orneriness in the shaping of a policy agenda. A politics of "traditional family values" took shape during the Reagan-Bush era. One of the first legislative proposals of the Reagan years was the draconian Family Protection Act; one of the last rhetorical engagements of the Bush White House was Vice President Dan Quayle's 1992 attack on the unwed motherhood of Murphy Brown, a fictional newscaster on a popular network television series. As the Republican Party and evangelical Christians made family a cause that bound them together, was it any wonder that queers would respond, "We are family, too"?[24]

The embrace of family by lesbians and gay men was more than a self-protective reaction to a homophobic opposition. It generated a platform of sorts, a cluster of issues loosely bound together conceptually under the heading of family. It provoked a decade of creative organizational initiatives. It sparked an intriguing inventiveness from a community striving to extend understandings of family to include queer folk. AIDS may have overshadowed this at the time, but the 1980s witnessed a widespread reclaiming of family among gays and lesbians.

One form of this creativity came from the National Center for Lesbian Rights. Lesbian couples raising children together faced a problem. The non-biological parent had no legal standing as a parent, since no state laws and no courts had ever recognized as parents of a child two individuals of the same sex. In case of the death of the biological mother, or legal challenges from the sperm donor, or the breakup of the couple, "the other woman" risked loss of access to the child, and the child risked loss of access to a woman who had filled the role of parent. In the early 1980s, lawyers at NCLR fashioned the notion of "second parent adoption," and soon lesbian couples were petitioning courts around the country for the right to have two women declared the parents of a child. Confronted with real families with a real problem, some judges responded flexibly. By the early 1990s, family court judges were creating, in effect, new law on the ground.[25]

Another imaginative response to the legal barriers to gay and lesbian family recognition was the invention of the concept of "domestic partnership." In the early 1980s, domestic partnership received its first incarnation as simple registries, created by municipalities, so that same-sex couples could achieve a modicum of legal recognition. Registration put couples on firmer ground if they confronted situations—in hospitals, for instance—in which the nature of their relationship needed confirmation. By the late 1980s, some municipalities were taking this a step further and extending spousal benefits, such as health insurance and family medical leave, to employees in same-sex domestic partnerships. Interestingly, many of these early DP measures were equally available to same-sex and opposite-sex couples.[26]

From my vantage point as a student of social movements, what made these policy innovations especially notable was that they were the tangible outcome of a much broader organizing impulse. By the late 1980s, one could find much evidence of community mobilizations taking shape around the concept of family. For instance, the National Gay and Lesbian

Task Force created a Families Project at the end of the decade. Because it was the national organization most committed to a philosophy of community organizing and had close ties to grassroots activists around the country, NGLTF's initiative in this area signaled that more change was on the horizon. The growing attention to the issue of children raised by gay parents provoked the formation, in 1990, of COLAGE (Children of Lesbians and Gays Everywhere).[27] Its members functioned not only as a support group for one another but also as an advocacy organization campaigning for fair treatment for queer families. Most dramatically, perhaps, these years witnessed an explosion of activism within the corporate world. Gay and lesbian employees and, increasingly, bisexual and transgender workers as well formed organizations at the workplace where they campaigned for, among other things, domestic partnership benefits. These efforts not only led to major shifts in the policies of corporate America but also brought changes in workplace culture. The last bastion of the closet was fast becoming a site of queer visibility.[28]

Where was marriage in this story? It would be a mistake to say that marriage never surfaced in the 1980s. At the massive March on Washington in October 1987, one of the unforgettable moments that weekend was the mass "wedding" of same-sex couples outside the Internal Revenue Service building. But the event was as much a public expression of love and commitment in the face of AIDS and American homophobia as it was a step in a campaign for the right to marry. Indeed, writing two years later in *Out/Look*, Tom Stoddard, the executive director of Lambda Legal, commented: "As far as I can tell, no gay organization of any size, local or national, has yet declared the right to marry as one of its goals."[29] In other words, marriage was a peripheral matter in the vibrant new family politics that lesbians and gay men had created by the early 1990s.

Beginning in the 1990s, a series of state-level court cases transformed the marriage issue from something of marginal concern to something front and center in public consciousness and political contention. This part of the story begins in Hawaii in 1991, when three same-sex couples filed a suit challenging their denial of marriage licenses. Although they lost their suit in the first round, in 1993 Hawaii's Supreme Court sent the case back and ordered the judge to reconsider. No such favorable outcome on the marriage issue had ever emerged from a court before. In 1996 a judge declared the ban on marriage unconstitutional, and a court in Alaska came to a similar conclusion. The rejoicing was short lived, since both states quickly passed constitutional amendments that preserved marriage as the union of a man and a woman. But the die was cast, and a corner seemed to have been turned. By 1996 the network of LGBT legal activists had dropped their skepticism about the wisdom of litigating marriage and decided to pursue cases in other states, at least selectively.

From the first favorable court ruling, in 1993, one can chart a fairly clear progression in the quest to obtain access to marriage for same-sex couples. First, in Hawaii and Alaska, court cases opened the door to marriage, but state constitutional amendments that legislators and voters overwhelmingly approved shut it firmly again. Next, in Vermont in 1999, a court declared that same-sex couples must have access to the *benefits* of marriage, and the legislature responded by creating a new legal status called "civil unions" in order to provide those benefits. Then, in 2003, the supreme judicial court in Massachusetts ordered access to marriage, and the state's liberal legislature did not intervene to block it. In a gesture saturated with symbolic significance, the first same-sex marriages in Massachusetts occurred fifty years after the US Supreme Court's historic ruling in *Brown v. the Board of Education*. California (at least temporarily) and Iowa also achieved marriage equality by way of litigation through the courts.

The year 2008 marked a significant shift in how the fight for the right to marry was conducted. That November, voters in California approved Proposition 8, a ballot initiative that overturned an earlier court decision allowing same-sex couples to marry, thus reinstating a marriage ban. Although a highly publicized legal challenge was quickly initiated, this taking away of a right already obtained, coupled perhaps with the mood of hope that Obama's election induced, finally began to provoke significant grassroots mobilizations to secure the right to marry. Beginning in 2009, some state legislatures for the first time took the initiative to provide equal access to marriage without the courts ordering them to do it. And, in 2012, advocates of marriage equality won at the ballot box, as Maine, Minnesota, and Washington all approved ballot initiatives. As of June 2013, thirteen states and the District of Columbia provided same-sex couples with the right to marry. And that month's Supreme Court decision invalidating the Defense of Marriage Act means that married couples in those states now have access to the full range of federal benefits.

Over these years, two other changes have accompanied this movement in the direction of marriage equality. First, the issue became widely debated and discussed; it is a staple of both popular culture and political discourse.

The lives of high-profile celebrities like Ellen DeGeneres put a public spotlight on the marriage issue, and both movies and, especially, television incorporate same-sex couples into their storylines. In 2012 both Vice President Biden and President Obama were able to express public support for same-sex marriage, something unimaginable just a few years earlier. Second, marriage has both replaced and overshadowed not only all other forms of LGBT family politics but virtually all other LGBT legislative priorities and issues as well. Whereas in the 1980s the opening up of recognized family forms to include something like domestic partnerships or civil unions would have seemed like wonderful progress, by 2012 the fact that a dozen additional states offered some legislatively enacted benefits to same-sex couples seemed to many activists not a victory but rather a queer version of the "separate but equal" doctrine.[30]

Recounting the history of movement activism and the marriage issue in this way, we seem to have a straightforward story of progress. We have moved across a half century, from a time when marriage and family seemed beyond the reach of lesbians and gay men to the emergence of a queer family politics and now to the legal recognition of same-sex marriage. The number of states offering marriage or couple benefits has grown slowly but steadily over two decades. Moreover, the way in which this has happened—from favorable court cases that were reversed by legislatures and voters, to favorable court cases that were not overturned, to legislatively initiated marriage equality, and now to voter-approved referenda—attests to movement in the direction of democratically chosen equality.

But such an interpretation would be only one part of the story. The Hawaii case unleashed something else besides movement toward equality. By 1996, as fears about the final disposition of the Hawaii case grew and the expectation that a court might order recognition of same-sex marriages sank in, a massive political mobilization in reaction against such an outcome took shape. One could say without exaggeration that a "moral panic" erupted. In 1996 Republicans introduced in Congress a so-called Defense of Marriage Act (DOMA). Just in case state courts were so reckless as to approve marriage for same-sex couples, these conservative politicians were taking no chances. DOMA specified that, under federal law, marriage was to be understood as the union of a man and a woman. If any states made marriage accessible to gays and lesbians, those couples would not be entitled to any of the benefits that federal law extended to the married. Social Security, federal tax breaks, benefits to the spouses of service members and veterans, and many more programs as well: none would be applicable to same-sex couples. The debate in Congress did bring some eloquent defenses of fairness and equality. Representative John Lewis of Georgia, one of the Freedom Riders of 1961, said the proposed legislation stank of "fear, hatred and intolerance" and should be called "the defense of mean-spirited bigots act." Nonetheless, DOMA passed both the House of Representatives and the Senate with overwhelming majorities. President Clinton, who fashioned himself a friend of the gay community, signed it into law.[31]

Congress was not alone in this resolve. In 1995 Utah's legislature passed a statute affirming that marriage was the union of a man and a woman. In 1996, the year Hawaii's courts declared the ban on marriage unconstitutional, the floodgates opened. Fourteen states, either through ballot measures or legislative enactment, reaffirmed what was now referred to as "traditional" marriage. In 2004, in the wake of the first marriages of same-sex couples in Massachusetts, twelve more states did the same. Significantly, the grouping of these measures in years that saw national elections meant that conservative evangelical voters had extra motivation to vote in high numbers, with terrible consequences for the political makeup of many state legislatures and governorships, as well as for the composition of Congress. In 2013, even as marriage equality was the law in thirteen states, almost all of the others have followed Utah's lead in explicitly defining marriage as a union of a man and a woman. Roughly thirty states have gone further. They have amended their state constitutions, often through ballot measures approved by overwhelming majorities of the voting population, to make clear that marriage is not for same-sex couples and that same-sex marriage is not the popular will.

Thus, a simple story of progress toward equality is not the only way to understand twenty years of fighting for marriage equality.

Matters of Strategy and Tactics: The Ghosts of Courtrooms Past

By the time of the national elections in 2004, when the issue of same-sex marriage jockeyed for headlines with news about war and terrorism, it was already becoming hard to remember that the LGBT movement had ever had a politics of family that was about anything except marriage. It was also becoming hard to recall that any strategy except litigation had ever been employed by the movement. Why did the field of queer family politics shift—some might say narrow—so dramatically in the course of little more than a decade? How did litigation for marriage become the magic bullet expected to deliver on the promise of equality? Why did one strategy and one goal replace many strategies and many goals? The rise to preeminence of court-based strategies was especially odd because the LGBT movement had never been litigation centered. Yes, there have been important court cases along the way. But, when one surveys the activist history of the past sixty years, what is most notable is how mass mobilization and militant activism have been central to our progress.

Underlying the decision to pursue the right to marry through the courts was an unspoken belief that goes something like this: "The courts are the place to go for the redress of grievances. When elected officials and public opinion are lined up against us, the courts can be relied upon to protect minorities from the tyranny of the majority. In fact, through the mechanism of civil rights litigation, the courts can be the engine of progressive social change." This assumption is so pervasive that it hardly needs to be articulated. It has been espoused by liberals and progressives, who endorse the idea, and by conservatives, who rail against it. The field of civil rights and public interest law has been constructed around it. Some of the best minds, some of the young people most committed to social justice, choose law as a profession out of the conviction that this is the way to change the world.

The source of this belief (a belief that would have been considered unusual for much of American history) is not difficult to identify. It emanates from popular understandings of two historic Supreme Court cases of the mid-twentieth century: *Brown v. Board of Education* (1954), in which the Court declared racially segregated public schools to be inherently unequal and hence unconstitutional, and *Roe v. Wade* (1973), in which the Court struck down state laws that banned abortion. Each of these cases is closely associated with social movements—the African American civil rights movement and the second wave of feminism—that deeply changed America. In fact, popular understandings see each case as somehow central to the success of their respective movements.

But to see these cases as provoking vast political upheaval on behalf of social justice badly misreads the historical evidence. The cases did not break new ground or map new territory. They did not take the law in new directions. Indeed, one could just as plausibly argue that these cases provoked the opposite of what they intended. Because of them, powerful reactionary movements had rallying points that allowed them to mobilize against racial and gender justice.

Take the *Brown* decision. When the Warren Court handed down its ruling, the forces already tending toward the demise of legally sanctioned racial segregation were compelling. Here are just some of them:

- Less than a decade earlier, the United States had fought a world war in which a primary aim was the destruction of a Nazi regime that rested on an ideology of Aryan supremacy. Fighting a war against racism abroad weakened acquiescence to racial hierarchy at home.

- Cold War foreign policy impelled the United States to seek the support of Africans and Asians in its struggle against the Soviet Union. Racial apartheid in the American South seriously weakened diplomatic claims that the United States represented the pole of freedom in a global fight with communism.

- In 1947 a civil rights commission appointed by President Truman released a report that outlined a comprehensive agenda to achieve racial equality. The White House itself seemed to be endorsing a racial justice platform.

- By the early 1950s, the Truman administration had committed itself to a thorough desegregation of the US Armed Forces, thus establishing racial equality as a desirable goal in a key national institution.

- Many northern and western states had already enacted civil rights laws prohibiting racial discrimination in a wide variety of arenas. Racial equality rather than racial hierarchy was becoming the formal legal norm.

- Increasingly in the years after World War II, "Jim Crow" came to be perceived as a regional practice, an artifact of southern life that was discursively cordoned off as deviant, as un-American.

In this environment, the Supreme Court's declaration that legally mandated racial separation was unconstitutional did not suddenly chart a new course for race relations. The Court aimed to consolidate a developing consensus, to add the force of the Constitution to powerful tendencies in

American life. It declared its principles so unambiguously in part because these tendencies already commanded judicial notice. As Jack Greenberg, one of the lawyers involved in the litigation, phrased it, "there was a current of history . . . and the Court became part of it."[32]

Notice also how the case had made its way to the Supreme Court. Since the late 1930s, the National Association for the Advancement of Colored People (NAACP) had litigated a series of cases designed to chip away, bit by bit, at the edifice of white supremacist law. By the early 1950s, the Supreme Court had provided civil rights forces with a number of victories. It had outlawed the exclusion of black voters from political primaries, racially restrictive housing covenants, separate seating arrangements in interstate transportation, and the denial of access to law school and graduate school education. While none of these cases had been a sure thing, Thurgood Marshall, the chief legal strategist for the NAACP, employed rigorous criteria when deciding whether to take them on. According to one of his assistants, "Thurgood had to be convinced of victory beyond a reasonable doubt before he said yes."[33] Thus, *Brown* was the last step in a carefully planned legal strategy that had moved forward one step at a time.

At first glance, the circumstances surrounding *Roe v. Wade* might appear very different from those attending *Brown*. As late as the mid-1960s, every state prohibited abortion. A law reform movement was slowly gathering force, but criminalization remained the norm. To some, the 1973 *Roe* decision seemed like "a bolt out of the blue," unexpected and without warning.[34] Thus, the case might seem to prove that, yes, the courts are our saviors and litigation is the way to go.

Behind this decision, however, lay more than a half century of change. Change had proceeded along two fronts that were thoroughly germane to the issue in *Roe*. First, among American women, contraceptive practice had spread until it was almost universal. Second, in the two decades before *Roe*, the Supreme Court delivered a series of decisions that took sexuality out of the Victorian era and placed it firmly within a modern sensibility.

By the time of *Roe*, Americans had already experienced a revolution in their practice of birth control. Partly this was achieved through the radical agitation of militant advocates of contraceptive freedom like Margaret Sanger. Women and their male allies disrupted public events, gave fiery lectures, risked arrest, and went on hunger strikes in order to end restrictions on access to birth control information and devices. By the 1940s, with the rise of organizations like Planned Parenthood, birth control became part of mainstream culture, a form of "family planning." Scientists investigated fertility control and entrepreneurs invested in it, provoking innovations like the birth control pill. Controlling fertility had become so normative that even American Catholics, in the face of papal edicts against contraception, employed artificial methods of birth control at the same rate as other Americans.[35]

Meanwhile, beginning in 1957 with *Roth v. U.S.*, the liberal Supreme Court of Chief Justice Earl Warren decided a large number of cases involving sexuality. Many of these concerned the issue of obscenity. Federal statutes dating from the nineteenth century had placed tight restrictions on the representation of sexuality in literature, the arts, popular culture, and the media. As understood by legislators, police, judges, and purity crusaders, these laws essentially equated sexuality and the erotic with obscenity. For decades, writers, artists, and publishers pressed against the limits of obscenity law; they changed social practice even as the laws constrained them. Finally, in the 1950s and 1960s, a string of cases challenging federal and state obscenity laws reached the Supreme Court. While the Warren Court never declared the regulation of obscenity to be unconstitutional, it sharply attenuated the connection between sex and obscenity. Its rulings made the depiction and discussion of sexuality a commonplace in American culture and social life. So much changed in these decades that, in 1970, a presidential commission actually recommended the decriminalization of pornography![36]

The Court's willingness to consider an issue like obscenity thus made it unsurprising when, in the mid-1960s, it began to rule on state laws that restricted access to contraception. In *Griswold v. Connecticut*, the Court not only invalidated a law that infringed on a married couple's ability to prevent pregnancy; it also framed its decision as a constitutional right to privacy. At least for married couples, the Court deemed fertility control—and, by extension, sexual expression—a liberty protected by the Constitution. In 1971 *Eisenstadt v. Baird* extended these principles to unmarried male-female couples.[37]

This was the environment in which the Supreme Court addressed the matter of abortion. By 1973, when the justices ruled on the constitutionality of state laws prohibiting abortion, contraceptive practice was normative, the Court had drawn some forms of sexual expression into the sphere of protected liberties, and sexual matters were an integral part of public culture in the United States. Add to these the facts that abortion had not always been criminalized in the United States (there were no anti-abortion laws at the time the Constitution was written) and that a number of states were already revising their abortion statutes. One can then see *Roe* not as a ruling on the frontier of constitutional law but as firmly located within the realm of common social practice and cultural values.

Thus, neither *Brown* nor *Roe* ought to be seen as decisions that placed the Supreme Court in the vanguard of social change. Instead, both decisions built on strong foundations in American society, culture, and law. They attempted to place a constitutional imprimatur on trends already well under way.

Although this interpretation is commonplace in scholarly writing about this era in American life, it is at odds with what we might call the "folk wisdom" about these decisions. For different reasons, both liberals and conservatives, the left and the right, have an investment in seeing these cases as radically innovative, as ruptures from the past. For progressives who, in recent decades, see themselves increasingly locked out of legislative majorities, the courts have sometimes seemed the last remaining hope for the survival of their political values. What the democratic process no longer seems to provide, the courts still promise. When prejudice, or inertia, or ideology, or electoral outcomes stand in the way, liberals turn to the courts to extend personal liberties and nurture the impulse toward social justice. Liberals applaud this view of the courts, and thus they stake their political capital on defending the courts against conservative encroachments.

Adopting the same view of cases like *Brown* and *Roe*, conservatives and the right condemn what they describe as an activist judiciary. They have used the rhetoric of "judge-made law" as a mobilizing tool to fire up their constituencies and extend their political power. They have had great success in resisting both *Brown* and *Roe*, not in the sense of overturning them but through legislative agendas and popular mobilizations that have significantly narrowed the impact of these decisions. For instance, one might reasonably trace the decline in support for public education, the collapse of tax revenues for it, and the rise of a charter school movement to conservative reaction to court-mandated integration. Likewise, one might also argue that the most significant factor in the consolidation of evangelical Christians as a political force was the Supreme Court's sudden elimination of abortion statutes. And, through its increasing domination of national electoral politics, the conservative right has succeeded wildly in making the federal judiciary more conservative than at any time since the early 1930s.

So, to say it again, liberals and conservatives both have it wrong. Especially when one considers Supreme Court rulings in historic cases, it becomes clear that the Court cannot be relied upon to push the nation in new directions. Instead, it moves and, by implication, shifts with the prevailing winds of history. When judicial decisions do seem to make new law that heads in the direction of justice and equality, they often provoke a sharp political counterreaction. In other words, there are no short cuts to social justice. Justice will come through mass popular mobilizations and the social consensus they imply.

Interestingly, the 2003 decision in *Lawrence v. Texas* confirms both the prevailing misunderstanding of what the Court does and this more modest view of the Court's role. The gay community hailed the ruling as a breakthrough that paved the way for the approval of same-sex marriage. The right denounced the ruling as a travesty that paved the way for the approval of same-sex marriage. Yet, if *Lawrence* tells us anything, it is that the Court takes a measured approach to the cases before it and is reluctant to step far out in front of public opinion and social values. As Justice Kennedy took pains to point out in his opinion, most states had already repealed their sodomy laws, the legal profession had been calling for repeal for a half century, and the European Court of Human Rights had already declared sodomy laws an infringement on basic human rights. Eliminating the remaining ones might easily pass unnoticed in the daily life of Americans. The *Lawrence* case closed out the books on sodomy laws. The Court was not ahead of its time but was catching up to its time.

The Court's decisions in June 2013 invalidating the Defense of Marriage Act and dismissing a challenge to a lower court's overturning of Proposition 8 in California both point to a measured approach to the issue.[38] Taken together, the decisions seemed to be saying, "Let the states decide." Presumably when enough states, through either legislative action or direct voter approval, have enacted laws permitting same-sex marriage, the Court will then intervene to put an end to the remaining prohibitions. How many states are enough, when that will happen, and whether those decisions will provoke successful right-wing mobilizations are all open to debate. But a "final" Supreme Court decision is likely to occur sooner rather than later if strategies shift from litigation to the mass mobilization of a community and its allies.

Moving against the Stream of History: Revolutions Demographic and Sexual

Tactics can be debated and changed. If court decisions provoke a popular reaction in the form of voter referenda that amend constitutions, a movement can try something else. Since 2008, when Proposition 8 in California overturned a court mandate in favor of same-sex marriages, most progress toward achieving marriage rights has come through lobbying and voter mobilization. A few Democrat-controlled, liberal-leaning legislatures have enacted marriage equality, and in three states the LGBT community was well enough organized that it could win marriage at the ballot box. For a few days, the Supreme Court's decisions on DOMA and Prop 8 monopolized the attention of the media and the public, but, day to day, the better part of the work around marriage was now being done by on-the-ground activists busy pursuing legislative routes to success and trying to mobilize mass constituencies.

But let's put the issue of tactics aside. There are other, far more unsettling reasons why prioritizing marriage has disturbed me. One of them I would phrase like this: in the deepest, most profound sense, the increasing primacy of marriage equality as a goal is moving *against history*.

At first glance, this statement might appear puzzling. In many of the marriage cases, for instance, historians have submitted friend-of-the-court briefs and testified in support of marriage equality. They have argued that marriage has been a continually evolving institution. Contrary to what "traditionalists" have claimed, historians have proposed that it is this very flexibility of marriage, its ability to adapt to changing times, that has allowed it to remain vital and relevant. Briefs submitted by historians have outlined major ways that marriage has changed over time: the end of "coverture," which was the legal principle that marriage absorbed a woman's identity into that of her husband, thus denying her rights and autonomy in the political, legal, and economic spheres; the end of laws banning interracial marriage, which had been commonplace for much of US history; and the rise in the 1960s and 1970s of "no-fault" divorce laws that, for the first time, made divorce easy to obtain for couples who wished to end their marriages. Each of these changes, and others like them, constitutes evidence that marriage has become more egalitarian and that it is more and more about the free choice of individuals to make—or to end—a commitment to another individual. From this historical perspective, one could say that marriage naturally evolves. It is no longer primarily about complex kinship networks, property, and inheritance; not primarily about the reproduction of the population; not about economic systems of production; and not about the enforcement of gender hierarchies. Marriage is now about the couple, their relationship, and their loving commitment to one another. So, why not the marriage of same-sex couples? Why not same-sex marriage as one more evolutionary change in the direction of egalitarianism, freedom, and individuality? Wouldn't that flow with the stream of history?

There is another historical trajectory that might point toward a very different set of political and legislative goals. This historical trajectory involves broad and deeply rooted demographic trends. It reflects fundamental shifts in social and economic structures. It stretches back across generations but has become especially apparent over the past fifty years. I am referring to a cluster of interrelated trends that revolve around what sociologists describe as the "deinstitutionalization" or "decentering" of marriage.[39] Over the past half century:

- The age of marriage has risen noticeably. In 1960 two-thirds of Americans in their twenties were married; now, less than one quarter of those in that age cohort are married.
- The divorce rate has dramatically increased. Fifty years ago, divorce was rare and unusual. Now it is commonplace.
- Cohabitation has become a widespread fact of life. From something scandalous and exceptional, it has morphed into a way of living that a majority of those under forty experience, sometimes more than once. The percentage of Americans with children who live together without marrying has risen twelvefold over the past four decades.
- Since 1960 the proportion of children born to unmarried women has increased eightfold, to more than 40 percent. An even larger percentage of children spend a good portion of their years living outside married-parent households.
- In 2010, for the first time, a majority of households in the United States no longer consisted of married couples. Only 20 percent of

all households are married couples with children. Less than half of all adult women live with a husband.

Although a very large proportion of the population still gets married, marriage figures much less centrally in the lives of more and more of us. It is increasingly disconnected, in practice and normatively, from childbearing and childrearing. Instead of marriage as the primary framework of life for adults and children, the living arrangements of heterosexual Americans have become bewilderingly varied. Over the course of a lifetime, an individual might move in with a partner; break up and find another partner; get married; have a child; get divorced; cohabit with someone else who also had a child (or didn't); break up again; cohabit again; marry again and become a stepparent. Throughout all this, every adult in this saga is likely to have been working for a living.

A succinct way of describing these changes is this: since the 1960s the lives of many, many heterosexuals have become much more like the imagined lives of homosexuals. Being heterosexual no longer means settling as a very young adult into a lifelong coupled relationship sanctioned by the state and characterized by the presence of children and sharply gendered spousal roles. Instead, there may be a number of intimate relationships over the course of a lifetime. A marriage certificate may or may not accompany these relationships. Males and females alike expect to spend their adult lives in the paid labor force. Children figure less importantly in the lifespan of adults, and some heterosexuals, for the first time in history, choose not to have children at all.

These changes are not aberrational, not temporary, and not reversible. Neither a decline in morality nor the cultural turbulence of the 1960s explains them. They were not caused by media that exploit sex. Instead, these changes are joined at the hip with long-term changes provoked by capitalist economics. As everything we need and consume in life has become something that has to be bought, virtually every adult has been forced into the labor pool. Not to work for wages is to be pushed into a life of poverty and hardship. Children are an economic burden, not an asset. Women's labor force participation is now virtually identical to that of men, with profound effects on whether, why, and when women marry and whether, why, and when they stay married.

These new "lifestyles" (a word woefully inadequate for grasping the deep structural foundations that sustain these changes) have appeared

253

everywhere that capitalism has long, historical roots. The decline in reproductive rates and the decentering of marriage have followed the spread of capitalism as surely as night follows day. They surface even in the face of religious traditions and national histories that have emphasized marriage, high fertility, and strong kinship ties.

If one needs more evidence that the new shape of social life is not a passing heterosexual phase, look at the dramatic failure of efforts to reverse these trends. Since the mid-1970s the most dynamic and aggressive force in American politics has been the evangelical Christian right. It has had the numbers, the money, the organization, and the passion that gay and lesbian organizations only dream of having. It can send people into voting booths like no other constituency in the United States. Evangelical conservatives have made issues of family and sexual morality the centerpiece of their message and mobilization. Because of them, abortions have become harder to get, an abstinence-only message has come to dominate sex-education curricula, and premarital counseling and vows of chastity have become widespread in certain sectors of the population. Yet, despite all this, the birth rate remains low, the young are still having sex and cohabiting, and divorce is commonplace.

Grasping the revolutionary change in the lives of heterosexuals in the past half century lets us put a whole different spin on the transformation in the status of gays and lesbians in the United States in the same time period. The huge steps toward visibility, acceptance, integration, and equality—and they have been huge—have come, fundamentally, because the life cycle of heterosexuals has become more like ours. We have made gains not because we have shown heterosexuals that we are just like them or because we have persuaded them to respect our "differences" but because many of them have become so much like us, or at least like what they imagined us to be, that they find us less threatening, less dangerous, and less strange. In other words, for the past several decades, our lives have been flowing with the most powerful currents of social, cultural, and economic change. We have been swimming with history, not against it.

Thus, the problem with the marriage issue is much more than a matter of unwise tactics that primarily helped a reactionary political force to coalesce, mobilize, and create another set of antigay laws that then had to be dealt with. The issue itself could be considered socially regressive, as well. In view of the real experience of more and more Americans, why are we not instigating broad-based campaigns to multiply the forms of family that receive recognition and institutional support? Why sustain a form of distributing to individuals benefits that rely on marital status—pensions, health insurance, survivor benefits, and the like—when that will exclude more and more Americans? Why not mount campaigns that move with the main currents of history and formalize the decentering of marriage that is occurring in practice? Wouldn't that advance equality and justice in more meaningful and expansive ways?[40]

Interestingly, almost all of the countries that first legalized same-sex marriage are nations that have already largely decoupled benefits and marriage. Could it be that the fastest way to marriage equality would have been to reduce the legal consequences of marriage to little more than a public expression of love?

A Question of Values

Proponents of same-sex marriage have presented their case as one rooted in values. The issue, they claim, is a clear matter of justice. Marriage is not just a public expression of love and commitment between two individuals. Instead, since the 1930s, public policy has made it a key vector for the distribution of benefits. One statement that circulated widely after Congress passed the Defense of Marriage Act, in 1996, was that there were something like 1,056 different federal benefits that marriage brought, and same-sex couples were excluded from all of these. So, yes, one can say that same-sex marriage is a matter of justice and equality.

But the matter is not so simple. In making marriage *equality* a central and overriding goal, the mainstream gay and lesbian movement has aligned itself with privilege and *inequality* on so many levels and in so many ways that it is staggering. Values that put the privileged first and that confirm privilege and inequality are everywhere to be seen in the campaigns.

Perhaps a place to start is with an observation about identity-based movements. In a *New Yorker* review of *When Everything Changed*, a history of the revolution in women's lives since the 1960s by Gail Collins, Ariel Levy made this striking observation: "Identity politics isn't much concerned with abstract ideals, like justice. It's a version of the spoils systems . . . try to get a bigger slice of the resources that are being allocated."[41] Or to put it the way that I do in classroom lectures: history teaches us that the benefits of identity movements are always unequally distributed. Movements based on racial and ethnic identities have won rights for all members of their group, but they have especially made it possible for some members of the group to climb the ladder of class privilege, leaving most others behind. The women's movement and the gay and lesbian movement have won rights for all women and all lesbians and gay men, but they have especially made it possible for some members of the group, especially those unencumbered by the weight of racial and class oppression, to climb the ladder of class privilege, leaving most others behind. The benefits of identity movements are not equally distributed.

To see this playing out of privilege in the campaigns for same-sex marriage requires a shift away from the rhetoric used by activists fighting for the right to marry. Rather than thinking of marriage for same-sex couples as providing access to benefits currently denied them, it might be more accurate and revealing to think of access to marriage as validating and sustaining privilege that one already has. Why do I claim that? Because marriage is not something randomly distributed across the population, with finding one's life partner or soul mate being the key factor in whether one marries. Instead, those least likely to marry are those nearest the bottom of the economic and educational pyramid; those most likely to marry are those with higher economic status and educational attainment. Marriage penalizes those who are struggling economically. For low-income families, marriage makes it harder to get access to public benefits. When working-class marriages end in divorce, the economic impact on adults and children is often devastating. By contrast, those who already enjoy the benefits of high economic status and educational attainment have many of the benefits that marriage allegedly brings. Marriage simply confirms and extends their already privileged status. A front-page *New York Times* headline in 2012 put it very succinctly: "Two Classes, Divided by 'I Do.' Marriage, for Richer."[42]

Values rooted in privilege come into play in so many ways in the campaigns for same-sex marriage. The issue was, for a decade and a half, prioritized and pushed forward primarily by organizations of lawyers rather than by grassroots organizations that mobilize communities. Despite the massive avalanche of antigay legislation that their cases provoked, legal organizations refused to give up on the issue because it proved to be, as one key legal activist told me, "a cash cow" for these organizations. The issue has been funded by the wealthy, by very large donors, and by foundations set up by wealthy Americans who have made marriage their cause. Many, notably, are Republicans who, the marriage issue aside, support a political party and candidates notorious for their commitment to deepening class inequality as well as policies that are overtly racist, sexist, and homophobic.[43]

Many of the arguments that proponents make for same-sex marriage and many of the examples used to demonstrate how wrong the lack of access to marriage is are rooted in class privilege. For instance, the *New York Times* ran a front-page article in 2009 on the cost to same-sex couples of being unable to marry. The reporters played out a variety of scenarios, but the bottom line was this: they made their case on the basis of a couple with a household income of $140,000 a year, a figure significantly above the medium income in the United States.[44] The Williams Institute of UCLA, perhaps the preeminent think tank in the United States on gay and lesbian issues, released a study showing the impact of the federal estate tax on same-sex couples. It reported that seventy-three same-sex couples pay, on average, $3.3 million a year more in federal taxes than would comparable heterosexual couples.[45] Is this unfair? Absolutely. Is it relevant to the 99 percent of us? No.

Then there are the ways that the marriage issue, in its unacknowledged and often unaware attachment to privilege, has a corrupting influence on academic research. For instance, almost every time there is a court decision or a legislative battle about same-sex marriage in a state, the Williams Institute releases a study, accompanied by a press release, announcing the economic benefits that the legalization of same-sex marriage will bring to that state. It provides statistics on the spending associated with the estimated number of yearly weddings of same-sex couples, the benefits that will accrue to local businesses, and the estimated sales tax revenues this will add to a state's treasury. The cost of failing to enact same-sex marriage, these studies are telling state legislators, is very high. In other words, the route to liberation has become the path of consumerist excess associated with the contemporary wedding industry.[46] In an effort to support the fight for access to marriage, the Gay and Lesbian Medical Association released a report in 2008, "Same-Sex Marriage and Health." "Dubious" would be a generous characterization of the claims it made that existing research demonstrated that marriage would improve the health of lesbians and gay men.[47]

Or take the way that marriage equality is often portrayed as something that must be pursued for the sake of children raised by same-sex couples. Almost every time I have spoken on the marriage issue in a form that expresses my skepticism about it, someone will raise his or her hand in the question-and-answer period and pointedly ask me, "Are you a parent?" When I say no, thereby presumably demonstrating that I am in no position to talk about the issue, the person who asked the question proceeds to explain how hard it is on kids to come from a family in which the parents can never marry. Or, in the words of the teenage son of two lesbians, after a court ruled against Prop 8 in California, "my family is finally normal."[48] I read statements like this, and I cringe. I hear the comments of parents in public forums, and I am frankly horrified at the values that are being supported. In an America where two out of five children are born to women who are not married and where an absolute majority of children spend a significant portion of their lives in households without two married parents, what moral logic would lead one to validate as normal and good only a family form that only a fraction of our children get to enjoy? Why are we not celebrating as a value the goodness of a broad variety of family structures and attempting to create public policy that affirms such variety? Instead, we have opted to open the gates of privilege to just a few more "normal" families.

A final example of what I consider the perverse values generated by the marriage issue involves what it has done to the rhetoric of the movement. The examples I could muster are legion, but here are two. Late in 2009, when the New Jersey legislature was considering bills related to the rights of same-sex couples, Steven Goldstein, head of Garden State Equality, told the press, "If we win marriage equality, it would be the fulfillment of our American dream. It would mean equality. This is really our lives on the line."[49] More recently, when President Obama declared that he supported marriage equality, Chad Griffin, the head of the Human Rights Campaign, announced solemnly, "For the millions of young gay and lesbian Americans across this nation, President Obama's words provide genuine hope that they will be the first generation to grow up with the freedom to fully pursue the American dream . . . the fight to secure marriage equality is the defining element of our generation's search for greater freedom."[50]

Rhetoric like this is not merely hyperbolic and stupid. It is dangerous. It encourages the belief that the marriage fight is the final battle and that we can all go home when it is over. Worse, it supports the strategic assessment that other issues are inconsequential. Take HIV/AIDS, for instance. For some, it has become quite inconsequential. If one is privileged enough to have a secure and generous health insurance plan that provides access to the latest extremely expensive treatment regimens, HIV infection is a manageable chronic condition. But, if you do not have those privileges,

HIV is an issue, unlike marriage, that really does put lives on the line. Or, if you are a well-educated female or male couple in your thirties or forties and have just gotten married, you probably do not carry in your sights the treacherous terrain in which many queer youth travel. Many are coming out at ever younger ages, when they are quite vulnerable to schools and peers—and sometimes parents—who are still deeply homophobic. If the resources and attention that have been expended on same-sex marriage in the past twenty years had been devoted instead to issues of youth, the schools, and the fight for comprehensive sex education curricula, we would be close to having homophobia pulled up by its roots. But, instead, the money has flowed to expensive legal campaigns and has had to be spent on ballot measures for an issue that, while emotionally powerful for many, is not at the structural foundation of homophobia and gay oppression.

The Power of Love

In the past decade, the marriage issue has eclipsed all other queer issues. It dominates public discussion; it dominates fund-raising appeals from organizations; it dominates the allocation of scarce resources. For all the reasons I have outlined, this state of affairs disturbs me greatly. The arguments against prioritizing the right to marry are so obvious to me, so easy to see, that I wonder why they are not obvious to everyone else. Am I delusional? Is there something consequential that I am missing?

There is something else to consider, something else of substance, though it is not substantial enough to make me shift my point of view about the campaign and the issue. Let me illustrate it with a story from the classroom.

In 1999, when the marriage issue had not yet risen to the prominence it now has, I began teaching at the University of Illinois at Chicago, in its Gender and Women's Studies Program. For the first time, I had the opportunity to teach undergraduate courses on gay and lesbian issues. In particular I was responsible for one titled "Sexuality and Community." It was intended to be a "Queer 101" class that introduces students to a range of issues and situates sexual and gender identity in contemporary society and culture.

As is always the case with a new course, the first time I taught it I scrambled to pull together a syllabus. I was looking for something to use on marriage. I had heard good things about *Chicks in White Satin*, a documentary film about two women who choose to have a public commitment ceremony—a wedding—in order to celebrate publicly their relationship. I did not have time to view the film before the semester started but took the good reviews on faith and included it.

The night before we were to see the film in class, I viewed it at home. I was appalled. I thought it was awful. It was short and chaotic. It jumped from scene to scene. The filmmakers could not even seem to hold the camera steady. I watched it thinking, "This is the worst piece of filmmaking I have ever seen!" But it was too late to come up with something different before our class met, and I resigned myself to the fact that it would not be one of our more successful meetings.

The next day, sitting in class with the lights out and watching the film again, I was astounded by the reactions of students. As the climax approached, more and more students were sobbing. Even some of the straight dudes were teary-eyed. The expressions of love, the conflicts with homophobic family members, the exchange of vows, the coming around of the mother of one of the lesbians, the dancing at the party afterward: all of it provoked intense emotional reactions. The amateurish filmmaking style that I had decried the night before now seemed like pure brilliance to me. The director had chosen to imitate the rough-edged style of home movies and videos, which of course is the way that most of us have seen family weddings. Since that first showing in class, I have become a great promoter of the film. I show it every time I teach the course, and it continues to provoke strong emotional reactions. Almost twenty years after it was made, *Chicks in White Satin* still works.

What lesson do I take from this, and how is this experience relevant to the campaign for access to marriage? We live in a culture in which we all are in love with "love." We yearn for love. We celebrate love. We give ourselves permission publicly to shed tears of joy for love.

On a wedding day, love joins not only the couple but the couple's whole world. Family members, friends, coworkers, neighbors, and anyone else connected to the couple get to join in the warm, fuzzy feeling of celebrating this public expression of a love meant to last forever. Weddings create bonds of identification, in this case between heterosexuals and homosexuals, in a way that few other things do. Job discrimination, the military exclusion policy, police raids of our bars and clubs, homophobic violence: none of these issues has rallied heterosexuals to our side in the way that marriage has. (The only comparable example I can think of is death, and, interestingly, AIDS for a time was the other issue that won over large numbers of heterosexual allies.)

What I have just said is almost never articulated in the same-sex marriage debate. Instead, proponents almost always frame it in terms of the benefits or describe it as a necessary and critical component of legal equality and full citizenship status. But, in truth, the benefits are not what drive the marriage fight. Nor is it about the legal status. It is about the power of love as an emotion to overcome the social divisions generated by homophobia and heteronormativity. And it is about the power of emotion, for better or worse, to overwhelm anything that resembles rational, intelligent thinking about political goals, priorities, and strategies. As a movement and a community, we could most likely have achieved the gains against homophobia if, like the lesbian couple in *Chicks in White Satin*, those of us in couples had all held a wedding and invited everyone we knew. In the meantime, we could have apportioned our resources toward the issues and campaigns that might have far more meaningfully challenged the oppressive, systemic inequalities that marriage will never touch.

Conclusion

Marriage equality will come. Whether it comes in five years, as some movement leaders were predicting after the Supreme Court rulings on DOMA and Proposition 8, or more distantly, after ballot initiatives or legislative action in many more states create a tipping point that induces another Supreme Court ruling, it will happen. It will happen in good part because marriage has declined in importance over the past two generations. When it does happen, it will not prove to be the final resting point on the long road to equality or the demise of homophobia and gay oppression. More than anything, it will mean that the heterosexual possessors of cultural, social, and economic privilege have opened their doors so that their gay and lesbian counterparts may enter as well. And, by the time it does happen, marriage equality will have consumed a huge amount of resources, from the labor of activists to the many tens of millions of dollars spent on the court cases, voter mobilizations, and lobbying campaigns.

Progressive queers need to be asking ourselves now, before marriage equality arrives, what will follow. How do we counter the message, which is already spreading, that marriage is the final fight? How can we take advantage of the political energy released in the course of the marriage battles so that we channel it beyond marriage to issues that will have a more substantial impact on the quest for justice, fairness, and equality? Are there issues that we can now be preparing and pushing so that we are well placed to take advantage of a post-marriage vacuum? Or, is it possible that the marriage campaign will have so mainstreamed "gay," so denuded it of its critical possibilities, that gay activism as a route to social and economic justice will be . . . history? Only time will tell.

Acknowledgments

Although in one sense these essays grow out of decades of research, writing, teaching, and social justice activism, they are also very much rooted in the experience and relationships of the past decade, during which I have lived in Chicago and taught at the University of Illinois at Chicago (UIC). There are many people from this stretch of time who deserve my thanks.

At UIC, I have been blessed with a succession of student assistants, both graduate and undergraduate, who have brought great skill and lots of enthusiasm to their work, thereby facilitating my research and writing in more ways than they know. Huge thanks go to Katie Batza, Vanessa Soleil, Lara Kelland, Zaiquiri Blair, Gabrielle Anderson, Stephen Seely, Jason Stodolka, Cat Jacquet, and Boyd Bellinger.

For many years, Mary Beth Rose and Linda Vavra have been the team that has made the Institute for the Humanities at UIC a splendid place for research, thinking, discussion, and writing. My two fellowship years there, one to work on the Bayard Rustin biography and another to work on Chicago's history, were extremely productive, in no small part due to them.

Thanks also go to Tracy Baim, the publisher and editor of *Windy City Times*, for giving me a community platform for my writing about episodes in Chicago's LGBT history. Mandy Carter's work with the National Black Justice Coalition, planning a ton of events around the country for the bicentennial of Bayard Rustin's birth, gave me opportunities to speak on Rustin and to consider the lessons his life offers today. Thanks specifically to Megan Carney and Martha Lang for the invitations to deliver keynote addresses at conferences on Rustin at UIC and Guilford College, respectively. And then, of course, there is Sue Hyde, conference organizer extraordinaire. For almost three decades she has been the driving force behind the Creating Change Conference of the National Gay and Lesbian Task Force. Invitations from her to address plenary sessions in 2005 and 2009 pushed me to pull together my thinking about the state of the LGBT movement in the twenty-first century.

My thanks also go to those editors who have invited me to contribute to a number of anthologies on history, social movements, and LGBT politics: Jill Austin, Nan Alamilla Boyd, Jennifer Brier, Jim Downs, H. N. Hirsch, Christopher Phelps, Craig Rimmerman, Horacio N. Roque Ramírez, and Clyde Wilcox. A special word of thanks goes to Richard Schneider, the long-time and amazing editor of the *Gay and Lesbian Review Worldwide*, who has consistently welcomed my contributions.

From the beginning, the University of Wisconsin Press has been a pleasure to deal with, and its staff has encouraged and facilitated my work on this volume. I especially want to thank Raphael Kadushin, Matthew Cosby, and Sheila McMahon.

Then there are the close friends and comrades whose support, conversations, intellectual insight, and affection make it possible for me to do the work I do: Ruth Eisenberg, A. Finn Enke, Nan Enstad, Estelle Freedman, Bert Hansen, Amber Hollibaugh, Jonathan Ned Katz, and Urvashi Vaid. Thank you all!

Finally, to Jim Oleson, my partner of more than thirty years, who has seen me through every book and every job change and every move: you're the best, and I'm so lucky. Thank you for every day that we have had together.

Notes

Chapter 6. Putting Sex into History and History into Sex

1. See Mary McIntosh, "The Homosexual Role," *Social Problems* 16 (1968): 182–92; Jeffrey Weeks, *Coming Out: Homosexual Politics in Britain from the Nineteenth Century to the Present* (London: Quartet, 1977); Kenneth Plummer, ed., *The Making of the Modern Homosexual* (London: Hutchinson, 1981); Jonathan Ned Katz, *Gay American History* (New York: Crowell, 1976); Esther Newton, *Mother Camp: Female Impersonators in America* (Chicago: University of Chicago Press, 1972); and Allan Bérubé, *Coming Out under Fire: The History of Gay Men and Women in World War II* (New York: Free Press, 1990).

2. Ann Snitow, Christine Stansell, and Sharon Thompson, eds., *Powers of Desire* (New York: Monthly Review Press, 1983), and Carole Vance, *Pleasure and Danger* (Boston: Routledge and Kegan Paul, 1984).

3. Jacquelyn Dowd Hall, "The Long Civil Rights Movement and the Political Uses of the Past," *Journal of American History* 91, no. 4 (March 2005): 1233.

Chapter 7. History, Social Movements, and Community Organizing

1. Amin Ghaziani, *The Dividends of Dissent* (Chicago: University of Chicago Press, 2008).

2. George Chauncey Jr., *Gay New York* (New York: Basic Books, 1994), and John Howard, *Men Like That* (Chicago: University of Chicago Press, 1999).

Chapter 8. If I Knew Then

1. *Sexual Politics, Sexual Communities: The Making of a Homosexual Minority in the United States, 1940–1970* (Chicago: University of Chicago Press, 1983; 2nd ed., 1998), and *Lost Prophet: The Life and Times of Bayard Rustin* (New York: Free Press, 2003).

2. See Jim Kepner, *Rough News, Daring Views: 1950's Pioneer Gay Press Journalism* (Binghamton, NY: Haworth Press, 1997).

3. See, for example, Nan Alamilla Boyd, *Wide Open Town: A History of Queer San Francisco to 1965* (Berkeley: University of California Press, 2003); Marcia M. Gallo, *Different Daughters: A History of the Daughters of Bilitis and the Rise of the Lesbian Rights Movement* (New York: Carroll and Graf, 2006); Martin Meeker, *Contacts Desired: Gay and Lesbian Communications and Community, 1940s–1970s* (Chicago: University of Chicago Press, 2006); and Marc Stein, *City of Brotherly and Sisterly Loves: Lesbian and Gay Philadelphia, 1945–1972* (Chicago: University of Chicago Press, 2000).

4. "Dreams Deferred: The Birth and Betrayal of America's First Gay Liberation Movement," in *Making Trouble: Essays on Gay History, Politics, and the University* (New York: Routledge, 1992), 55. The essay originally appeared in *The Body Politic* in February 1979.

5. Elizabeth Lapofsky Kennedy and Madeline Davis, *Boots of Leather, Slippers of Gold: The History of a Lesbian Community* (New York: Routledge, 1993).

6. Twin Cities GLBT Oral History Project, *Queer Twin Cities* (Minneapolis: University of Minnesota Press, 2010).

Chapter 22. Remembering Bayard Rustin

1. Jacquelyn Dowd Hall, "The Long Civil Rights Movement and the Political Uses of the Past," *Journal of American History* 91, no. 4 (March 2005): 1233.

2. Susanna McBee, "Organizer of D.C. March Is Devoted to Non-Violence," *Washington Post*, August 11, 1963, A6; *Life*, September 6, 1963.

3. Details about Rustin's career in this and the following paragraphs come from my biography of Rustin, *Lost Prophet: The Life and Times of Bayard Rustin* (New York: Free Press, 2003). The quotation comes from my interview with David McReynolds, now on deposit at the Swarthmore College Peace Collection.

4. John Lewis with Michael D'Orso, *Walking with the Wind: A Memoir of the Movement* (New York: Simon & Schuster, 1998), 217.

5. Reminiscences of Bayard Rustin: Oral History, 1987, Columbia University Oral History Collection.

6. Quoted in *Lost Prophet*, 180.

7. Ibid., 71.

8. David K. Johnson, *The Lavender Scare: The Cold War Persecution of Gays and Lesbians in the Federal Government* (Chicago: University of Chicago Press, 2004).

Chapter 24. Some Lessons from *Lawrence*

1. *Lawrence v. Texas*, 539 U.S. 558 (2003). For a recent history of the case, see Dale Carpenter, *Flagrant Conduct: The Story of "Lawrence v. Texas"* (New York: W. W. Norton, 2012).

2. *New York Times*, June 27, 2003, p. 1.

3. Alan Bray, *Homosexuality in Renaissance England* (London: Gay Men's Press, 1982), 114.

4. Evan Thomas, "The War over Gay Marriage," *Newsweek*, July 7, 2003, pp. 38–45.

5. *San Francisco Chronicle*, June 29, 2003, p. A4.

6. Chad Graham, "Changing History," *Advocate*, January 20, 2004, pp. 36–39.

7. Lisa Leff, "Gays Joyful, Relieved over Court Ruling," Associated Press, June 26, 2003, as distributed over lgbt-politics@yahoogroups.com, accessed June 26, 2003.

8. *Los Angeles Times*, June 27, 2003, p. A31.

9. Ibid.

10. Thomas, "The War over Gay Marriage."

11. Ted Olson and Todd Hertz, "Opinion Roundup: Does *Lawrence v. Texas* Signal the End of the American Family," *Christianity Today*, June 30, 2003, http://www.christianity today.com/ct/2003/juneweb-only/6-30-11.0.html, accessed September 22, 2013.

12. Quoted in National Gay and Lesbian Task Force, "Know Thy Enemy: A Compendium of Recent Quotes about the Supreme Court Sodomy Ruling and the Same-Sex Marriage Backlash," July 30, 2003.

13. *Lawrence v. Texas*.

14. *Newsweek*, July 7, 2003.

15. Graham, "Changing History."

16. *New York Times*, November 19, 2003, p. A24.

17. *Los Angeles Times*, June 28, 2003, p. A21.

18. *Lawrence v. Texas*.

19. Ibid.

20. Ibid.

21. *Bowers v. Hardwick*, 478 U.S. 186 (1986).

22. Ibid.

23. The "Brief of Professors of History" may be found under the title "The Historians' Case against Gay Discrimination," July 3, 2003, http://hnn.us/articles/1539.

24. Ibid.

25. Ibid.

26. *Lawrence v. Texas*.

27. *Roth v. United States*, 354 U.S. 476 (1957).

28. *Griswold v. Connecticut*, 381 U.S. 479 (1965).

29. *Eisenstadt v. Baird*, 405 U.S. 438 (1972).

30. *Lawrence v. Texas*.

31. Ibid.

32. Ibid.

Chapter 25. Rethinking Queer History

1. The Stonewall raid and subsequent rioting have been treated at great length. One of the earliest accounts is in Donn Teal, *The Gay Militants* (New York: Stein & Day, 1971).

The most detailed account is David Carter, *Stonewall: The Riots That Sparked the Gay Revolution* (New York: St. Martin's, 2004). Other discussions include Dudley Clendinen and Adam Nagourney, *Out for Good: The Struggle to Build a Gay Rights Movement in America* (New York: Simon & Schuster, 1999); Martin Duberman, *Stonewall* (New York: Dutton, 1999); and David Eisenbach, *Gay Power: An American Revolution* (New York: Carroll & Graf, 2006). For a description written soon after the events, see *New York Mattachine Society Newsletter*, July 1969, pp. 21–25.

2. Jerald E. Podair, *The Strike That Changed New York: Blacks, Whites, and the Oceanhill-Brownsville Crisis* (New Haven, CT: Yale University Press, 2002).

3. For coverage of the student protests at the City College of New York, see *New York Times*, April 23, 1969, p. 31; April 26, 1969, p. 15; April 27, 1969, p. 66; April 29, 1969, p. 30; April 30, 1969, p. 28; May 8, 1969, p. 46; May 9, 1969, p. 28; May 16, 1969, p. 50; May 17, 1969, p. 31; and May 19, 1969, p. 33.

4. See the works cited in note 1, this chapter.

5. *New York Times*, April 8, 2009, p. 20.

6. For accounts of what followed in the years after Stonewall, see Teal, *The Gay Militants*, and Clendinen and Nagourney, *Out for Good*. See also Dennis Altman, *Homosexual Oppression and Liberation* (New York: Avon, 1971); Sidney Abbott and Barbara Love, *Sappho Was a Right-On Woman* (New York: Stein & Day, 1972); Toby Marotta, *The Politics of Homosexuality* (Boston: Houghton Mifflin, 1981); and Chris Bull, ed., *Witness to Revolution: The "Advocate" Reports on Gay and Lesbian Politics* (Los Angeles: Alyson Books, 1999).

7. On these older discourses and the early efforts of academics to respond to gay liberation, see *The Universities and the Gay Experience: A Conference Sponsored by the Women and Men of the Gay Academic Union* (New York: Gay Academic Union, 1974). A scanned version of these proceedings can be found online at http://www.rainbowhistory.org/pdf/73 conference.pdf, accessed September 8, 2013.

8. Martin Bauml Duberman, Martha Vicinus, and George Chauncey Jr., eds., *Hidden from History: Reclaiming the Gay and Lesbian Past* (New York: New American Library, 1989). On the rhetoric used by gay liberationists and lesbian feminists, see Karla Jay and Allen Young, eds., *Out of the Closets: Voices of Gay Liberation*, 20th Anniversary Ed. (New York: New York University Press, 1992). For examples of historians referencing this rhetoric, see John D'Emilio, "Capitalism and Gay Identity," in *Powers of Desire: The Politics of Sexuality*, ed. Ann Snitow, Christine Stansell, and Sharon Thompson (New York: Monthly Review Press, 1983), 100–112, and George Chauncey, *Gay New York: Gender, Urban Culture, and the Making of the Gay Male World, 1890–1940* (New York: Basic Books, 1994). An important early effort by an activist to research and present history is Jonathan Katz, *Coming Out!* (New York: Arno Press, 1975), a play based on historical documents that played in cities around the United States in the early and mid-1970s. Katz eventually developed this into the influential documentary collection *Gay American History: Lesbians and Gay Men in the U.S.A.* (New York: Thomas Crowell, 1976).

9. John D'Emilio, *Sexual Politics, Sexual Communities: The Making of a Homosexual Minority in the United States, 1940–1970* (Chicago: University of Chicago Press, 1983).

10. Other discussions of the homophile movement include Marcia Gallo, *Different Daughters: A History of the Daughers of Bilitis and the Rise of the Lesbian Rights Movement* (New York: Carroll & Graf, 2006); Martin Meeker, *Contacts Desired: Gay and Lesbian Communications and Community, 1940s–1970s* (Chicago: University of Chicago Press, 2006); David K. Johnson, *The Lavender Scare: The Cold War Persecutions of Gays and Lesbians in the Federal Government* (Chicago: University of Chicago Press, 2004); Nan Alamilla Boyd, *Wide Open Town: A History of Queer San Francisco to 1965* (Berkeley: University of California Press, 2003); and Marc Stein, *City of Brotherly and Sisterly Loves: Lesbian and Gay Philadelphia, 1945–1972* (Chicago: University of Chicago Press, 2000).

11. Elizabeth Lapovsky Kennedy and Madeline D. Davis, *Boots of Leather, Slippers of Gold: The History of a Lesbian Community* (New York: Routledge, 1993).

12. Other community studies include Esther Newton, *Cherry Grove, Fire Island: Sixty Years in America's First Gay and Lesbian Town* (Boston: Beacon Press, 1993); Stein, *City of Brotherly and Sisterly Love*; Boyd, *Wide Open Town*; and Brett Beemyn, ed., *Creating a Place for Ourselves: Lesbian, Gay, and Bisexual Community Histories* (New York: Routledge, 1997).

13. Allan Bérubé, *Coming Out under Fire: The History of Gay Men and Women in World War II* (New York: Free Press, 1990).

14. Eric Garber, "A Spectacle in Color: The Lesbian and Gay Subculture of Jazz Age Harlem," in Duberman, Vicinus, and Chauncey, *Hidden from History*, 318–31.

15. Linda Gordon, *Heroes of Their Own Lives: The Politics and History of Family Violence, Boston 1880–1960* (New York: Viking, 1988).

16. Boyd, *Wide Open Town*.

17. John Howard, *Men Like That: A Southern Queer History* (Chicago: University of Chicago Press, 1999).

18. Some examples of books that use Chicago, either wholly or as a key recurring example, are Arnold Hirsch, *Making the Second Ghetto: Race and Housing in Chicago, 1940–1960* (Chicago: University of Chicago Press, 1983); Robin Bachin, *Building the South Side: Urban Space and Civic Culture in Chicago, 1890–1919* (Chicago: University of Chicago Press, 2004); Margaret Garb, *City of American Dreams: A History of Home Ownership and Housing Reform in Chicago, 1871–1919* (Chicago: University of Chicago Press, 2005); Adam Green, *Selling the Race: Culture, Community, and Black Chicago, 1940–1955* (Chicago: University of Chicago Press, 2007); James Grossman, *Land of Hope: Chicago, Black Southerners, and the Great Migration* (Chicago: University of Chicago Press, 1989); Lizabeth Cohen, *Making a New Deal: Industrial Workers in Chicago, 1919–1939* (New York: Cambridge University Press, 1990).

19. See David K. Johnson, "The Kids of Fairytown: Gay Male Culture on Chicago's Near North Side in the 1930s," and Allen Drexel, "Before Paris Burned: Race, Class, and Male Homosexuality on the Chicago South Side, 1935–1960," both in *Creating a Place for Ourselves: Lesbian, Gay, and Bisexual Community Histories*, ed. Brett Beemyn (New York: Routledge, 1997), 97–145.

20. See Chris Albertson, *Bessie* (New Haven, CT: Yale University Press, 2003); Stephen Bourne, *Ethel Waters: Stormy Weather* (Lanham, MD: Scarecrow Press, 2007); Sandra Lieb, *Mother of the Blues: A Study of Ma Rainey* (Amherst: University of Massachusetts Press, 1981); and Frank C. Taylor, *Alberta Hunter: A Celebration in Blues* (New York: McGraw-Hill, 1987).

21. Angela Y. Davis, *Blues Legacies and Black Feminism* (New York: Vintage Paperback, 1999), 3–4, 8.

22. Lyrics in ibid., 200.

23. *Chicago Defender*, February 18, 1928, p. 7.

24. Lyrics in Davis, *Blues Legacies*, 238. For the ad, see *Chicago Defender*, September 22, 1928, p. 7.

25. Quote from *Chicago Defender*, October 22, 1938, p. 19.

26. On the Cabin Inn, see *Chicago Defender*, March 30, 1935, p. 8; May 1, 1937, p. 20; July 10, 1937, p. 10; and May 28, 1938, p. 19.

27. *Chicago Defender*, December 26, 1936, pp. 3, 20.

28. For examples of the language used, see *Chicago Tribune*, March 26, 1950, p. 5; March 30, 1950, p. 1; July 27, 1950, p. 14; and October 5, 1951, p. 15.

29. On Chicago's earliest history of cross-dressing laws, see William N. Eskridge Jr., *Gaylaw: Challenging the Apartheid of the Closet* (Cambridge, MA: Harvard University Press, 1999), 27–28. The city council amended the law so that it prohibited cross-dressing only for the purpose of concealment in 1943. See *Chicago Tribune*, January 9, 1943, p. 1; January 21, 1943, p. 3; and January 26, 1943, p. 9.

30. On the killing of James Clay, see *Chicago Defender*, November 28, 1970, p. 1, and *Chicago Sun-Times*, November 26, 1970, p. 46.

31. *Chicago Tribune*, August 31, 1973, p. 1.

32. *Chicago Tribune*, January 10, 1949, p. 1; January 22, 1949, p. 9; February 5, 1949, p. 4.

33. *Chicago Tribune*, December 31, 1951, p. B7.

34. *Chicago Tribune*, March 27, 1962, p. B5.

35. *Chicago Sunday Sun-Times*, April 26, 1964, p. 1, and *Chicago's Sunday American*, April 26, 1964, p. 1.

36. *Chicago Tribune*, August 16, 1973, p. 2.

37. *Mattachine Midwest Newsletter*, December 1966, p. 3, copy in Gerber/Hart Library, Chicago.

38. Ibid. For examples of other discussions of the police, see *Mattachine Midwest Newsletter*, April 1966, p. 7–8; May 1966, p. 4; July 1966, p. 3; and August 1966, p. 3. For an account of the work of the Mattachine Midwest, see John D. Poling, "Standing Up for Gay Rights," *Chicago History* 33 (Spring 2005): 4–17, and Poling's master's essay, "Mattachine Midwest: The History of a Chicago Gay Rights Organization, 1965 to 1986," Department of History, Illinois State University, 2002.

39. Accounts of activism in the early 1970s can be found in *Chicago Gay Liberation Newsletter* and *Chicago Gay Alliance Newsletter*, both in Gerber/Hart Library, Chicago.

40. Mike Royko, *Boss: Richard J. Daley of Chicago* (1971; reprint, New York: Plume Books, 1988), 125, and Adam Cohen and Elizabeth Taylor, *American Pharaoh: Mayor Richard J. Daley, His Battle for Chicago and the Nation* (New York: Little Brown, 2000), 7.

41. *Chicago Tribune*, December 31, 1972, p. 1; May 14, 1972, p. 1; November 22, 1972, p. 5.

42. *Chicago Tribune*, August 16, 1973, p. 2.

43. *Chicago Tribune*, May 10, 1967, p. 1.

44. *Chicago Defender*, January 5, 1970, pp. 1, 3; *Chicago Tribune*, May 16, 1970, pp. W2, W6; *Chicago Defender*, August 25, 1971, pp. 1–2; *Chicago Tribune*, August 25, 1971, pp. 1, 12.

45. *Chicago Tribune*, October 28, 1972, p. 1.

46. *Chicago Tribune*, November 22, 1972, p. 5, and December 31, 1972, p. 1.

47. *Chicago Sun-Times*, December 29, 1972, p. 1.

48. *U.S. v. Braasch*, 505 F. 2d 139.

49. *Chicago Tribune*, October 11, 1973, p. 6.

Chapter 26. The Campaign for Marriage Equality

1. *New York Times*, May 7, 1993, p. 14.

2. See, for instance, such texts as Theodore Roszak, *The Making of a Counter Culture: Reflections on the Technocratic Society and Its Youthful Opposition* (Garden City, NY: Doubleday, 1969), and Shulamith Firestone, *The Dialectic of Sex: The Case for Feminist Revolution* (New York: William Morrow, 1970).

3. Terry Gross, interview with John Waters, on National Public Radio, "Fresh Air," February 25, 2004, http://www.npr.org/templates/story/story.php?storyId=1700561.

4. *Lawrence v. Texas*, 539 U.S. 558 (2003).

5. For analyses of the *Lawrence* decision, see Dale Carpenter, *Flagrant Conduct: The Story of "Lawrence v. Texas"* (New York: W.W. Norton, 2012), and Harry Hirsch, ed., *The Future of Gay Rights in America* (New York: Routledge, 2005).

6. *Newsweek*, July 7, 2003, pp. 38–45.

7. David G. Savage, "Ruling Seen as Precursor to Same-Sex Marriage," *Los Angeles Times*, p. A21.

8. *Boston Globe*, June 11, 2003, p. 1, and *Toronto Sun*, June 18, 2003, p. 7.

9. *Lawrence v. Texas*.

10. *New York Times*, November 19, 2003, A24; *Los Angeles Times*, June 28, 2003, A21; Chad Graham, "Changing History," *Advocate*, January 20, 2004, pp. 36–39.

11. See David K. Johnson, *The Lavender Scare: The Cold War Persecution of Gays and Lesbians in the Federal Government* (Chicago: University of Chicago Press, 2004).

12. On the homophile movement, see John D'Emilio, *Sexual Politics, Sexual Communities: The Making of a Homosexual Minority in the United States, 1940–1970*, 2nd ed. (Chicago: University of Chicago Press, 1998); Marc Stein, *City of Sisterly and Brotherly Loves: Lesbian and Gay Philadelphia, 1945–1972* (Chicago: University of Chicago Press, 2000); Elizabeth A. Armstrong, *Forging Gay Identities: Organizing Sexuality in San Francisco,*

1950–1994 (Chicago: University of Chicago Press, 2002); and Nan Alamilla Boyd, *Wide Open Town A History of Queer San Francisco to 1965* (Berkeley: University of California Press, 2003).

13. For a recent account of the 1960s that captures how tumultuous the era was, see Maurice Isserman and Michael Kazin, *America Divided: The Civil War of the 1960s*, 3rd ed. (New York: Oxford University Press, 2008).

14. There is not yet a satisfying book-length account of the gay liberation era. For aspects of it, see Stein, *City of Brotherly and Sisterly Loves*, and Armstrong, *Forging Gay Identities*, as well as Dudley Clendinen and Adam Nagourney, *Out for Good: The Struggle to Build a Gay Rights Movement in America* (New York: Simon & Schuster, 1999). See also Terence Kissack, "Freaking Fag Revolutionaries: New York's Gay Liberation Front, 1969–1971," *Radical History Review* 62 (Spring 1995): 104–34, and Justin David Suran, "Coming Out against the War: Antimilitarism and the Politicization of Homosexuality in the Era of Vietnam," *American Quarterly* 53 (2001): 452–88. Important accounts from the era are Dennis Altman, *Homosexual: Oppression and Liberation* (New York: Avon 1971), and Karla Jay and Allen Young, eds., *Out of the Closets: Voices of Gay Liberation*, 20th Anniversary Ed. (New York: New York University Press, 1992).

15. For aspects of the 1970s, see Dennis Altman, *Coming Out in the Seventies* (Boston: Alyson, 1981); Bonnie J. Morris, *Eden Built by Eves: The Culture of Women's Music Festivals* (Los Angeles: Alyson Books, 1999); and Karla Jay and Allen Young, eds., *Lavender Culture* (New York: New York University Press, 1994).

16. For accounts of this earlier history of lesbian mothers, see Daniel Winunwe Rivers, *Radical Relations: Lesbian Mothers, Gay Fathers, and Their Children in the United States since World War II* (Chapel Hill: University of North Carolina Press, 2013), and Lauren Jae Gutterman, "'The House on the Borderland': Lesbian Desire, Marriage, and the Household, 1945–1979," PhD dissertation, New York University, 2012.

17. Jay and Young, *Out of the Closets*, 32, 333, 365, and 258.

18. Keith Hartmann, *Congregations in Conflict: The Battle over Homosexuality* (New Brunswick, NJ: Rutgers University Press, 1996), 79–89.

19. For a discussion of the Washington case, see Gary L. Atkins, *Gay Seattle* (Seattle: University of Washington Press, 2003), 127–28; for Chicago, see John D'Emilio, "Marriage, Chicago-style," October 28, 2009, http://www.windycitymediagroup.com/lgbt /CHICAGO-HISTORY–Marriage-Chicago-style/23285.html, accessed June 18, 2013.

20. On the Sharon Kowalski case, see Karen Thompson and Julie Andrzejewski, *Why Can't Sharon Kowalski Come Home?* (San Francisco: Spinsters/Aunt Lute Press, 1988), and Casey Charles, *The Sharon Kowalski Case: Lesbian and Gay Rights on Trial* (Lawrence: University of Kansas Press, 2003).

21. The literature on AIDS is vast. Some important works that discuss the impact of the epidemic in the 1980s and early 1990s are Cindy Patton, *Sex and Germs: The Politics of AIDS* (Boston: South End Press, 1985); Dennis Altman, *AIDS in the Mind of America* (New York: Anchor/Doubleday, 1986); Simon Watney, *Policing Desire: Pornography, AIDS and*

the Media (Minneapolis: University of Minnesota Press, 1987); the ACT UP/NY Women and AIDS Book Group, *Women, AIDS, and Activism* (Boston: South End Press, 1990); Martin P. Levine et al., eds., *In Changing Times: Gay Men and Lesbians Encounter HIV/AIDS* (Chicago: University of Chicago Press, 1997); Cathy J. Cohen, *The Boundaries of Blackness: AIDS and the Breakdown of Black Politics* (Chicago: University of Chicago Press, 1999); and Jennifer Brier, *Infectious Ideas: U.S. Political Responses to the AIDS Crisis* (Chapel Hill: University of North Carolina Press, 2009).

22. For writings by gays and lesbians of color from this era, see Joseph Beam, ed., *In the Life: A Black Gay Anthology* (Boston: Alyson, 1986); Juanita Ramos, ed., *Compañeras: Latina Lesbians, An Anthology* (New York: Latina Lesbian History Project, 1987); Essex Hemphill, ed., *Brother to Brother: New Writings by Black Gay Men* (Boston: Alyson, 1991); Makeda Silvera, ed., *Piece of My Heart: A Lesbian of Color Anthology* (Toronto: Sister Vision Press, 1991); and Cherrie Moraga, *Waiting in the Wings: Portrait of a Queer Motherhood* (Ithaca, NY: Firebrand Books, 1997). For the perspective of gays and lesbians outside large urban centers, contrast Edmund White, *States of Desire: Travels in Gay America* (New York: E. P. Dutton, 1980) with Keith Hartmann, *Congregations in Conflict*.

23. For discussions of the move toward parenting in this era, see Kath Weston, *Families We Choose: Lesbians, Gays, Kinship* (New York: Columbia University Press, 1991), and Mary Bernstein and Renate Reimann, eds., *Queer Family, Queer Politics: Challenging Culture and the State* (New York: Columbia University Press, 2001).

24. On the conservative family politics of the era, see Didi Herman, *The Antigay Agenda: Orthodox Vision and the Christian Right* (Chicago: University of Chicago Press, 1997); Godfrey Hodgson, *The World Turned Right Side Up: A History of the Conservative Ascendancy in America* (Boston: Houghton Mifflin, 1996); and William Martin, *With God on Our Side: The Rise of the Religious Right in America* (New York: Broadway Books, 1996).

25. See Nancy D. Polikoff, "Raising Children: Lesbian and Gay Parents Face the Public and the Courts," in *Creating Change: Sexuality, Public Policy, and Civil Rights*, ed. John D'Emilio et al. (New York: St. Martin's Press, 2000), 305–35, and the website of the National Center for Lesbian Rights, http://www.nclrights.org.

26. David L. Chambers, "Couples: Marriage, Civil Unions, and Domestic Partnership," in D'Emilio et al., *Creating Change*, 281–304.

27. See its website, http://www.colage.org.

28. On workplace activism, see Kitty Krupat and Patrick McCreery, eds., *Out at Work: Building a Gay-Labor Alliance* (Minneapolis: University of Minnesota Press, 2001).

29. "Why Gay People Should Seek the Right to Marry," *Out/Look* 6 (Fall 1989): 12.

30. The marriage issue has generated a huge scholarly and popular literature. Two of the most recent books on the subject are Michael J. Klarman, *From the Closet to the Altar: Courts, Backlash, and the Struggle for Same-Sex Marriage* (New York: Oxford University Press, 2013), and Mary Bernstein and Verta Taylor, eds., *The Marrying Kind? Debating Same-Sex Marriage within the Lesbian and Gay Movement* (Minneapolis: University of Minnesota Press, 2013).

31. Defense of Marriage Act, HR 3396, 104th Congress, 2nd Session, *Congressional Record* 142 (July 11, 1996): H 7444; *Washington Post*, July 13, 1996, p. A1, and September 11, 1996, p. A1.

32. Quoted in James T. Patterson, *Brown v. Board of Education: A Civil Rights Milestone and Its Troubled Legacy* (New York: Oxford University Press, 2001), 72.

33. Ibid., 13.

34. Kristin Luker, *Abortion and the Politics of Motherhood* (Berkeley: University of California Press, 1984), 126.

35. For histories of birth control activism in the twentieth century, see James Reed, *From Private Vice to Public Virtue: The Birth Control Movement and American Society since 1830* (New York: Basic Books, 1978), and Linda Gordon, *Woman's Body, Woman's Right: A Social History of Birth Control in America* (New York: Grossman, 1976).

36. *Roth v. United States*, 354 U.S. 476 (1957); Commission on Obscenity and Pornography, *Report* (New York: Bantam Books, 1970). See also Whitney Strub, *Perversion for Profit: The Politics of Pornography and the Rise of the New Right* (New York: Columbia University Press, 2010), and Leigh Ann Wheeler, *How Sex Became a Civil Liberty* (New York: Oxford University Press, 2012).

37. *Griswold v. Connecticut*, 381 U.S. 479 (1965), and *Eisenstadt v. Baird*, 405 U.S. 438 (1970). For a detailed discussion of the legal history that led up to *Roe*, see David J. Garrow, *Liberty and Sexuality: The Right to Privacy and the Making of Roe v. Wade* (New York: Macmillan, 1994). For a more critical evaluation of these cases, see Marc Stein, *Sexual Injustice: Supreme Court Decisions from Griswold to Roe* (Chapel Hill: University of North Carolina Press, 2010).

38. The cases in question, both decided on June 26, 2013, are *United States v. Windsor* and *Hollingsworth v. Perry*.

39. For an overview of this interpretation, see Andrew J. Cherlin, "The Deinstitutionalization of American Marriage," *Journal of Marriage and Family* 66 (November 2004): 848–61.

40. For a fuller elaboration of this argument, see Nancy D. Polikoff, *Beyond (Straight and Gay) Marriage: Valuing All Families under the Law* (Boston: Beacon Press, 2008).

41. Ariel Levy, "Lift and Separate," *New Yorker*, November 16, 2009.

42. *New York Times*, July 15, 2012, A1.

43. On the association of wealthy Republican donors with the campaign for same-sex marriage, see *New York Times*, May 14, 2011, A15; June 26, 2011, A1; February 6, 2012, B1; and March 24, 2012, p. 1.

44. Tara Siegel Bernard and Ron Lieber, "The High Price of Being a Gay Couple," *New York Times*, October 2, 2009, p. 1.

45. Michael D. Steinberger, "Federal Estate Tax Disadvantages for Same-Sex Couples," http://williamsinstitute.law.ucla.edu/research/economic-impact-reports/federal-estate-tax-disadvantages-for-same-sex-couples/, accessed May 23, 2012.

46. These studies are accessible at http://williamsinstitute.law.ucla.edu/category/research/economic-impact-reports/, accessed May 23, 2012.

47. See http://glma.org/document/docWindow.cfm?fuseaction=document.view Document&documentid=146&documentFormatId=236, accessed May 23, 2012.

48. Quoted by Karen Ocamb in a posting on www.bilerico.com, February 8, 2012.

49. See http://www.bloomberg.com/apps/news?pid=newsarchive&sid=aLjNm6 ptlC_4, accessed May 23, 2012.

50. Lisa Keen, "Obama Comes Out in Support of Marriage Equality," *Windy City Times*, May 16, 2012, p. 4.